g/m : [ordered] a few amounts

etc/ou :

veteran

Pathena

¶ VIN

wire . goes

Fleet st black hole

wire s cam : Marples — wire got lost

w. Clarksno dad edd Reveille 57—70
                    (born 1956)

golf and head

court : Jewish

Fagan : Lucas' farewell

boxer — libel payment avoided

wrong man on Jeno i/view

Left tdwds absent minded

A FEW GROSS WORDS

A
FEW GROSS
WORDS

The Street of Shame, and My Part in It

Cyril Kersh

S I M O N & S C H U S T E R
LONDON • SYDNEY • NEW YORK • TOKYO • TORONTO

First published in Great Britain by
Simon & Schuster Ltd in 1990

Simon & Schuster Ltd
West Garden Place
Kendal Street
London W2 2AQ

Simon & Schuster of Australia Pty Ltd
Sydney

British Library Cataloguing-in-Publication Data available
ISBN 0–671–71029–X

Typeset in 11/13.5 pts Trump Mediaeval by Selectmove Ltd, London
Printed and bound in Great Britain by
Richard Clay Ltd, Bungay, Suffolk

Contents

Foreword   ix

ONE   A Few Gross Words   1

TWO   Exploding Herring Shock Horror   5

THREE   Buy Him Up! He's Going To Hang!   17

FOUR   Of Thrift And The After Life   29

FIVE   A Legend In His Own By-Line   43

SIX   Monkey Brains And Mayhem   54

SEVEN   El Vino Veritas   66

EIGHT   The Tragedy Of Gerald Kersh   81

NINE   Another Shock Horror – The £10
Lunch   95

TEN   The Man Who Cut Stalin 110

ELEVEN   Play Up, Play Up And Pass
The Scotch 130

TWELVE   Some Of My Best Friends Are
Jewish 142

THIRTEEN   The Queen's Bed And Tuxedo
Junction 159

FOURTEEN   Call A Strike – There's Rind On My
Bacon 177

FIFTEEN   If You're Dead Please Let Me Know 190

Epilogue 206

To the memory of some great journalists:
Stuart (Sam) Campbell, Michael (Mike)
Christiansen, Arthur (Tony) Helliwell,
G. W. (Tony) Clarkson, Willi Frischauer,
Allen (Pip) Andrews and Brian Checkley.

Among the living, grateful thanks to
that most excellent of family
physicians, Martin Johnstone.

Foreword

For the most part, popular Sunday journalism celebrated the emerging freedoms of the post-war world in robust style. In the context of the time, from the late forties to the sixties, it was outrageous, amoral, reprehensible – and enormous fun – staffed by innocents, reprobates, opportunists, bemused old-timers, and one or two true gentlemen who had lost their way or were seduced by fiver-clutching fingers beckoning from one of idealism's back alleys.

This book is by no means an attempt at the history of those years. Equally, an autobiography would be an impudence. What I have set out to do is record, not necessarily in precise chronological order, my hopefully funny (in the main) reminiscences of those wicked days from joining *The People* to taking early retirement from the *Sunday Mirror*.

The liveliest years in journalism, they are worth remembering not only for their stories and characters, but because today's popular newspapers had their origins, as it were, in the loins of those irresponsible years.

Today there are guidelines, frequently broken, for self-discipline. During much of the time I am writing about there was no such code, yet while we quite savagely exposed villains and villainies, the world was not yet ready for us to hound adulterers who happened to be famous. (Except, as it were, by proxy, when in *The People* we would quote stories published abroad about loose-living Britons, then castigate the evil, shameless (etc.) publications concerned and demand denials and/or retractions.)

The French writer, Alphonse Karl, said: 'The more things change the more they are the same.' Simplistic, but there's a truth in it. It is only a matter of degree.

Such is the way of Fleet Street, far too many of the people about whom I write are now forgotten, not even preserved in saloon bar mythology. Equally, newspapers – daily and Sunday – that had their years of glory: the *News Chronicle*, *Daily Sketch*, *Sunday Dispatch*, *Sunday Chronicle*, *Sunday Empire News*, *Reynolds News* and *Daily Herald*. Magazines, too, including the great *Picture Poet* and its not-quite-so-good rival, *Illustrated*, the superb (in its day) *Lilliput*, *John Bull* (in the post-war years a sort of *Saturday Evening Post*), the old, pocket-size, *Men Only*, *Picturegoer* for film fans – and many more.

If this book adds no more than an amusing footnote to even the postscript of marginalia it will have served its purpose.

*　　*　　*

Memory is a fickle jade, but I have done my best to be accurate with names, dates and places where they are uncheckable. On only a few occasions have I deliberately changed names where not stated: to avoid a widow unnecessary embarrassment; to save someone from possible reprisals by what might be termed a hostile management. That sort of thing.

But nothing of consequence.

ONE

A Few Gross Words

My grandmother, and from time to time various uncles, aunts and cousins, lived above the family bakery in Askew Road, Shepherd's Bush.

Life there centred on the Front Room, a shadowy mini-museum of shabby Victoriana and remembrances of yesterday's prosperity. I recall its detail as vividly as the conversation which took place there one Saturday just before the outbreak of war. (It had to be Saturday, the day of the week my uncles, flour-dusty from the bakery, sat together for lunch prepared by my mother.)

Lew, the youngest and most handsome, was the family artist and gentleman: not only a delicate icer of cakes, he could play 'Over the Waves' on the family's upright piano, and when he broke the little finger of his right hand it set crooked, giving an impression of aristocratic elegance when he drank tea. He was also the only uncle with more than three teeth.

Uncle Dave, the eldest and a bachelor, slept in obsessive secrecy with nine cats behind the locked door of a ground-floor storage cupboard. No one in living memory had entered the cupboard, which was rumoured to hold undreamed-of treasures including a vast collection of books, the contents of which were the subject of much ribald conjecture. (In the event, his death revealed no treasures other than vintage silk shirts and underwear and collections of cigarette cards, while the rumoured pornography proved to be his father's prayer books and rabbinic commentaries.)

A superb baker and pastrycook whose hobby was converting old broomsticks into rolling pins, he was credited with wide-ranging medical knowledge, and swelled visibly when addressed as Doctor Dave. Although his prescriptions were limited to iodine and Sloane's Linament (external) and Ex-Lax (internal), his advice was much sought after by those members of the family who, doubtless by coincidence, died young.

Among his eccentricities was the conviction that, because they wanted repossession of his cupboard, the family were in a plot to poison his food – a belief which, when voiced, had long been responded to with dismissive shrugs from my aunts and uncles, but still provoked near-apoplexy from my mother who was high in culinary skills but abysmally low in dismissive shrugs.

Uncle Sam was acknowledged to be the family's business genius. The logic of this must have been that while one (or even two) bankruptcies could be attributed to bad luck, it needed genius to be responsible for seven. Over the years that followed my grandfather's death a small fortune must have been paid to sign-writers changing the name on the fascia above the shop in Askew Road.

Sam was also the family's intellectual since, apart from buying the *News Chronicle* daily and a complete set of papers on Sunday, he subscribed to *The Freethinker* and could prove that he wasn't a Jew. 'I'm English by birth. You follow? It's what they call my nationality. English. I'm also an atheist. Because there isn't no bloody God. If there was would I be bloody bald with no teeth? You follow? So if I'm English with no religion, how can I be a bloody Jew?'

I cherish the memory of Uncle Sam opening a tin of frozen eggs, cutting himself in the process, then displaying his bleeding finger to the bakehouse staff with a triumphant: 'And some people say there's a God!'

The impeccability of his I-can't-be-a-Jew reasoning was questioned only by my mother's *sotto voce*: 'Go tell Hitler.'

It was Uncle Sam that Saturday who asked me: 'What you going to do when you leave school?'

Since it was the sort of question calculated to make a 13 year old squirm, I squirmed, then managed a hesitant, 'I wouldn't mind being a writer.'

Uncle Dave, who had been jabbing suspiciously at a boiled potato, lifted his fork, scratched his stubbled chin with it, then waved it at me. 'You, a scholarship boy, can't write yet?'

'Of course I can write,' I protested.

'Don't argue with your uncle, you toerag!' my mother shouted, digging at my ribs with an elbow. 'If your uncle says you can't write, you can't. And that's that.'

'But I can. Didn't I write a letter the other day for you to the landlord about the rent?'

'Rheumatism,' my mother explained apologetically, displaying her swollen knuckles.

'Letter writing,' said my grandmother. 'They still do it?'

'Do what?' Uncle Sam demanded.

'In the old days,' his mother explained, 'there was people who'd write letters for you for sixpence or a shilling. Yiddish. Polish. Marvellous they was. Like that cousin of Morrie Rosen who could also do English. But I didn't know they still done it.'

'Not letter writing,' I explained. 'I meant . . .'

'Not books, I hope,' Uncle Lew interrupted. 'We've already had enough with one in the family. The shitpot.'

My mother flushed at this reference to my brother, Gerald, whose first novel, *Jews Without Jehovah*, had been banned after libel actions brought by my uncles and various cousins. (Irrespective of the morality of their behaviour, the book was certainly highly libellous. It was also very funny.)

My mother patted the air with her hands. 'He meant well,' she said, feebly defensive.

Uncle Dave paused from sniffing at a segment of stewed beef to mutter: 'Meant well. But what's the good of the well without the water?'

Silence as we attempted to work out the significance of this pronouncement. Then Uncle Sam looked pointedly at his brother and said: 'Of course, you know all about books, don't you? God alone knows what scandal if we got bloody raided. You follow?'

'Raided? Like with air raids?' asked my mother, appalled. 'You mean if there's a war and Hitler air raids, it's because of Dave's books?'

Uncle Dave grinned, then laughed; an unnerving sight since it caused his tooth to vibrate in its gum.

An *oi veh* of despair from Uncle Sam. 'We're not talking about bloody Hitler (may his boils fester) but bloody books.' To me: 'So if not letters, not books, what you going to write? What's left?'

'N-newspapers?' I ventured.

A triumphant bellow from Sam. 'Newspapers I know about. I read. Regular. They got words. Long words. You follow? And you can write them?' He turned to his mother. 'May God strike me down bloody dead and then cripple me for life if I lie, they got some words even I don't understand. Even me! You follow?' When my grandmother shook her head: 'What I mean is that, if even I don't understand, how can this stinker write words for me not to understand? You follow?'

Uncle Lew said: 'So OK. Words is writing. Just like writing is words. What matters it who's going to buy? Who's going to buy words?'

'Right,' said Sam, banging a fist on the table. 'You've hit the bloody nail on the whatsit.' To me: 'You'd be better off learning a trade. You know that? You'll know where you stand. Like the baking. Every day I know how many quartern bread to bake. How many gross of fancies. How many chocolate gatters. How many gross of rolls and cakes. You follow? That's logic. Common sense. People need bread and cakes. What they call the staff of life. But words?'

'Maybe he's already got,' said my grandmother.

'Got?' Sam frowned. 'Got what?'

'An order,' my grandmother replied patiently.

'Order for what?'

'A few gross words,' said my grandmother.

TWO

Exploding Herring Shock Horror

Fate played a succession of dirty tricks on my mother during her middle years. She was 45 when I was born (my eldest sister, Annette, was old enough to have been my mother). Four years later my father died, leaving my mother penniless and quite unable to cope with a small boy and two other children of school age during a grief-obsessed menopause.

My father, Hyman, had won cups and medals for his skills as a master tailor, and counted among his clients such worthies as the Royal physician, Lord Dawson of Penn, and Lord Howard de Walden, who owned much of London's Marylebone. Yet he died poor at 50, for although he made superb suits he sold them with no regard to practical profit margins. He was to have become a Freemason but never got round to it, and among my mother's many regrets was that, had her husband joined the Worshipful Brothers and then died, we would have been kept in champagne-bubbling luxury for the rest of our lives.

We lived above and below the shop and workroom at 18 Blandford Street, off Baker Street, and to this day my admiration of Georgian building is tempered by memories of a damp, gaslit basement with its rat-frequented kitchen, absence of a bathroom, an outside lavatory and the lumping of buckets of coal up steep flights of stairs. When my father died we moved into Pereira Mansions on Shepherd's Bush Green with Uncle Max and Aunt Esther and their daughter Eva.

Our next years were determined at Askew Road one Saturday when Uncle Sam said to my mother: 'You're a wonderful cook, Leah. You should open a boarding house.' The subject came up at the next family poker game, and Uncle Aaron knew someone who knew someone who had a kosher boarding house at Westcliff-on-Sea in Essex, the contents and goodwill of which she was prepared to sell for next to nothing since she had made a sufficient fortune in no time at all to retire to Worthing. (As nobody in the family had been to Worthing, and were not even certain where it was situated, it was accepted to be the sort of place to which the Rothschilds retired.) So, at Uncle Sam's urging, the Millers scraped together the £150 for the fixtures and fittings of 23 Cobham Road in that mud and pebble dominated resort on the Thames estuary which, because of its proximity to the East End, was filled with kosher hotels and boarding houses. (Gentiles preferred neighbouring Southend.)

On the day of our departure the members of the family who came to Fenchurch Street Station to shout 'Good luck' might just as well have cried 'Bon voyage, Titanic,' for the decision to give my mother charge of a boarding house topped the list of Uncle Sam's many commercial absurdities.

As others mitigate grief with drink or drugs, my mother assuaged the misery of widowhood by cooking. She came to believe that anyone not actually in the process of eating or expressing a desperate craving for nourishment was critically ill, with food the only cure. People on diets were mentally unstable and had to be saved from themselves. Her kitchen was a gastronomic iron lung.

To add to the problem, my mother was a superb cook with absolutely no business sense. She wanted to play the hostess. Feed people. Make them happy. After all, whether they realized it or not, it was for their own good – apart from a refusal being a brutally wounding criticism of her culinary skills.

One of her weapons was blackmail. 'Of course you'll have another piece of fish. I made special. Fresh. When I bought it this morning it was winking at me. Have a small piece' – pointing to a vast middle cut of fried plaice.

'But I just can't eat any more.'

'Can't?' her voice rising. 'What do you mean, can't? There's no such word. So sure I should live you'll have another piece of fish. May I never leave this room alive if you don't. I take my dying oath on it.'

An appalled: 'Ssssh! You mustn't say such things.'

'So I've said them . . . You want I should die? Have a black year?'

'Of course not!'

'Then eat the fish.'

If not blackmail, bizarre rationalization. A memorable example with her sister, Dora Gassman: 'Have another piece of cheesecake, Dora. Good for you. . . Too fat for your stomach? What's this with a stomach? Since when have you had a stomach, and what do you mean, too fat? Since when has cheese been fat? Butter is fat. Chicken fat is fat. Beef fat is fat. But cheesecake? And even if it is fat (and I'm admitting nothing mind you), you mean to say your stomach was there in the kitchen watching when I made it? I've never heard such rubbish. Have another piece of cheesecake. Better for the stomach than all the medicines.'

Generally she had no problems at Westcliff. As her reputation spread, people wrote virtually begging to spend a week or two at Cobham Road. Others were rumoured to go without food for days to build suitable appetites for her sixpenny Sunday teas: combinations and permutations of fried and gefilte fish; white, brown, rye and black bread and butter; smoked salmon; chopped, pickled and smoked herrings; jams, marmalade and honey; hard-boiled eggs and chopped eggs and onions, sardines, anchovies and salads; a vast selection of home-made cakes and biscuits.

The more people ate, the more pleasure it gave my mother – and the greater became her debts. Yet she could not accept her poverty except as an additional punishment for unknown crimes she had committed against an implacable God. 'Why else am I suffering? Tell me,' she would demand of nobody in particular after an eighteen-hour day of toil. 'Why else am I a widow with ungrateful children and arthritis? . . . So what did I do? Eh? I've lived a decent life, but everywhere I'm punished, left, right and centre.

'Now, as if I didn't have enough aggravations. I'm up to my eyes in debt. The place has been full all season. People were

7

even sleeping on the floor. It was packed out. I should be rolling in money, but I'm broke. What have I done to deserve it? Can nobody explain?'

Explain? It was useless to talk about profit margins or, more simply, that she gave her guests food and other services in excess of those for which she charged. 'How can you begrudge somebody a crust of bread and jam and somewhere to sleep? You mean I'm near bankrupt for giving someone a tiny piece of fish and a biscuit? I've never heard such rubbish.'

Other problems were endemic to boarding houses: guests who stole linen and cutlery . . . Demands to know why Mrs So-and-so had the breast of chicken and I got the leg ('When they invent chickens with no legs, no wings and ten breasts then everybody will have breasts. In the meantime you've got to take turns. In any case the legs are marvellous for the health. Especially the phlegm. You haven't got phlegm? That's because you had the leg. Be grateful.') . . . Dispute about bills . . . Who was served first at mealtimes . . . And so on.

One incident was so outlandish few people believe its telling and, until now, I dared write only as fiction in *The Diabolical Liberties of Uncle Max.* Yet it happened, I promise you, and became something of an East End legend.

It began with the soup (almost certainly chicken soup), which one of the newly arrived guests, a Mrs Mordisch, would not drink because it gave her heartburn. My sister, Sylvia, who waited at table, called my mother. Despite her blandishments, bullying, shrill threats of self-destruction and pleas to Mr Mordisch to make his wife see sense, Mrs Mordisch was adamant, and as other guests became angrily impatient for their food my mother, purple with rage, returned to the kitchen. If that was not aggravation enough, later in the day Miss Kemlett was taken ill and asked for a doctor to be called.

My mother's reflex was a sneer. 'Doctors! What do they know? I'll warm some soup.' Her hand went to her mouth. 'I hope you're not insinuating. Suggesting it was something you ate. Because if so . . .'

'No, no, no,' Miss Kemlett interrupted impatiently. 'Nothing to do with food. I get spasms from time to time. I'll explain to the doctor.'

'Spasms,' my mother echoed. 'Spasms. Is that like the dropsy? Because if so I'll cook you . . .'

'The doctor!' Miss Kemlett yelled.

My mother, frightened now, kicked me on the ankle and screamed: 'Why are you standing there like a stuffed dummy when the poor woman's dying? Go fetch the doctor!'

Dr Fox's medications included an injection which needed to be repeated last thing at night after Miss Kemlett had taken sleeping tablets, but which he could not administer himself since he would be at Southend General Hospital. But there was no need to worry. My brother was at Cobham Road for a couple of days, so who better to give the second injection? After all, Gerald was an extremely fit young man who, between trying to sell his novels and short stories, worked as an all-in wrestler and night club bouncer. His party trick was to clasp a sixpence between his teeth and with the strength of a thumb bent it to an angle of 90 degrees. In any case, Dr Fox explained, Miss Kemlett would be in a drugged sleep and wouldn't suffer from any unskilled inaccuracy. So he showed Gerald how to fill and use the hypodermic, collected his fee from Miss Kemlett and departed, leaving my brother pale and trembling.

The trouble was that for all his physical strength I knew that Gerald was utterly terrified by the very sight of a hypodermic, although he was too proud to admit the fact. So that night in the kitchen he was literally dripping sweat and shaking as he filled the syringe. Then, after much lip licking, he took a deep breath and watched by myself, Sylvia and our knuckle-biting mother rushed out of the room, along the corridor and up the stairs.

A series of shrieks, followed by a confusion of furious screaming and shouting, told us that in his panic Gerald has crashed into the wrong bedroom.

Of the chaos that dominated the next hour or so I recall my mother's weeping, Mrs Mordisch's groans and her husband swearing on his children's lives that he'd report us to the police, sue us for every penny and write to the *Jewish Chronicle*, the Jewish Board of Guardians and his member of parliament. At some point my mother managed to interrupt to sob: 'It was an accident. And for such a tiny needle you'd make such a big fuss? Make me bankrupt? Send me to prison – me, a poor widow without a husband?' When, after more in the same vein, she added: 'I'll take it off the bill. No, better still, forget the bill,' something like order was restored.

Mrs Mordisch did not seem to suffer from the injection and Miss Kemlett did not seem to suffer from its absence. But what brought the events of the day together to make them part of the marginalia of legend (and, indeed, ensures that the story is still told, albeit with a variety of different names) was the version spread around the East End by Mrs Mordisch with its concluding: 'I'm telling you straight, that Leah Kersh is mad. A fanatic. If you go to stay there do me a favour – no, do yourself a favour – and drink the soup. If you don't, she'll send someone in the middle of the night to stick it up your bum.'

We left Westcliff soon after the outbreak of war. The move back to Askew Road was motivated in part by my mother's horrendous debts, partly because she thought London would be safer: she had visions of German battleships sailing up the Thames estuary and 'bombarding us to smithereens in our beds. We'll be better off in London.' Mainly however, her decision to move was determined by the primal reassurance offered by the communal womb of Family – although, after a few months, we moved to the ground floor and damp-oozing basement of a house in Vinery Villas on the fringes of St John's Wood, a crumbling cul-de-sac that trembled every time a tube train thundered under its foundations.

Even with Sylvia and myself at work my mother was seldom lonely: at up to 500 yards trained ears could hear a match being struck to light the cooker. She was spared breakfast, but at lunch, tea and supper times neighbours would call 'just for a minute to see how you are' and remain to bloat themselves with food. (My questions as to how she managed, despite rationing, were met with wrathful replies on the lines of 'Mind your own business, Nosey Parker,' although coffee, poultry and fish were among unrationed foodstuffs, and Askew Road helped out with bread and cakes from the shop, and flour, sugar and fats from the bakery's allowances.)

Our neighbours were a heterogeneous collection. There was Martin Williams, dispensing chemist and psychic, who was one of my mother's favourites since he could foretell the future from playing cards, tea leaves, the palms of hands and bumps on the head. Most important, he received astral vibrations with their assurances of eagerly listened-to predictabilities: health, wealth and happiness – plus the imminent death of Hitler in excruciatingly painful circumstances. Like all compulsive crossers of fingers and touchers of wood, my mother was spellbound by Williams, conveniently forgetting his failures as she eagerly grasped at a new ephemera of hope, aware that when the chemist's vibrations were weak, food rapidly strengthened them.

There was the Belgian Walter Magnée, once European Graeco-Roman Heavyweight Wrestling Champion, now a hypochondriac ex-film actor whose greatest role had been doubling for Charles Laughton in the wrestling scene in *The Private Life of Henry the Eighth*. He, at least, earned his keep by doing odd jobs around the place. Between visits he was a lonely feeder of pigeons in Regent's Park, where he sat clutching an envelope crammed with photographic glory.

He lodged at Number One with Mrs Seymour, a tough old Irishwoman so concerned with letting rooms that her own sleeping place was an armchair in the kitchen. The natural corollary for other residents in the street was that Mrs Seymour had reached the stage when she had to sleep in the kitchen whether she liked it or not – the chair was stuffed with a huge sum of money she dared not bank in case the Inland Revenue learned about it. This belief was strengthened with the coming of the blitz. The rest of us spent at least some nights in the local shelter, while Mrs Seymour refused to leave her heavily bolted and padlocked kitchen, even though the reverberations from the anti-aircraft guns in Hyde Park and on Primrose Hill caused bits of Vinery Villas to fall off. As my mother put it, with a wink and a smile: 'She's made her bed and now she's got to lie on it.'

Her smugness turned to rage when bombs fell on Marylebone Station's goods yard and the blast, while leaving Number One intact, caused the collapse of our bathroom and scullery. Emergency repairs by the local council meant bricking-up the holes and moving the bath, cooker and sink into our kitchen. Apart from causing understandable grief, it solved the problem of her freeloaders: there was no longer room to accommodate more

11

than my mother, Sylvia and myself (if I sat on the plywood-lidded bath.)

How then, to satisfy my mother's obsessive need to feed the masses? It did not take her long to arrive at the answer: without her expertise the family at Askew Road must surely be dying of starvation. She discounted the women there ('What do they know about boiling a potato?'), and so began a daily, arthritis-defying journey to Shepherd's Bush to cook lunch, a ritual that was to continue until, nearing 80, the onset of cancer forced her to leave them to famish.

*   *   *

My schooling had ended at 14 when we left Westcliff. In London I first worked at W. H. Smith bookstalls, where I spent so much time reading I was unaware of thefts from stock on display. I quit when I realized that even reasonably calculated weekly deductions from my 13 shillings-a-week salary for these depredations would take me years to repay. Next to Askew Road as a sort of odd-job boy: an act of charity since it was obvious I'd never make a baker. Then to an engineering factory where my incompetence with a micrometer meant that all my lathe-turned aircraft brake blocks had to be scrapped. So to an illegal toy factory in a Charlotte Street basement; its owner, Eli Hurwitz, had no licence to buy wood or paint. Next, doing the books (me, the master innumerate) for a drunken woollen merchant off Regent Street. And so on, until I was summoned for service with the Royal Navy towards the end of 1943.

I could never master Morse or semaphore or the art of tying complicated knots and so, despite three-and-a-half years of Fighting For Those Things We Hold Dear, I ended the war with the rank of Acting Able Seaman – promoted from Ordinary Seaman only because the captain of HMS *Penn* was ashamed to have a sailor with this minimal rank aboard his battle-scarred destroyer.

This came later. Having completed my basic training and a gunnery course at Whale Island, I was shuffled between various shore bases, including an ex-army barracks at Gosport – a relatively elegant and spacious, flat-roofed, one-storey building with a wide balcony helping to keep cool the basement where the horses had been quartered. It was an anachronism, explained by the transposing of the Edwardian architect's plans. Somewhere on the Indian sub-continent soldiers were pig-sweating in a claustrophobic red brick building intended for Gosport. Transferred to Royal Naval Barracks Portsmouth I received a letter from my mother in which, after the inevitable hopes that I was being a good boy and keeping warm, she told me that she had posted me a salt (schmaltz) herring of which she knew I was very fond, and which she doubted (rightly) were often served where I was stationed.

Coincidentally I was in London a couple of days later on embarkation leave. Then back to Portsmouth (no herring) before a troopship took me to Colombo and a train to Trincomalee. After some weeks there I joined the destroyer *Redoubt*. When that old lady returned to England it was back to Trinco before joining another destroyer, HMS *Penn*.

One day, after shooting at things in the Malacca Straits, we returned to Trinco to find that mail had arrived. Mine included a brown paper parcel addressed in my mother's handwriting. It took me the best part of a minute to realize that it was the missing Schmaltz herring. The damn thing had been following me through all manner of climates for the best part of a year.

I sniffed at the package. There was no noticeable smell: as was her fashion, my mother had wrapped the fish in vast quantities of greaseproof paper.

Curious, I undid the string, probed the inner wrappings – and was hit by the mephitis of rotten fish plus a gassy hiss. Stomach on the turn, I threw the package overboard, but it had barely cleared the rail when it exploded, and if that terrifying noise were not enough, my nearby shipmates and myself were sprayed with the truly disgusting stink of the gas and, since we were wearing only shorts, particles of decomposed herring were embedded in our faces and torsos.

The stench spread throughout the ship as we carried it to our various messdecks, and despite the scrubbing of clothes and bodies it took weeks to clear. The monsoon season did not deter some members of the crew from sleeping on the upper deck. It also took our bodies some time to be rid of the herring fragments since the only means we had of digging them out were our fingernails and pins supplied by the Sick Berth Attendant. Occasionally I still sniff at myself fancying a vestigial trace of herring. I was not very popular, but they couldn't find anything with which to charge me.

I am convinced to this day that had I not thrown the package overboard I'd have made a short paragraph in Naval memorabilia as the only British sailor to have been blown to pieces by a salt herring.

We spent Christmas '45 in Bombay. On Christmas Eve signal flags and bits of bunting were strung across the messdecks, but nobody was feeling particularly festive since all we had to drink apart from the daily tot of rum was near-bubbling lemonade: the sun had turned the ship into a cellular oven. I was quick to agree when one of my messmates (I'll call him Jock as he might now be a pillar of Glaswegian respectability) said: 'Come on, Kersh, we'll go ashore for a drink.' We found a *gharri*, made tilt-the-wrist drinking signs, and were trotted to a place labelled Monjini.

It was a vast, bleak, characterless box of a place: grey-greased walls and ceiling, a bare floor, the only furniture overdue-to-be-scrubbed wooden tables and benches reeking of a composite of raw alcohol, tobacco and sweat. The customers, all drunk, were a shouting (occasionally brawling) confusion of language and colour. It was something from an over-the-top B-film. There may be scores of such establishments around the world's seaports. I don't know, but I'll wager that Monjini's had something unique: a string quartet.

At the end of the room furthest from the bar two violins, a viola and a cello, played by four middle-aged European ladies with white hair and wrinkled faces, scratched out excerpts from popular musicals of the twenties and thirties. Who were they? How did they come to be scraping away, enervated and off-key, in Monjini's? And, as an added humiliation, behind a curtain of chicken wire to protect them from the empty bottles hurled from time to time by their audience?

While I have fantasized many an answer to the mystery, one thing I do know: after an hour or so drinking the raw (and doubtless illegal) alcohol that passed for Indian whisky, I spilled some on the table and lighted a cigarette. A multi-coloured flame

14

spurted into the air and Jock and myself were thrown out for what I assumed to be attempted arson.

'Let's go and eat something,' I suggested.

'Let's find a woman,' Jock countered.

'Not in Bombay!' I cried. 'Anywhere but Bombay. Let's eat.'

Another *gharri*. It was only when I saw a street name, Grant Road, that I realized we were in an area strictly out of bounds to Service personnel. The driver took us past the 'cages' – iron-barred, dim-lit windows behind which ragged whores displayed drooped and faded attractions – and drew up outside a house with its door open and a tiny, beaming and beckoning Indian at the foot of a gloomy staircase.

'Come on!' Jock yelled as he rushed towards the door.

Since he was past argument I said: 'I'll wait here' and paid off the *gharri*. Then a thought: 'What if a patrol comes along and asks me what I'm doing? How do I explain without betraying Jock?'. . . I followed him up the stairs where I discovered the establishment's madame who was sympathetic: I was not the first person to find himself in this predicament. She took me to her parlour where she told me she was half-Indian, half-Zulu, and was managing the brothel only to earn money to complete her studies for degrees in philosophy and economics. She had studied at . . . I never did know, for at that moment a mighty tattoo was hammered on the parlour door.

'Sod it, we've been raided,' I groaned and wondered: 'Who is likely to believe that I am in a brothel about to commit no greater misdemeanour than discuss Kant's *Critique of Pure Reason* with its manageress?'

The door opened to reveal the diminutive Indian, who was pushed aside by Jock who gave a drink-slurred explanation that the girl with whom he was to have passed an ecstatic ten minutes had been stolen from him by an RAF corporal. 'Does it matter?' I reasoned. 'In a place like this? There must be other girls. Is there much difference between them?'

'Let's find the bastard and kill him!' Before I could remonstrate further, another of the brothel's undersized staff appeared at the end of the corridor. 'He'll do!' Jock shouted as he rushed to the unfortunate man and began beating him into what was likely to be pulp. The man's screams brought others to the rescue, and since Jock was now getting the worst of it I went, reluctantly, to his aid.

It was an unmemorable sort of brawl – until what seemed to be the entire population of Bombay descended on us. After much beating we were thrown down the stairs. I tottered to my feet and saw at the top of the stairs a grinning Indian waving a small knife. I tugged at Jock's arm and drew his attention to the knife.

We patted ourselves. Blood. Mine.

To convince people that I was Mr Innocent when stabbed in the arse in a Bombay brothel has never proved easy.

Jock managed to find his way back to the ship, but I have no memory of the rest of that night. I awoke next morning spreadeagled in the dockyard without my cap or shoes. It is safe to assume that the latter had been stolen as I lay there.

Back aboard *Penn*, the officer of the watch took one look at my filthy state, closed his eyes and said that as it was Christmas Day he would not put me on charges for being adrift, being improperly dressed and anything else he could think of. Since we didn't carry a surgeon, he sent me to our parent ship, HMS *Mayina*, for my wound to be treated. Having spent the war amputating and sewing, the doctor I saw was contemptuous of my torn buttock. 'A bit of catgut should do the job,' he said, plainly annoyed at having his Christmas troubled by such trivia, and put in three stitches without the benefit of anaesthetic.

I was so hungover the pain barely registered.

I was demobbed early in 1947 and my noble career really began.

THREE

Buy Him Up!
He's Going To Hang!

Before joining the Navy I had spent a few months on *The People*. Early in 1943 Gerald, who had achieved fame with his book about the Coldstream Guards, *They Die with Their Boots Clean*, was able to provide an escape from a succession of jobs that not only bored me, but at which I was inept. He introduced me to Harry Ainsworth, editor of *The People*, who gave me a job as a trainee journalist at £3 a week. I managed to get a couple of stories published before my call-up.

While the war correspondents led a precarious existence, working in Fleet Street during the war seemed to be a bit of a doddle. Quite apart from the stories told to me by others, it certainly appeared that way in 1943. Newsprint rationing was severe, so papers were thin, and much of the news came from official communiqués. Other stories were frequently emasculated by the Ministry of Information, lodged in the London University building in Bloomsbury. Some maverick news did get into the newspapers: the *Daily Express* demanded the end of rationing, and the *Sunday Pictorial* sent reporter Susan Garth and a bunch of incredibly scruffy down and outs to Park Lane so that when the air-raid siren sounded they could ask at the Dorchester if they could use the hotel's air-raid shelter. They couldn't. That sort of thing.

My brother wrote a weekly column in *The People* under the pen name Piers England, much of it about Czechs with names like Ladislaw Kobra and Karel Manet, and Yugoslavs called Marko and Janez. All were heroic members of the Resistance, even if some were legless and/or armless because of German atrocities. Their tales of derring-do were described in powerful detail, although it was never clear how Gerald obtained these inspiring exclusives from occupied Europe.

Some papers kept a solicitous eye on Our Servicemen, but for the most part the meagre space available after news from the front lines and speeches of the day was devoted to tips and wrinkles on the best way to cook the newly introduced snoek (the South African name for barracouta), how to substitute for stockings (stain your legs with old tea leaves), how to keep warm in the absence of coal, gas or electricity (wrap yourself in newspapers), and how to beat clothes rationing by converting your husband's best suit into a two-piece costume. (Don't worry, he'll get a new one when he's demobbed.)

In terms of being called up for the Services there was a grey area: men in a certain age bracket could avoid call-up if their employers could present a satisfactory case to show that with the younger men conscripted these older hands were vital to the running of an essential civilian service (e.g. newspapers). *People* reporter Stanley Buchanan ('Bucky') came into this group, and Harry Ainsworth told him one Saturday that it had been agreed that he could be spared conscription. Bucky was delighted and went in search of beer and any scotch that was to be had.

The problem was that one of Bucky's Saturday tasks was to walk down Bow Street to the Waldorf Hotel and bring back the Editor's supper – a tureen of soup on a silver tray – before H.A. retired to the basement air-raid shelter. On this occasion, when Bucky returned from his pub crawl, Harry Ainsworth wanted to know what had happened to his soup. The normally meek, but now well-stewed, Buchanan replied: 'I'm a reporter, not your bloody butler.'

A fortnight later he was in the Army.

At the time of my early days on *The People* a favourite meeting place for the young who liked to think they were bohemian and intellectual was the Coffee An' in an alleyway next to St Giles' Church on the opposite side of Charing Cross Road to Soho. We could spend an entire evening over a threepenny cup of coffee as we resolved the world's political, religious and artistic problems.

A relatively small room of a place, its walls covered with sexy, if crudely executed, murals, it was managed by a sad, sallow man with badly peroxided hair, and owned by Boris Watson, a Russian who later opened the Mandrake Club in Soho and then a chess club in the Strand.

The Coffee An' attracted some adults, including a local villain called Henry who appointed himself our (unpaid) protector and carried a cut-throat razor in his breast pocket. When he popped in on his rounds he'd produce it, announcing: 'Boys and girls, do not fear. I've got little Louis here.' (Unfortunately he wasn't there the night when three or four very drunk Canadian soldiers staggered in and, discovering they couldn't buy alcohol, decided to compensate by wrecking the place. An amiable second-lieutenant in the Royal Army Pay Corps (his eyesight precluded more active service) bravely approached them and said: 'I say! I'm an officer and I'm ordering you', but got no further as one of the Canadians broke a chair over his head.)

The Coffee An' comes to mind now not because of its would-be artists and poets and film directors and fashion designers, but because of the few I met there who did make it, among them Wolf Mankowitz, Lucien and Clement Freud, and John Mortimer. Over in Charing Cross Road, Paul Hamlyn, today a millionaire and probably the biggest and most powerful name in British publishing, sold second-hand books by stacking them along the window ledges of shops closed for the day.

Fame being what it is, the names remind me of the faces, while a hundred other excellent chums are reduced to nameless blurs. Equally, since at the time we were all adolescent nobodies, what is there to remember? I do recall that the Freud brothers were extremely shy. I recollect Lucien as slight and ungainly although, even then, we teenagers accepted him as a fellow-genius; while the chubby-cheeked Clement Freud was delighted when he was taken on by the Royal Court Theatre's restaurant as a trainee chef.

With most of the young bucks in the Services, conversation on *The People*, apart from the war and news of where cucumbers were to be found in Covent Garden or which pubs had Scotch on sale, centred on reminiscence.

A favourite story concerned Conrad Philips (father of Conrad Philips the actor), who had edited the *Daily Mirror*'s 'Parliament of Youth' column. Decorated with Conrad's youthful and noble profile, the 'Parliament' was typical of the *Mirror*'s frivolous, if immensely popular, nonsense of the day, and was aimed at those whom Conrad referred to as 'fellow youngsters' – a sort of stopgap between the kiddies' strip cartoon 'Pip, Squeak and Wilfred' and the paper's adult readership. It posed such questions as: Should everyone be put to sleep at 50? Should we allow MPs over the age of 20, and a prime minister older than 25? There was, apparently, furious debate among Conrad's readers, with over-forties chipping in their selfish two-penn'orth.

Then, as war loomed, Conrad's topic for the week was a thundering, unequivocal address to teenage girls: IF YOUR BOYFRIEND ISN'T A TERRITORIAL GIVE HIM UP! So powerful was his rhetoric that at least two of his *Mirror* colleagues, Brian Murtough and Cyril James, joined the Territorial Army – and were among the first to be summoned to the colours.

On the day of their farewell party one of them was inspired to ask: 'Why aren't you coming with us, Conrad?'

After much hum and haw the voice of Britain's youth had to admit that he was too old. Brian and Cyril never forgave him.

After the war, when I came to know him, Conrad worked for one of the Kemsley newspapers and tripped and fell when he caught his heel in the worn carpet at the group's headquarters in Gray's Inn Road. He was away sick for several weeks, reappeared wearing a corset that encased him from neck to hips, and sued for damages since he was crippled for life. An old friend of his, Tony Clarkson, who knew Conrad's eye for the main chance, asked him what he'd do if he won his case. Conrad's reply became the punchline of what is now a cliché of a joke: 'I'll go to Lourdes and get a miracle cure.'

He won, and he did.

The *Daily Mirror* and its sister paper, the *Sunday Pictorial*, were the pre-war fun papers, filled with japes and wheezes. Example: 'Can a woman hatch an egg?' They found a female willing to take a clutch of eggs to her bosom, although I don't know the result of the experiment. Photographer Frank Charman told me of stunts which he claimed were invented by Pic editor, Hugh

Cudlipp (who put the responsibility back on Frank). For instance, to announce an early spring, a tortoise was shown on a lawn – the readers were not to know that it had been woken from its hibernation in the oven in Frank's kitchen. . . The stunt, one hot summer, of frying an egg on the pavement – spray the egg with methylated spirits, light a match, and the egg will soon sizzle, the flames of the meths not registering in the picture . . . The shipwreck when Frank bought a rocking chair and persuaded the wife of one of the missing fishermen to pose looking at it, handkerchief to eye to justify the headline: THE EMPTY CHAIR. (For good measure Frank bought a framed print of a storm at sea for the background wall.)

More seriously, the *Mirror* and *Pictorial* did warn of Hitler when most papers averred: 'There will be no war!' (This didn't prevent the *Express*'s Lord Beaverbrook from building an air-raid shelter in his back garden.) Most papers favoured appeasement, particularly the *Daily Mail* whose proprietor, Lord Rothermere, was a notorious fascist sympathizer.

The *Mirror* was proud of its, albeit clothed, pin-ups. The *Daily Sketch* responded with 'All The News and Pictures Fit To Print'. They had bishops to support them. Around 1938 the *Sunday Pictorial*, under Hugh Cudlipp, published what was claimed to be the first topless model in a newspaper. Mind you, it is still difficult to tell the sex of the model because of the amount of concealing cherry blossom. Those were the days of the magazine *Health and Efficiency*, ostensibly for nudists. The men exposed nothing except an occasional buttock, and the re-touching of the pictures of the women meant not only the absence of pubic hair but their inability to urinate or enjoy normal sex. (I think they also lacked nipples.)

In the newspapers the word 'love' euphemized 'sex'. For 'kiss', as in 'Would you kiss on a first date', read 'Would you bonk?' Women didn't have periods; if you wanted to be bold you would refer to 'the lunar influence'.

Pre-war series were on the lines of 'Unsung Heroes of the Trenches' . . . 'The History of Madame Tussauds' . . . 'The Titanic' . . . 'The Romance of Lloyds of London' . . . 'Famous Murder Cases' . . . 'Hero Balloonists of the American Civil War'. If it was competitive it was also cosy.

The *Sunday Express* continued to publish such series well into the 1960s, and I remember saying to its then features editor one Saturday lunchtime in the El Vino wine bar in Fleet Street: 'Why don't you do a series on Unsolved Hansom Cab Mysteries?'

He dragged me to a corner, his eyes gleaming. 'Have you got it, or written it? I need something for the week after next.' I had to tell him that it was a joke. 'Oh no it isn't,' he assured me. 'I'll get someone on it right away.'

The main thrust of pre-war circulation battles had little to do with news and pictures and series, and more to do with free gifts to regular readers. The Works of Bernard Shaw were offered, and Shaw's prefaces to his plays. Canteens of cutlery, free insurance and silk stockings were also to be had, as were other items of clothing.

I recall my mother subscribing to the *Daily Herald* in order to obtain their souvenir volume of the world's events in pictures during King George V's twenty-five years on the throne. The idea behind these promotions was that after taking the paper for some weeks or months new readers would become hooked on it. But most weren't. The trouble was that when my mother – along with thousands of other readers – had subscribed to the *Herald* for long enough to obtain her book, she switched to the *Daily Mail* (or maybe it was the *News Chronicle*), which was offering free boots of which I had a pressing need.

*　　*　　*

The Fleet Street to which I returned was at the beginning of a revolution. With the end of newsprint rationing, competition was reestablished. Not with pap and free gifts (in any case shortages and rationing precluded the latter), but with an aggressive brashness that reflected the revolution in attitudes brought about by the war. Which is why Odhams, who owned the paper, brought Renton Stuart (Sam) Campbell to *The People* as managing editor from the *Sunday Pictorial*, which he had edited while Hugh Cudlipp was overseas editing newspapers for the Forces.

Sandy-haired, bespectacled, slightly stooping, invariably dressed in a three-piece brown suit, Sam surveyed the world with a puzzled half-smile and wrinkled forehead as though bemused by life's frailties and villainies, the exposure of which gave him the reputation of being Fleet Street's finest investigative editor. A younger Alec Guinness could have played him to perfection. Sam was also a hypochondriac: the only man I've known whose office contained a table devoted to, and completely covered by, pill boxes, medicine bottles, tins of tablets, nasal inhalants and throat sprays.

Those were the days when eight popular Sunday newspapers were battling for circulation: *News of the World, People, Pictorial, Dispatch, Graphic, Empire News, Sunday Chronicle* and *Reynolds News*. Those were also the days when newspapers could buy criminals' memoirs as part of normal trading. Indeed, solicitors queued to auction the stories of their soon-to-be-hanged clients in exchange for the defence costs. With so many rivals in the field, bidding could be brisk.

Not that the popular Sundays were particularly aggressive to begin with, except for campaigns on behalf of homeless ex-servicemen, demands that we should send no more precious food to the Krauts and the Eyeties (who were making fortunes selling it on the black market), and so on.

Then the *Sunday Pictorial* shocked thousands when it published a poll: 'Should Our Future Queen Marry Prince Philip?' Why not? He was a Greek, not yet a British Citizen. Predictably the majority of replies said, 'Yes, if they are in love,' but the poll itself was denounced by many as an unwarranted intrusion and horsewhip-deserving near-treason. (Mind you, most of Fleet Street were envious of the *Pic*'s daring.)

The *News of the World* ran a different sort of survey. They'd long had the reputation of being Fleet Street's 'dirty' newspaper, pandering to the most prurient among the country's lumpenproletariat. Decent people didn't have it delivered to their homes. If they bought it they did so surreptitiously, and read it in private, and then only if it was concealed inside the covers of a 'decent' newspaper. It specialized in a round-up of the week's court cases – murders and sexual scandals, particularly crimes involving clerics and choirboys, scoutmasters and cubs, teachers and pupils, and similar aberrancy. Interlaying this material, to give the paper some quasi-respectability, were columns devoted to Unclaimed Money (from Wills), Missing Persons, a page of sheet music and lyrics ('Gather round the family pianist'), a fashion competition, and a yawn of a feature by a Conservative MP hard up for a few pounds.

Soon after the war (so Sam Campbell told me), with the formula basically unchanged, if truncated, the editor said, reasonably enough: 'Morals and manners have changed with the war. So what do our readers really want? Let's find out.' A survey was arranged: men (a fatal mistake as it proved) were employed to visit newsagents and obtain the names of regular readers on whom they then called. Husbands were generally at work, so housewives opened their doors to strange men who asked: 'What do you like best in the *News of the World*?'

Understandably, not one was prepared to reply: 'I'm very fond of the rape, and my old man is keen on the buggery and them stories about fathers and their daughters and things.' Instead, replies were on the lines of a nervous: 'We're both very keen on the Unclaimed Money – no harm in hoping, is there? – and them Missing People, and the sport, and that MP who writes, and the fashion contest, and the letters' . . . and so on. Not a syllable about sex in any form.

When the survey was processed, the editor looked at the result and cried: 'You see! People aren't interested in that sort of thing any more! It's old hat. Starting this week we'll drop all the sex. All of it – even bestiality and flashers in the park. Instead we'll give a whole page to Unclaimed Money, build up the letters into another page, give sport more space and turn Missing Persons into a two-page spread. Likewise the fashion competition. But no more sex. Understood?'

For two weeks the editor's orders were obeyed. Meticulously. At the start of the third week the *News of the World* had a new editor, things returned to what passed for normal and, at its peak, reached a circulation of about 8,500,000 copies a week.

Then the *News of the World* had to deliberately cut back its print run because its huge circulation meant it was losing money. The explanation is simple enough: the more copies you print, the more costly newsprint you use. The bulk of a newspaper's income comes, not from the cover price, but from advertising. Yet there is a limit to the amount you can ask advertisers to pay. Thus if you continue to add to your print run over and above your advertising revenue you lose money.

The *News of the World* still keeps its commanding lead in the market, although there has always been keen competition for second place. *The People* was the first to 5,000,000, then the *Sunday Pictorial* took over the lead.

Another folly of the day was down to *Daily Mirror* editor Sylvester Bolam. This was in 1949 when acid bath murderer John George Haigh was arrested. The *Mirror* went way over the top for calling him both a murderer and a vampire. Haigh was indeed hanged . . . later. At this stage he'd only just been apprehended. Found guilty of contempt of court, the unfortunate Bolam served three months and the *Mirror* fined a hefty (for the day) £10,000.

The *Empire News* (or was it the *Sunday Chronicle?*) purred with self-satisfaction when it bought the memoirs of Albert Pierrepoint, the hangman, for what was claimed to be a record fee. Pierrepoint must have had a fascinating tale to tell, only he couldn't tell it. He'd signed the Official Secrets Act and the paper wasn't allowed to publish a word. Mischievously, the Home Office didn't invoke the Act until the week of publication – although, in fairness, the paper should have been aware of the Act before they signed up Pierrepoint. Contractually, however, they had to pay the hangman.

Fleet Street's popular papers, urged on by rivalry, grew progressively bolder as they hyped themselves into the belief that nothing succeeds like excess. Charles Eade, editor of Rothermere's *Sunday Dispatch*, bought the serial rights in Katherine Windsor's *Forever Amber* and serialized it over umpteen weeks. It did the circulation enormous good. Although today it could be a harmless subject for O-level English (were it more literate), at the time it was considered to be very near the knuckle and almost earned Charles Eade Randolph Churchill's utterly meaningless title of Pornographer Royal (it was Coronation year), but the accolade went to the editor of the *Daily Graphic* for his alleged scraping-the-barrel attempts to out-Mirror the *Mirror*.

When Bishop Barnes of Birmingham wrote a book questioning the Bible's miracles, no newspaper wanted to know, except the *Sunday Pictorial*, which serialized it. Later Malcolm Muggeridge and John Grigg (formerly Lord Altrincham) caused furores when they attacked the Royal Family. The *Guardian, Observer* and *New Statesman* were to publish (maybe with self-conscious defiance) that 'infamous word' from *Lady Chatterley's Lover.*

If there was much fun in those post-war years, there was also a great deal of hard work. The print unions were greedy – managements huffed and puffed like the Grand Old Duke of York as they led their troops to the brink and then caved in. The National Union of Journalists was badly organized at this time and had no branch at *The People* (despite its sister paper, the *Daily Herald,* being the official voice of Labour). There was no minimum wage on *The People*, pensions (if any) depended on the management's paternalistic whims, and there was nothing to prevent arbitrary firing – particularly if you moaned too much to Sam Campbell at having to work all hours of the day, seven days a week. The comedy – and a very common one in Fleet Street – was that in his early days with the Mirror Group Sam had the reputation of being a militant trouble-maker. As they sing to the tune of 'The Red Flag':

> You can stick the Red Flag up your arse,
> I've got the foreman's job at last.

After a few years I was promoted to be *The People's* news and features editor. This meant that for most of the week I was gathering and writing news stories and features, adapting books for serialization in the paper, and rewriting other people's not very good material, as well as sending my reporting staff (all three of them) on stories. On Friday afternoons my desk became the News Desk as I sorted out material from staff and freelances for Sunday's paper. This role continued from early on Saturday morning until 5.30 p.m. when I went down to the composing room as stone sub, making sure stories fitted into their allotted spaces, rewriting headlines, and so on. Then a few beers and a sandwich, and at 9 o'clock when H.A. and Sam went home I was in charge of the paper and a couple of subs and reporters until 3.30 on Sunday morning when, if there was nothing happening, the composing room closed down. I got an extra payment (2 guineas, I think) for this, plus my taxi fare home, which I turned into profit: having the master set of keys for the night I slept on the carpet (the only one in *The People*) in Harry Ainsworth's office.

When the art and picture editor was away, I fitted another role into my Saturdays: rushing from time to time from my desk to the art room to select pictures for the paper, measure them up and send them to the process department. Fortunately the paper had some lively messenger boys to help us, including Charlie Wilson, now editor of *The Times*. During holidays I also had to squeeze in film and theatre reviews and, so help me, a sports column on a couple of occasions.

If it was sweatshop journalism it was also an unrivalled crash course in aspects of journalism other than writing.

One man who had a tougher time than me on Saturdays was on *Reynolds News*, a paper kept alive, even in those boom years, by hand-outs from the Co-op. He was the only man left on the paper after early evening on Saturdays. When (if) the phone rang with a freelance offering a story, and if the story was wanted, he had to go to the relevant typewriter, put on the earphones and take down the dictated story. Then he went to his own desk, edited the material until it was suitable for publication, took it down to the composing room, decided what it would replace, waited until it had been set and then made sure it fitted into the page.

What gave the situation its piquancy was that the man who had to cope with all these minutiae was Bill Richardson, the paper's editor.

The circulation war among the popular Sundays was exhilarating knockabout, but the time was to come, around 1960, when the *Empire News*, *Sunday Chronicle*, *Sunday Dispatch* and *Reynolds News* all died. The *Sunday Graphic* hung on for a few more years. Their deaths were due, in varying degrees, to a concatenation of circumstances. Bad managements were unable to cope with the greed and intractability of the print unions. Bad editorship and shortage of money resulted in bad newspapers. Television took away people's interest in reading, and commercial TV also took away much of the advertising life-blood. Ownership of motor cars and new prosperity meant that people could escape from the need to have a lie-in on Sundays and read the papers.

This is something of an over-simplification. A thorough examination and analysis of events would take volumes. Has taken volumes. With more volumes to come.

*   *   *

My first assignment after my return to *The People* could well
have been my last. A famous star of show business – I'm pretty
sure it was Jack Buchanan – married one Saturday for what was
said to be the first time. 'Rubbish,' said Harry Ainsworth. 'He's
been married before. Years ago. You ask Cousins. He was there.
I'll give you his phone number.'

John Addison, the news editor, who was present added: 'And
be quick about it. It's almost press time.'

I telephoned Mr Cousins. At first he couldn't remember who
Jack Buchanan was. When I told him that Buchanan was a great
star he remembered. 'And according to Harry Ainsworth you
were at his first wedding.'

After a long pause: 'Was I?'

'Please try to remember,' I begged. After a long silence, and
terrified now of missing that deadline, I got panicky and yelled:
'You now know who Jack Buchanan is! He got married today
and says he's never been married before! But apparently he was,
about thirty ago years! And you were at the wedding, but can't
even remember! For God's sake try!'

After more badgering he gave a squeal of delighted remembrance. 'Jack Buchanan! Of course I was at his wedding. I was
his best man!'

'Good God!' Fairly calmly: 'Please tell me something about it.
Who did he marry? Where was he married? How did you come to
know him? That sort of thing.'

'Oh, I can't tell you that. I remember Jack Buchanan, and I
remember being his best man. For the moment I can't recall
anything else. Now if you phone back tomorrow I'll try and . . .'

'A fat lot of good you are,' I interrupted and rang off.

It was only later that day I discovered that the Mr Cousins
to whom I'd been offensive was A. G. Cousins, chairman of our
owners, Odhams Press.

Fortunately I heard no more about it.

FOUR

Of Thrift And
The After Life

Visitors who used the men's lavatory at *The People*'s editorial offices in Long Acre were frequently startled to find themselves sitting in sudden and total darkness. Embarrassed apologies for blown fuses and power cuts concealed the fact that editor Harry Ainsworth had been on his rounds. A substantial shareholder in Odhams, he had an Exocet capacity for homing in on any economies that could boost dividends. Since he had little else to do at the tail-end of his career, with Sam Campbell effectively running the paper, he was not only a compulsive extinguisher of electric lights but scavenged wastepaper baskets for sheets of carbon paper and typewriter ribbons that might contain a residual paragraph of reproductive life, as well as rummaging for paper clips, elastic bands, pencil stubs and envelopes with unfranked or foreign stamps.

He also kept a needle-sharp watch on editorial expenses, including his own when he felt he wasn't receiving value for money.

The first time he took me to lunch was at the Connaught Rooms, next to the Masonic Temple in Great Queen Street. In the bar he announced in his slow Lancashire: 'We'll 'ave 'alf a bottle of that South African 'ock with the meal.' To me: 'You don't know anything about wine, do you?' Without waiting for an answer: 'So that's all right. And since it's dangerous to mix grape with grain, 'ave a beer to start.'

I asked for half a bitter. Having heard that it was the new fashionable drink, H.A. ordered a half of lager and lime for himself, sipped it and said to the barman: ''Ow much do you charge for the lime?'

'Tuppence, sir.'

'There's no tuppenceworth in this,' said H.A. firmly and gulped down a third of his glass. 'Now fill it up with lime and I'll 'ave a proper two-penn'orth.'

With a slightly trembling hand the barman did so and joined me in hypnotic fascination as H.A. took a swig from his glass. His eyes glazed, and as though by some process of osmosis the lime began to yellow his puckering cheeks. 'C-can't let the buggers swindle you,' he gasped as he bravely managed another sip. Blinking back lime-coloured tears, he placed the glass on the bar and croaked: 'Let's go and eat.'

'Don't you want to finish your drink?' I asked. 'It's a pity to waste it.'

'Waste' drained the lime from his cheeks. 'You're right, Kersh. You 'ave it.'

'Half of bitter's enough for me,' I lied.

Harry Ainsworth looked regretfully at the half-glass of what was now lime and lager, took sixpence from a waistcoat pocket for a tip, then put it back. 'You finish it, lad,' he told the barman with a gracious pat on the man's arm, and led me to the dining room.

At the table, as the waiter hovered, H.A. asked: 'Do you 'ave a proper breakfast?'

'Always,' I assured him. 'Eggs, or smoked haddock or kipper. That sort of thing.'

H.A. nodded approvingly. 'Must 'ave a good breakfast. Sets you up for the day.' Putting down the menu: 'Means you don't need a big lunch. It's bad to stuff yourself in the middle of the day, so what do you want to eat?'

I fell for it, primarily I suppose because he was the editor and I was a junior reporter/feature writer. 'The fixed menu will do me fine: soup and steamed plaice.'

Another approving nod. 'Good lad. I didn't 'ave time for breakfast this morning, so I'll 'ave the oysters and a well-done steak.'

On another occasion I had lunch with H.A. at the Waldorf. I found him at a table in the bar on which were five glasses, four containing liquids, the fifth empty. 'Have a drink,' I said. 'But what exactly is it?'

'It's what they call a Bronx. It's made of gin, dry vermouth, sweet vermouth and orange juice.' He tapped his nose. 'But if I order the ingredients separately and mix them myself I can make the orange juice last for two. Saves thruppence.'

Develop this sort of thing into a dedicated philosophy and you are on the Yellow Brick Road to riches. Or, in the case of Harry Ainsworth, greater riches.

This is not to deny that in his day H.A. was one of Fleet Street's more distinguished editors. His reign must have been something of a record: thirty-five years from 1925, even if in most of the post-war years he was only nominally editor while Sam Campbell did the work. He took over at the age of 37 and made innovations echoed in the popular Sunday press to this day: big headlines, more and larger pictures, extensive sports coverage and the personalized stories he liked to describe as 'vignettes'.

He is credited with inventing the Prize Crossword Puzzle. The first prize was £1,000 – if anyone could win it. Half the clues were straightforward, the remainder in the category of: 'You may have one at home.' Alternative solutions were provided: CAT, RAT, MAT, HAT, and readers were assured that a panel of academics met weekly to decide the appropriate answer. Allowing for a score of such clues, it was small wonder that their permutations guaranteed columns of analysis in *Competitors' Journal*. There was also a football contest, an ingenious forerunner of the Pools, for which the reader had to forecast the results of no fewer than eighteen matches to win. It is not known whether anyone ever did.

His greatest coup in this field was the introduction of free insurance for Registered (i.e. regular) Readers. From £1,000 payable to the next of kin of a Registered Reader and his wife killed in a railway accident, compensation scaled down to £3 a week for up to six weeks for total disablement caused by an accident in the home. Thus a particularly horrendous rail crash which was the lead story in all the Sunday papers gave *The People* the exclusive headline: LUCKY READER LOSES LEG TO WIN £250.

Most important of all, Harry Ainsworth was the first editor to serialize personal memoirs rather than the fiction popular at the time. He bought the confessions of the blackmailing lawyer in the sensational Mr A Case, involving a Maharaja's 'dalliance' while in London; 'Nurse Edith Cavell by A Priest Who Knew Her'; 'Stories of the Royal Family by A Court Photographer'; 'The Cases of Marshall Hall KC'; 'People I have Known by Arthur Roberts (comedian)'; 'The Memoirs of Earl Lonsdale' – and so on, each running for interminable weeks over innumerable pages.

Since H.A., Fleet Street series have changed in degree rather than substance. They were suspended during and immediately after the war because of the shortage of newsprint, and I remember Sam Campbell assuring me in 1947 that, even when paper rationing ended, series would be part of a pre-war scene dead and beyond recall. Two months later I adapted a book for him – *Eastern Approaches*, the wartime memoirs of Sir Fitzroy Maclean – which spearheaded *The People*'s onslaught on the Sunday newspaper series war.

Harry Ainsworth's pride may have been hurt when Sam came, but he didn't exactly starve. When H.A. moved from *John Bull* to become editor in 1925 the circulation of *The People* was 250,000. For years his income, apart from salary, was geared to the paper's circulation figure – until sales reached something around the 5 million mark and his pay cheques became so colossal that Odhams had to buy him out. During the war he again edited *John Bull* (as an extra) but never lost the additional income. He had an interest in a literary agency (from which he bought much of his material), and had holdings in such diverse enterprises as a Tunbridge Wells-based insurance company and the Southend-on-Sea waterworks. He was also reputed to forgo certain salary increases in exchange for Odhams stock, which did him no harm when take-over time arrived.

Add to this his meticulous prudence when it came to expenditure. . .

Every November a reporter had to write a story about the dangers of Guy Fawkes Night. A certain fireworks manufacturer had to be quoted as issuing the warning, and H.A. received a package of fireworks for his grandchildren. . . When there were three evening papers at a penny each, and they were delivered late to the office, H.A. would miss his train rather than buy his own set. . . He switched off his car engine and free-wheeled downhill to save petrol. . . He once advanced my brother Gerald £200, a 'personal loan' for which my brother was so grateful I never had the heart to tell him that Sam Campbell asked me from time to time when the series was coming for which the firm had paid a £200 advance. . . Review copies of books (other than those that could provide free feature-length reviews) had to be stacked in his office for periodic purchase by a neighbourhood bookseller.

Part of the job of writer Arthur (Tony) Helliwell was to provide a weekly homily under the heading 'Life's Little Problems by The People's Friend'. (When war broke out it was retitled 'Life's Big Problems'.) It was the sort of thing you read today in *War Cry*: 200 words of anecdote in which Jesus Christ had to be mentioned at least once in its hortative Christianity.

Tony became a war correspondent, giving distinguished service in the Mediterranean and Burma. During a particularly hairy convoy run to Malta he received a signal from Harry Ainsworth: RUNNING SHORT OF LIFES PROBLEMS STOP PLEASE ADVISE STOP. Tony told me he was inclined to cable back: SOD YOUR PROBLEMS STOP GOT MY OWN, but he didn't when a further cable from H.A. reminded him that 2 guineas of his salary was down to 'Life's Big Problems'. Being aboard ship he was able to explain the situation to the officer in charge of censorship, but it was somewhat different in Burma.

He crossed the Irrawaddy River with the Fourteenth Army and the censor behind the lines received a report for transmission to London which had as a postscript to that famous battle a dozen paragraphs which began: 'I met Old Bob sitting on a stile by my parish church. He told me he had planted an acorn for his great-grandchildren to see grow into an oak tree . . .' and which ended: 'Anyone who thinks the spirit of Britain is wavering should come to Oxfordshire to see Old Bob's confident promise of our free and noble future.'

Tony told me: 'I had the most bloody awful time with that censor. He was convinced I was sending coded messages. And who could blame him? After all, in the blood and mud and shit of the Burma Campaign who was going to believe I had to file 200 words of parish magazine pissology? In the end they refused to transmit it but John Addison reprinted the ones I'd written before the war, and since H.A. didn't notice, I continued to get my two guineas.'

Little is known of H.A.'s private life except that he lived in Leatherhead, Surrey, with his wife Bella, had two attractive daughters, played golf, had played cricket, was a devoted Christian particularly in observance of precepts of thrift and good husbandry (he knew the true meaning of the axiom Jesus Saves), and his idea of a spectacular evening's entertainment was to attend a Masonic function or watch TV with a carefully measured Dubonnet at his elbow. It was also supposed that H.A. owned a dog since reporters took it in turns to go to Soho to buy him horsemeat. I was dropped from the rota when I took to charging him for taxis there and back, necessitated by my anxiety not to be away from the office for too long.

H.A. also had a sense of occasion: when King George VI died we all had to wear black ties on the day of his funeral.

One thing that frequently overspilled into his working life was Harry Ainsworth's obsession with spiritualism and kindred magics. (It is said that the only item in his newspaper that he read thoroughly was Edward Lyndoe's astrological forecast.) On one famous occasion he came into the News Room – an act indicative of the magnitude of the occasion – and waved a letter at news editor Charles Rowe. 'There's a bloody good story 'ere, Rowe,' he said with the wink that, for H.A., signified wild excitement. He went on to explain how a psychic healer in Brighton removed appendixes merely by the laying on of hands. No anaesthetic, no knife, no scar, no anything. One minute the appendix was there, then – abracadabra! – it wasn't; a sort of Cosmotic surgery. 'The man's performing miracles,' H.A. concluded. 'Go and see him. Go yourself. Do an interview.'

Charles thought it prudent to tell Sam Campbell what he'd been asked to do. To Charles' astonishment Sam chortled: 'It's a corker! H.A.'s right, the man's a bloody miracle worker. But why come to see me? Moral scruples? If you've got moral objections, say so Charlie. You've got to believe what you write. . . for as long as it takes to write it. And this won't take long, will it? So go ahead.' He rubbed his hands. 'It's going to be the best story until the bloody Second Coming.'

Utterly baffled by Sam's unequivocal enthusiasm for the story, Charles said: 'OK' and started to leave the office. As he reached the door Sam cackled and added: 'By the way, chum, make sure you get before and after X-ray pictures.'

Charles did obtain them and they were taken to a Harley Street radiologist. 'There's no doubt about it,' said that eminent gentleman. 'In one X-ray there is an appendix. In the other there isn't.'

'Bloody hell!' Charles shouted, 'it *is* a miracle.'

'There's just one wee problem,' added the specialist. 'They're X-rays of different abdomens.'

Harry Ainsworth raged: 'They'll say anything, them 'Arley Street quacks,' but his fury, together with his interest in the story, evaporated when he saw Sam's proposed headline: ARREST THIS EVIL MAN . . . CRUEL SPIRITUALIST CONS THE SUFFERING.

Harry Ainsworth's passion for spiritualism was shared by A. C. 'Pat' Duncan, chairman of Odhams in the fifties. One of the two most momentous happenings in Duncan's life occurred at a seance where he was told that, although (as he put it when relating the story) his union had not been blessed with fruit in this world, a daughter had been born to his dear lady and himself 'on the other side'. The processes of this extra-dimensional breeding were never explained, but just as there is belief in spirit writing so Duncan was convinced in its psychographical equivalent, and a medium, guided by Gainsborough, regularly went into trances for him and his dear lady to draw (and sell) updated sketches of their occult offspring. (From time to time there was whimsical debate in the Long Acre pubs as to how Duncan worded his will or gave the address of the Duncans' next of kin.)

The other momentous event came when, via this truly surrealist artist, Duncan – and then H.A. and the legendary Hannen Swaffer – met the world's greatest psychic, coincidentally a Mrs Duncan. Now for years H.A. had tried to interest my brother in spiritualism, without success, but when Gerald learned the name of Mrs Duncan's spirit guide he could not wait to attend a seance in the front room of her suburban semi. 'But you must swear not to tell anyone the guide's name,' said Harry Ainsworth. 'Publicity would be disastrous. You swear?'

Gerald swore. They shook hands on it, H.A.'s Freemason-trained thumb cracking my brother's knuckles.

At first, Gerald told me, the seance followed a familiar pattern. After envelopes containing donations to assist Mrs Duncan in her charitable works had been left on a table, a couple of mood-setting hymns were badly and self-consciously sung. Then nervous and heavily breathed anticipation from his companions as Mrs Duncan sat rigid in her chair, eyes closed, hands grasping its sides as her face became contorted in what seemed to be some kind of pain . . . Agonized gurgles, then a great groan of ecstasy as she relaxed and said: 'He is coming. The Master is coming. . .' Gerald noted that Duncan, Ainsworth and Swaffer were frozen in their chairs, open-mouthed and goggle-eyed.

After some seconds a deep bass voice came from Mrs Duncan's mouth: 'It is I, ze Mastair. I bring you ze blessing of ze Lord and we vill recite Iz prair . . Our Farzair which art in 'Eaven, 'Allowed be zy name. Zy Kingdom come . . .' After they had recited The Lord's Prayer, the voice continued: 'Ze future 'olds a good picture for zoze oo believe. For zoze of you oo 'ave face all will be tip-top. Do you 'ave ze question you vish to ask?'

In a shaky voice Duncan said: 'Er. . . Lord. . . Master. . . Your Divinity. . . How is my daughter?'

'Everyzink iz tip-top. 'Ave face. Zair is much vickedness in your world, but 'ave face and you can conquer. Over 'ere iz 'Eaven. 'Ave face and when ze time comes you vill also be in 'Eaven. Any ozzer questions?'

H.A. asked about a certain share on the Stock Exchange and Swaffer wanted to know how Sophie Tucker was getting on. Both received the same sort of reply as was given to Duncan. (It is to be supposed that the nature of the questions was governed by the fact that more weighty topics had been dealt with at previous meetings.) Then my brother said: 'May I ask the Master a question?'

'Ask,' boomed the voice.

'Your last words on the Cross were "*Eli, Eli, lama sabachthani*". Aramaic. However, as the Lord Jesus Christ, You must know, in all manner of fluency and accent, the tongues of all mankind. So I wonder if You would be so gracious as to explain why You speak English like Maurice Chevalier.'

Gasps of horror from Duncan, Ainsworth and Swaffer. The voice said: 'Zair is an unbeliever 'ere,' and a few seconds later Mrs Duncan came out of her trance with a shudder and stammered: 'Is something wrong? I feel very bad vibrations. Very bad. The Master is unhappy about something. You had better leave.'

At subsequent seances, despite the absence of Gerald, the trio had to be content with the guidance of Confucius. It was only when H.A. said pointedly that 'paying to get services from some bloody Chink is good money down drain' that, by happy coincidence, Mrs Duncan was able to re-establish her rapport with Jesus Christ.

But until this Second Coming my brother was treated as though he had been responsible for the second crucifixion. Swaffer refused to talk to him, Duncan suggested to H.A. that it might be an idea to employ him only if absolutely necessary, while Ainsworth accepted free lunches from Gerald only if there was a week's advance notice.

Remembering Harry Ainsworth always ends up with stories of money, and for me his most masterly financial stroke involved Stanley Buchanan, the bald, bemused, bespectacled Scottish reporter who was a compulsive chewer of paper. (I am convinced that the blockage in his bowel which caused his death was papier mâché.)

The incident occurred when Bucky, fortified by several pints of bitter, went to see H.A. with the complaint: 'It's not fair, Mr Ainsworth.'

'What isn't, laddie?' asked H.A. as he filed his nails. (As other people's clothes have dandruff or cigarette ash, H.A.'s had nail dust.)

'What's not fair is that the other reporters are getting 13 guineas a week, and I'm only paid 13 pounds. I'm doing the same job as them. The same work. It's very embarrassing.'

H.A. nodded. 'Um. . . Aye, laddie, I can see that.' I can visualize his face creased in sympathy and his nodding head synchronized with puffs of air through pursed lips. Finally: 'You're right, Bucky. It is embarrassing. And I don't want you to be embarrassed. So I'll tell you what to do. Tell the others you *are* getting guineas. I'll back you up.'

When the Mirror Group took over Odhams, H.A. and Pat Duncan were the first casualties. (Rumour has it that H.A. refused to go, until the day he arrived at Odhams to discover that his office had been turned into a typing pool.) When H.A. died in 1965 leaving relatively little, some said that he'd parcelled out his wealth during his lifetime in order to escape death duties. Others insisted that he became a spiritualist in the hope of being reunited with it on the other side.

*　　*　　*

During the hunt for John Christie, Stanley Buchanan was arrested three times because of his fleeting resemblance to the Notting Hill Gate mass murderer.

That excellent author and *Observer* critic, Maurice Richardson, bore an uncanny likeness to the unpopular Randolph Churchill. One night, after much drinking, Maurice was hit by the fresh air outside El Vino and collapsed in the gutter. Traffic thundered past. Pedestrians strolled past. Then a couple of Randolph's *Evening Standard* colleagues saw the inert figure.

First journalist: 'We'd better help that fellow up.'

Second journalist, peering at Maurice: 'Sod that. It's Randolph.'

First journalist: 'So it is,' and each gave the unfortunate Maurice a hefty kick in the ribs and walked on.

Later, passing policemen were seen dragging Maurice to the other side of Temple Bar where they dumped him, as was common practice: another drunk became the responsibility of the Met's coppers instead of the City of London's. (It happened in reverse, of course, but the City got the better of the exchanges since Fleet Street had more drunks to offer than Aldwych and the Royal Courts of Justice.)

At around this time – late forties, early fifties – I had occasion to be mistaken for the famous.

As a member of the Burma Star Association I was nagged regularly by Frank Owen (part creator of the Association and its Mayfair club, distinguished editor of the South East Asia Command newspaper, *Phoenix*, and at this time editor of the *Daily Mail*) to attend Burma Star reunions at the Albert Hall. I didn't go, because I wasn't grabbed by the thought of reminiscences of old battles, bottles and bullshit. But when one year Frank added, 'Come to the room behind my box where the drinks are free', I went.

The room was packed, mostly with former Far East top brass including Admiral Power and General Rees, who I certainly didn't know but recognized. I had a couple of drinks and was about to enjoy myself, when Dai Rees came over and said: 'Were you with the Fourteenth Army?'

'No sir,' adding gratefully: 'I was in the Navy.'

For all his short stature (he was known as the Chota General) he had a compensatory voice. His: 'Power, I've an old shipmate of yours here!' had the admiral pushing his way through from the other side of the room.

Power glared (or maybe just stared) at me. 'What's your name?'

'K-Kersh, sir.'

'What were you on?'

'D-destroyers, sir.'

He frowned, concentrating, as he tried to place Kersh among his destroyer commanders. I was now attempting to blink away the sweat, but before he could ask another question and I had to admit that I'd been demobbed with the rank of Acting Able Seaman, General Rees came up with someone else to introduce to the admiral. I sidled out.

Where now? Tony Helliwell had told me that in the basement there was always an Artists Bar for the Reunion's cabaret, the nostalgic coming-together of artists who had entertained the troops in South East Asia. After a few drinks there with Tony and various now-forgotten or half-forgotten stars I decided it was time to go. But as I reached the door – literally then – Colonel Robbins, another active member of the Burma Star Association, arrived to announce: 'The Chief of the Imperial General Staff would like a word with the artists.'

It was still sufficiently close to my Service days for me automatically to freeze to attention as *the* great hero of Burma, Field Marshall Sir William Slim, medals clanking, came to the door and stopped just inches away from me. I was petrified.

Adopting his famous legs astride, hands behind back pose with his prognathous head set forward and at an angle, he looked me straight in the eye and said: 'I want to thank all you artists for coming here tonight. I want to thank you for all the work you did for the troops in the past. And I know – yes, know – that should the occasion again arise, you will come forward to do your bit. Again, thank you.' Slim extended his hand. I shook it. He about-turned and marched off followed by Colonel Robbins.

Why had he picked on me when, according to Tony Helliwell, the true artists behind me were jumping up and down in silent fury, pointing at themselves? Was it because I was the first face he saw?

According to Frank Owen's enquiries it was because he thought I was Jewish comedian Izzy Bonn.

A story told by Slim and passed to me by Frank Owen:

When Slim first became Chief of the Imperial General Staff he went to his room at the War Office, looked around, and saw on the wall framed instructions as to what to do in the event of fire. Among the prolix officialese was the order to go into the corridor and shout: 'Fire!'

Slim decided to try it out. 'Fire!' he cried. 'Fire!'

Two minutes later an aged messenger arrived with a bucket of coal.

As editor of the *Daily Mail* Frank Owen was involved in at least one of life's twist-in-the-tail dramas.

A veteran *Mail* reporter, Montague Smith, became so crippled by some ailment that he had to be brought to the office by car, then painfully make his way on crutches to his desk in the news room. Not unreasonably perhaps, Frank said to news editor Lindon Laing: 'We must retire him. He's been a great journalist over the years, but we just can't have a cripple on the reporting staff. It's ludicrous. We'll retire him with a generous pension. He'll be grateful.'

'He will not be grateful, mister.' (Lindon Laing called everyone mister.) 'He's an obsessive journalist. Like an alcoholic too old to be cured. Take his job away from him and he'll die. Literally.'

'But he's a cripple. We'll be doing him a favour.'

'He won't know that.'

The argument raged all that day and into the next – by which time Montague Smith had come to hear of what was going on and wept. Then Lindon Laing had an idea: 'Don't pension him off, mister. But it's winter. Snow and ice. Cold and slippery. So let us tell Monty to take some time off and that he doesn't *have* to come in until the weather's better. In the Spring. But say that his desk is always there. By then he'll have got into the habit of staying at home. After all, he's an old man.'

'Brilliant!' Frank exclaimed.

Lindon Laing was so delighted he took Montague Smith for a drink.

Next morning, because of the ritual of the years, Montague Smith went to the office as usual, only to remember, as he arrived, that he didn't have to be there that cruelly cold morning. On the other hand he'd been told he could come in whenever he wanted: his desk and telephone would always be there. So what the hell? He sat at his desk reading the papers – until he had a call from Frank Owen.

After his drink (or two) with Montague Smith, Lindon Laing had caught a train home. For some reason – the police deduced that he'd wanted to vomit – he'd stuck his head outside the carriage window and struck it on a projection in a tunnel.

Thus the twist in the tail: by coming to the office that morning Montague Smith was given the task of writing the obituary of the man who had saved his journalistic life.

Endpiece

Tony Helliwell's problems with 'Life's Problems' were to have reminiscent echoes with Patience Strong's 'Quiet Corner' in the *Sunday Mirror*. For years, going back to the 1930s on the *Sunday Pictorial*, Miss Strong contributed weekly, God-permeated verses under the 'Quiet Corner' heading, and when she suffered a long illness the *Sunday Mirror* agreed with her agent to reprint her pre-war poetry.

Here is a pastiche, made up as I went along, and without pause for breath as it were, and since it is not a bad imitation of the sort of stuff she wrote week after week, year after year, it is understandable that no one noticed that the poems had appeared before:

God is in His heaven while we are here below,
And as about our daily tasks so happily we go,
We give our thanks to Him above for helping us along.
He is our one and only hope. To Him we sing our song . . .

Et cetera, et cetera.

What makes Patience Strong's 'Quiet Corner' a fascinating item of Fleet Street memorabilia is how the sub-editor handling her material could easily check whether or not her verse scanned: invariably – absolutely no exceptions – it could be sung to the tune of 'MacNamara's Band'.

FIVE

A Legend In His Own By-Line

For one reason or another Kirschenblatt becomes Kersh, Feinstein – Phillips, Cohen – Coe, Winogradsky – Grade and Berkowitch – Birkin. But Boris Sienkiewicz remained defiantly Sienkiewicz, arguing that as a descendant of Henry K. Sienkiewicz, Nobel Prize-winning author of *Quo Vadis*, his name would add lustre to any publisher who had the courage to add him to his list. The trouble was that Boris's 'slices of life', as he called them, caused even the strongest publisher's reader to scratch, reach for the air freshener and take a heavily disinfected bath as he shuddered through novels featuring, in graphic and meticulous detail, suppurating tramps, refuse-tip whores, sub-normal alcoholics and disabled child molestors.

I met him when I was news and features editor of *The People* (this was in about 1952) and he came to the office with a story he'd discovered during researches into certain of the more bizarre happenings at Parker Street dosshouse in Covent Garden.

The teller of the tale was a former squadron leader who, while stationed near Secundehabad during the run-up to India's independence in 1947, had an inspiration: why give India to the Indians when you could sell it to them? He evolved an elaborate scheme which convinced wealthy locals that independence meant the country was up for sale and that he was the King's representative for the disposal of land in the area. Payments to be made in gold, in exchange for Deeds signed personally by His Majesty. (There would be a short waiting time for these since King George VI was up to his eyes signing them.)

The squadron leader collected hundreds of thousands of pounds in gold selling small farms and villages, then ambitiously sold Secundehabad airfield. The proud new owner mentioned the deal to his nephew, a newly qualified barrister.

Newly qualified barristers are notorious for their probing curiosity.

For reasons of political and diplomatic expediency, the affair was hushed up. After an *in camera* court martial the squadron leader was cashiered and sent to jail for 'grave misconduct'. The off-the-record explanation circulated around Secundehabad was 'Buggery. So for God's sake be discreet.'

Now he was an alcoholic dossing in Parker Street where he'd met Boris, to whom he offered a fifty-fifty deal to write and sell his memoirs.

After I'd had the story checked out, I took it to Sam Campbell (*The People*'s managing editor was still not yet officially its editor).

Sam read the story and beamed. 'It's a corker, chum.' I glowed. As' Corker' or 'Womb trembler' was the highest praise Sam could award a story, so 'chum' meant that the recipient was in favour for at least half-an-hour.

'How much does he want for it?' Sam asked.

'A thousand. He's got to split with the squadron leader.'

'Give him two-fifty.'

'Five hundred.'

'They'll take three-fifty. Christ chum, they're living in a bloody dosshouse.'

'Sienkiewicz isn't.'

'Who?'

'Boris Sienkiewicz. He wrote it,' I explained.

'See? . . . Sien? . . . God's bloody trousers! We can't have a by-line like that in the paper.'

'It's his name.'

'It's not one he's likely to have invented,' Sam retorted. 'You can have a by-line like See-wassisname in the *Observer*. They'd love it. Foreign. Obscure. Unpronounceable. Right up their street. I can see it across five columns on page one. But this is *The People*, chum. Think of your mum in her cottage trying to pronounce it.' (My mother still lived in her damp basement in the ineptly named Vinery Villas, but Sam was of the belief that all mothers of *People* readers lived in cottages.)

He flicked through the pages of the story again. 'Anyway, it'll need a lot of work on it.'

'It's very funny,' I ventured.

'That's it, chum,' Sam said approvingly. 'You've got it. What's wrong.' His voice became solemn. 'Crime, vice and evil aren't funny. They must be exposed. Rooted out. Published as a warning to others. Here's a man in the service of His Majesty, a man of high rank, ordinary soldiers dying, and this evil swine is conning innocent wogs out of their francs or coconuts or whatever they use out there . . . Oh no, it isn't funny. We'll expose him. That's what your Sheffield bus driver wants, isn't it?' (As their mums lived in cottages, so *People* readers were Sheffield bus drivers.)

'He's exposed himself,' I pointed out.

'Don't worry, chum; we'll expose him,' Sam assured me with a wink. He looked at his watch, tut-tutted and searched among the medicines on the table by his desk.

It dawned on me. 'Tommy Webb.'

Sam nodded and swallowed a variegated selection of pills and tablets. 'But don't tell that whatsit.'

'Sienkiewicz.'

'God, what a bloody name. Why doesn't he change it?'

'He's proud of it. His great-great something or other wrote *Quo Vadis*.'

Sam frowned. 'A bloody Papist?'

'It was a novel.'

'Fiction, eh? Don't worry, we'll turn it into fact.'

To borrow Sam Campbell's immortal phrase, I made an excuse and left.

Sam Campbell's early *People* triumphs included 'I Took A Lorry Ride To Shame', in which an anonymous and fictitious young lady warned other girls of the perils of hitch-hiking from Birmingham to London. It makes tame reading by today's standards, as does the report 'by a famous Harley Street specialist who must remain anonymous for professional reasons' that the flushing of railway train lavatories caused a higher incidence of polio among people who lived near railway tracks. But they were powerful stuff in the context of their time.

Harry Ainsworth hated them. He would have preferred series about clairvoyance, telepathy and spiritualism, or on the lines of 'What Life Has Taught Me' and 'If I Had My Time Again' by bishops who started as bootblacks, missionaries who were once burglars, and urchins whose hard work made them millionaires: Horatio Alger-flavoured Incitation to Self-improvement via the Christian Ethic.

Then came Sam's really big one: how the Messina brothers were living on the immoral earnings of a small army of Mayfair whores. Other popular Sunday papers, including the *Pictorial*, had thundered about the 'Maltese brothers'; Sam Campbell took the decision to name them and document their activities.

Gathering the evidence was to prove a Homeric undertaking. Sam put Duncan (Tommy) Webb in charge of the operation, assisted by staff and freelance reporters, crooked policemen and firms of private detectives.

Despite his smiling Irish charm and lively eyes twinkling behind thickly rimmed glasses, Tommy was a difficult man to get along with. Like so many crime reporters, his movements were shrouded in irrational mystery, and he spoke in coded, almost monosyllabic whispers. I recall a conversation at The Falstaff in Fleet Street between Tommy and Willy Jones of the *Daily Herald* which went almost exactly like this:

'See Chummy?'

A nod.

'Good?'

'Promised.'

'Still . . .?'

'Same one.'

'Exclusive?'

Another nod.

Tommy scratched his chin.

Willy tapped his nostril.

'No double cross?'

'You-know-who was also there.'

'Trust him?'

A shrug.

'Sensational.'

'Worth money.'

'Price?'

A shrug.

This went on for what seemed hours. I discovered later that they were discussing the advisability of putting a pound each way on a tip one of them had been given for the three-thirty at Epsom.

A recording of Tom Webb's pillow talk would have made fascinating listening.

The People's exposure of the Messinas was a major coup for Sam. It also made Duncan.Webb something of a legend in his own by-line, which, in turn, led to certain eccentricities.

On one occasion, driving with Tommy on an empty stretch of the Brighton road, he made an elaborate diversion because 'the Messinas are following. They've sworn to get me.' There was the night we left the Enterprise in Covent Garden and a well-known vegetable wholesaler staggered across the road from the Kembles Head, gave Tommy a great hug, muttered a scotch-thickened: 'The Mesheshinas shent me. Bang! Bang!' roared with laughter and tottered off into the night. Tommy ran back to the office to telephone the Press Association. Next day the *Daily Mail* ran the story: 'Journalist attacked by mob of Messina thugs.' He was also known to send himself telegrams warning him not to go to Shepherd Market that night because the Messinas were waiting for him.

What mattered was that having created Duncan Webb, as it were, Sam Campbell had to keep the legend alive. Thus Tommy reported dramatically of how, armed with an automatic pistol, he rowed round a remote Adriatic island in pursuit of Burgess and MacLean who escaped him by minutes. He investigated the diamond smugglers of Sierra Leone in a series that contained the memorable passage: 'The jungle was now so hot I would have welcomed the cooling breath of a leopard on my neck.'

Sam Campbell bought up all manner of villains and rewrote their stories as major Duncan Webb investigations. Sometimes Webb himself was astonished to read whose confessions he had obtained that week. So it came as no surprise to see the squadron leader's story presented as ANOTHER DRAMATIC DUNCAN WEBB EXCLUSIVE.

It began: 'After years of investigation I have finally completed my dossier on one of the most evil men in the annals of crime.'

(Alongside, a picture of Tommy in broad-brimmed black trilby, sucking at his pipe, frowning through his glasses, chest-deep in dossier.)

'At last, despite Air Ministry secrecy and obstruction, I can reveal how a senior R.A.F. officer perpetrated a fiendish and diabolical plot that netted him a vast fortune from the suffering poor in India.

'When I finally tracked him down to a seedy dosshouse some-where in London and confronted him, he shuddered visibly and confessed all.' (Montage picture of pipe-smoking, trilby-hatted, bespectacled Duncan Webb pointing an accusing forefinger at a grey, unidentifiable down and out.) 'I'm glad the truth has come out at last,' he sobbed. 'Only you could have found me, Mr Webb. Now I want to tell you my shameful tale as a warning to other squadron leaders tempted by a foul lust for tainted gold. . .' (*The People* really did read like that, even then.)

Great stuff – until Boris Sienkiewicz saw it. After bewilderment came the near-apoplectic rage. It was his story, not Duncan Webb's. It had been completely rewritten without his know-ledge or consent. Had the series appeared as written, and with his by-line, it would have made him famous. Publishers would be queuing at his door. In any case, the story had been falsified and he and the squadron leader would sue *The People* for every penny we possessed. . .

Sam Campbell took it in his stride. 'They didn't sign a con-tract, did they?'

'No.'

'There you are then, chum. All we did was common *People* practice in adapting the story to our style. There's been no com-plaint from the villain, has there?'

'No. I paid him his share in cash and got a receipt in full and final settlement. By now half the money's in the Kembles Head till. It's Sienkiewicz I'm worried about. Apart from suing he's threatening to march around London with a sandwich board accusing *The People* and Tommy of being liars, cheats and God alone knows what else.'

'If he does, get Bow Street to arrest him.' Sam closed his eyes and his face wrinkled in thought: he was plainly visualizing the sandwich board. As he opened his eyes, unwrinkled his face and reached for a box of pills: 'We don't really want trouble though, do we chum? Let's give him a job. As an ape.' (To Sam, all reporters were 'apes'.)

'He's not really a journalist.'

Sam beamed. 'Great. I'll fire him after a month's trial.'

'I'm fairly sure he'd rather starve.'

'Ungrateful bastard.'

A couple of weeks later I was walking through Leicester Square when I heard a fearsome shriek. I turned (as did others) to face a fist-shaking Boris. 'Revenge!' he hissed. 'I'll have my revenge!' Had he then made the Sign of the Cross instead of a two-fingered salute it would have been a moment worthy of Robert Taylor in the appalling film of great-great Henryk's epic novel.

Of other series that came along, the most memorable, for a number of reasons, was bought from a prostitute-cum-black-mailer who had found God and was anxious to make public confession of her sins before entering a nunnery. It cost *The People* the huge sum (for those days) of £5,000 – in cash. She wanted to donate the money in anonymous packages to various charities before taking her vows. Duncan Webb wrote the story after lengthy interviews in the office and at her Lancaster Gate flat. It was meaty stuff, and she signed every page of manuscript to confirm that its contents were accurate – although this was not to inhibit Sam Campbell, in the course of rewriting it, from inserting various well-known (if anonymous) peers of the realm, distinguished clergymen and famous stars of the silver screen. ('She's not likely to get a copy of *The People* in a bloody nunnery, is she chum?') To complete the package, photographs were taken of the lady lying on her bed drinking champagne, adjusting a stocking in Hyde Park and puffing at a cigarette in a foot-long holder while wearing a mink coat we'd hired for the day, with Brompton Oratory in the background.

It was a great series, one that would run for weeks. The first instalment was headlined: WOMAN OF THE NIGHT FINDS GOD – THANKS TO DUNCAN WEBB, and, after a brief précis of her evil life and redemption, flashed back to her childhood in a Wiltshire rectory, her private school education, her life among the local aristocracy and her service in the Wrens. Next Week: HOW I BEGAN MY LIFE OF SHAME.

Splendid stuff, and much of it true. A Mrs X did live in that block of flats at Lancaster Gate (although a floor above our client); she was the daughter of a clergyman, she had been to a private school, she had been (indeed still was) closely involved with the Wiltshire aristocracy, and she had served as a Wren officer. The only problems that she was not, and never had been, a blackmailing prostitute – as a solicitor's letter was quick to point out. On the contrary, she was a highly respectable widow devoted to good works and on the point of marrying a barrister who was also a Conservative candidate guaranteed a safe seat at the next by-election.

Sam's normal reaction to threats of legal action was uncomplicated: he'd send back a one-sentence letter giving the name of our solicitors, Simmons and Simmons, and their address in Bishopsgate – and hope for the best. After a few pills and tablets he'd explain: 'Look chum, they're not likely to sue. They can't afford it. It's defensive. It looks good if somebody says to them: "What's all this I read in *The People* about you?" and chummy replies: "I'm suing them for libel." Sounds good, doesn't it?'

Most libel actions resulted from Sam being a great writer of what he called his 'witty' or 'human' headlines. I was once involved in eight libel actions, all at the same time, not because of stories I'd written but because Sam had rewritten them to suit such headlines.

To be fair, he did have pre-publication consultations with the office lawyer, Hugh Davidson. 'If we have to pay,' he'd ask, 'what'll it cost?'

Hugh Davidson, a shrewd Scot, would work it out. 'If they do go ahead we could probably settle out of court for two thousand' (or whatever his estimate).

Sam would decide whether the story was worth the sum mentioned, on top of what he might have already paid. If it wasn't, he'd amend the headline.

On this occasion he realized he was beaten, even without legal advice. The damage had been done. The complainant's fiancé was a barrister and a court case would have warranted a fearsome sum in costs and damages (apart from unpleasant publicity). The paper had been cleverly set up by the woman living on the floor below Mrs X, and who had borrowed her name and background.

A cheque for considerable damages (Sam would never reveal how much) was sent to Mrs X's solicitors.

Duncan Webb wanted to call in the police to track down our now-vanished client and our £5,000. Again aware of unpleasant publicity, this time if a prosecution got to court, Sam vetoed the suggestion. 'Let's put it down to experience,' he said, shaking his head at the venal wickedness of post-war society. 'Where have all the Christian virtues gone?' he sighed as he reached for his Benzedrine inhalant.

The incident faded into memory and was half-forgotten until, some two years later, I received a letter from Leonard Coulter, our man in New York. He told of a meeting in a bar with a woman who, hearing he represented *The People*, and being full of vodka, told him of a great trick she had played on the paper by pretending to be a blackmailing whore while she was, in fact, nothing of the sort. But, Coulter wrote, she said she'd been able to fabricate the story thanks to her boyfriend who had inspired her to do it. 'She told me who it was, but you know how difficult those bloody Polish names are. I think it was Boris something.'

I thought it wiser to say nothing to either Sam Campbell or Tommy Webb.

A libel action that did get to court was brought by Randolph Churchill to whom, *The People* had referred as 'a paid hack'. Churchill wrote a letter of protest, which *The People* published – except for a vital last paragraph in which the paper admitted being in the wrong and apologized for it. So Churchill sued and was awarded £5,000.

Needless to say, it was all down to Sam, but the man named in the writ was the luckless editor, Harry Ainsworth.

Another of Sam Campbell's judgements . . .

Billy was an amiable barber, part-time musician and drug addict who I first knew during the war when he deserted from the RAF and worked as a drummer with various short-handed bands until his inevitable arrest. We met again in post-war Soho just before he was arrested for possession of marijuana. I visited him at Chelmsford Prison where he was cutting hair (taking him some cigarettes which I had to hand to the warder in the visiting

room and which Billy swore he never saw again). On his release
he came to see me at *The People* where he told me that for a time
one of his fellow-prisoners had been atom spy Klaus Fuchs.

'He was a nice bloke. Wrote me a poem. You can have it. I
owe you one.' Billy handed me a verse written in pencil on a
sheet of toilet paper. I thanked him, bought him a couple of
gins, gave him a fiver and took the poem to Sam Campbell.

'Poetry?' said Sam. '*Poetry*?!' and I knew then that it was
doomed never to appear in the paper. He frowned from behind
his desk and continued: 'Fuchs. That's a couple of years ago,
eh chum? . . . Poetry!' Sam rolled his eyes, groped for the first
tablets within reach, swallowed one and again said: '*Poetry*! You
want me to publish a poem by some intellectual traitor? This
isn't the *Observer*, or the *New Statesman and Nation*, or that
magazine. . .'

'*Poetry Today*?' I suggested.

Sam glowered. 'Don't tell me you read poetry.'

'Only on lavatory walls.'

Sam nodded. 'That's where these poets train. They're all sodo-
mites. No chum, just tear it up.'

I didn't. I tucked it away with other papers and then completely forgot about it until I came across it while checking
something for this book. It goes:

> To Billy
>
> Thus let your scissors serve men's vanity:
> What people truly want, that they deserve.
> Yet in the execution of their wish
> Remain your cunning scissors' artful master,
> And let discretion, sympathy and grace
> Guide their keen edge with beauty's noble aim.
>
> Klaus

It's not all that bad.

*   *   *

The Sienkiewicz story caused reactions when I told it to the
family at Askew Road. Hearing the name, Uncle Sam said: 'A
Yiddisher fellow, eh? Polish.'

'His family was originally Polish,' I replied 'but he's a Catholic.'

'A convert?' asked my mother, appalled.

'No, his family have always been Catholics. Not all Poles are Jews.'

'If they was,' said my grandmother, 'We wouldn't have had to run away from them.'

'That's it!' Sam cried triumphantly. 'You've hit the nail on the whatsit. So OK, it's a Polish name. But it's got to be a Yiddisher Polish name, because whoever heard of Polish Christians coming over here to escape the pogroms? You follow?'

'His family was probably converted to Catholics under torture,' said Uncle Dave. 'I read about it. The Imposition.'

'The Inquisition was in Spain,' I said.

'Don't contradict your uncle!' my mother shouted.

'Spain. Poland. What difference?' Uncle Lew demanded. 'The bastards are everywhere.'

'So you got books on torture, eh?' said Sam to Dave, frowning.

'Also books on how to deal with food poisoning,' Dave retorted.

Lew's wife, Katie, sighed. 'Here we go again with his poisoning.'

'Don't take notice,' said my mother, recognizing storm clouds.

'So you're taking his side!' Sam shouted – and Sienkiewicz was forgotten as the conversation dissolved into the familiar pattern of a table-thumping quarrel.

SIX

Monkey Brains
And Mayhem

Since Sam Campbell's amorality was absolute, he regarded himself as being highly moral. Stories in such publications as *Confidential*, the *New York Enquirer* and *France Dimanche* from which rival editors shuddered away or, at best, approached with circumlocutory euphemism, Sam turned into page one evangelism. The formula was simple:

'Buckingham Palace must waste no time before denying the monstrously wicked story now circulating in America about Princess Margaret and famous comedian Danny Kaye. These filthy guttersnipes have the effrontery to suggest. . .' Then followed a verbatim repeat of the fantasies of the journal concerned, ending with a thunderous: 'THESE EVIL LIES MUST BE DENIED IMMEDIATELY!'

I wrote more variations of that story than I care to recall involving film stars, politicians, sportsmen, the aristocracy and other public figures.

One I didn't write concerned Princess Margaret's romance with Group Captain Peter Townsend. *The People* was the first paper to get the news. . . But was it true? Surely not. On the other hand. . . Since there was no way of telling, and since the Royal Family were sacrosanct (apart from the Duke of Windsor), Sam solved the problem in typical fashion:

'It is high time for the British public to be made aware of the scandalous rumours about Princess Margaret asserting that the Princess is in love with a divorced man and that she wishes to marry him.' Naturally, *The People* demanded a denial from the

Palace since such a marriage 'would fly in the face of Royal and Christian tradition'.

It was left to the *Mirror* to follow this with its famous poll: 'Should Princess Margaret be allowed to marry him?' and was condemned by the Press Council because the poll was 'contrary to the best traditions of British journalism'.

Among the Council members who condemned the *Mirror* was Harry Ainsworth.

Sam was a powerful preacher of morality and its concomitant, sincerity. From time to time he would lecture his reporters on the need to believe, to write from the heart. As he once put it to me, feet on desk and toying with a mosaic of variegated pills: 'If you don't believe in what you're writing when you write it Cyril, you'll communicate your lack of faith to the readers. You won't get wombs trembling if you sound insincere, chum.'

Thus I was in something of a quandary when, having written a story positively throbbing with sincerity about the outrageously high percentage of bread and fat shown by analysis to be contained in the sausages of a famous grocery chain, Sam asked me the following week to write a piece on the dangers to health of sausages made with too much meat, stressing that it was far wiser to purchase sausages with a generous percentage of fat and bread. Various doctors (anonymous for professional reasons) were to be quoted confirming this, with the previously offending product cited as an exemplary example.

It transpired that after the first story the grocers concerned threatened to cancel their advertising not only with *The People*, but with all of Odhams Press, which meant the *Daily Herald* and a vast magazine empire that included *Woman, John Bull, Ideal Home, Illustrated* and *Picturegoer*. The loss of revenue would have been enormous, and sufficient boardroom muscle had been applied to compel Sam to run this second story.

I learned about this later; at the time all I knew was that I was being asked, within a period of seven days, to write a story diametrically opposed to the earlier one. 'How', I asked news editor Charles Rowe, 'am I supposed to be utterly sincere, convinced in my own heart, of a story that takes such a contrary line?'

Charlie, occupied at the time with the runners at Epsom, shrugged. 'Better ask Sam.'

I did. Sam sighed and looked at me with the expression of combined pity and suppressed rage common among Fleet Street editors when dealing with idiots (i.e. members of the staff who questioned their genius). 'What I said was that you must be sincere while writing the story. That's what I'm always telling people. How long is it going to take you to write it? Half an hour?' His hands trembled as he snarled: 'Can't you be bloody sincere for even half a bloody hour?'

I tried, but my heart wasn't in it. Not that it mattered: Sam's rewrite contained enough apostolic fervour to convert *People* readers to completely all-fat sausages for a fortnight.

After his distinguished career as a war correspondent, Arthur (Tony) Helliwell returned to write the 'Follow Me Around' column. Devised by Harry Ainsworth, it was intended in those austere times to expose London's post-war spivery and the excesses of the capital's black market-oriented night life. As it turned out, the spivs were referred to by nicknames (Robert the Razor, Vodka Roy, Cucumber Bill), while that part of the column devoted to the night life of which Tony was inordinately fond contained so many plugs for club owners it became known as the Railway Column (puff. . . puff). None the less, thanks to Tony's writing, it made entertaining copy, and Tony, always nattily dressed in waisted suits, starched collars and Windsor-knotted ties, and with his pencil-line moustache, one-size-too-small trilby hat and halitosis, became something of a name in the land.

Those were the glum years when nobody going abroad could take more than £25-worth of foreign currency unless they could demonstrate that vital overseas trade negotiations were involved. From time to time Tony Helliwell would investigate the British who visited such places as Monte Carlo, the Venice Lido and Miami. Those on essential business – boxing promoters, bookmakers and night club owners – were named and praised for their self-sacrificial suffering when they would rather be on the rainswept beaches of Brighton and Scarborough; evil (if anonymous) villains and their women lapping up the sun on black market foreign currency were severely castigated. Occasionally Tony went further afield, and on one trip visited Hong Kong from where he filed his famous Monkey Brains Scandal.

It told of the bizarre ritual practised by an aged (if anonymous) Chinese millionaire in the dining room of his heavily guarded mansion. His guests were also enormously wealthy and, like their host, worried about waning sexual prowess. They would sit round a table on the surface of which a series of holes had been bored. Beneath the table were servants holding young, live monkeys. At a signal the monkeys were lifted so that the tops of their heads protruded through the holes. These were sliced off in the manner of boiled eggs and the aphrodisiac warm brains spooned out and eaten.

A sensational report, it led to a furious outcry from Britain's animal lovers, and an even more vociferant protest from the affluent and influential citizens of the Crown Colony. Via the Colonial Office, their trade centre in London and gleeful rival newspapers, they protested that the story was a disgusting, insulting, revolting, gutter journalistic lie. Who was the evil millionaire who practised such barbaric acts? Name him, they cried, or retract the outrageous libel on the good name of the people of Hong Kong.

This proved to be difficult: the story had been sold to Tony for cash by a local freelance who now denied ever having met Helliwell. Sam Campbell, although nettled by the furore, had no intention of sending Tony back to Hong Kong to find proof of the story. 'He'll get murdered by opium crazed savages. They've got those Tongs out there. Secret societies. Did you see that picture with Edward G. Robinson? He was the hatchet man from Sacramento. Had a little chopper up his sleeve to kill people with.' I stared at Sam, astonished that he had ever been to the cinema and, more important, that he was concerned about the possible death of a member of his staff. After all, wouldn't it make a corking womb trembler? He brought me back to earth when he added: 'Cost us a bloody fortune in insurance for his widow. No, what we'll do is get support over here. Ask the Chinks in London about it. They'll know.'

It is a regrettable fact that when Fleet Street's stars are in trouble because of a story they are rarely asked (or volunteer) to get themselves out of it. That is left to others. So Stanley Buchanan and I were told to interview Chinese in London to corroborate the Monkey Brains Scandal. (Such was the eclectic structure of *The People* at the time, only a month's wages would have been due to next of kin if drug-crazed hatchet men chopped off *our* heads.)

In those days there was no Chinatown in the Gerrard Street area of Soho. I recall a few restaurants in the area (Ley On's, the Shanghai and the Universal come to mind), but the largest Chinese community was centred around Limehouse in dockland. So Bucky and I went there. Well, we meant to go there, but when we reached Aldgate at the edge of the East End, Bucky said: 'Sod this for a lark.' He tore a corner from the *Evening News* in his pocket and chewed at it. The effect was calming, but not sufficiently so. 'Let's have a pint.'

Over a beer in a pub near Aldgate East underground station Bucky peered into his glass, its surface covered with *Evening News* pulp, and said with an aggression never shown in the office: 'I've got a wife and son waiting for me at Epsom, so why should I get my head chopped off by some Chink just to prove some bloody story I didn't even write? These docks are worse than Glasgow's. Do you know that? My father was a foreman at the docks there. Do you know why foremen up there wear bowler hats and need a good sense of smell? Because the rivetters drop red-hot rivets on the foreman's head, and the foreman had to be able to smell his bowler burning before the rivet falls through the top of the hat to the top of his head.' With a mournful nod: 'And I haven't even got a bowler hat. I should have kept my tin hat from the army. I could have bought thousands of them. War surplus. Could have made a fortune. All you do is polish the insides and they become bowls for electric fires. Too late now.'

I shared a sigh with him and said: 'So you haven't got an electric fire or a tin hat or a bowler hat. What do you want to do?'

'What do you reckon?'

'Turn round and go to Soho?'

'I'd rather have a woman.'

'Plenty in Soho.'

Bucky shook his head. 'All got pox. And what makes you think the Chinks in Soho haven't got hatchets?'

'More likely to be razors.'

He shuddered. 'So what do we do?'

Although I was a reasonably efficient investigative journalist in those days, I shared Bucky's lack of stomach for the assignment, and my absence of enthusiasm was reinforced when he tore another strip from the *Evening News* and said: 'Ever been in the kitchen of a Chinese restaurant? I have. Sam wasn't wrong about the hatchets. Little shiny ones. They use them for everything: chopping, slicing, carving. Bloody clever really – except it could be our balls... Let's have another drink.' After I'd ordered them he continued: 'and what makes Sam think that Chinky waiters in Wapping know what goes on behind the barbed wire of a millionaire's mansion in Hong Kong?'

I agreed. 'In any case, they were probably born over here or came pre-war from Peking and Shanghai.'

Over more drink we talked ourselves out of continuing our enquiries. 'So what'll we do?' Bucky asked finally.

A couple of whiskies provided me with the answer. 'Members of London's Chinese community trembled and paled (can Chinese pale?) when we mentioned the loathsome monkey brain cult. Terrified of the vengeance of the dreaded Tongs, they swore us to anonymity as green fingers of fog ... '

'What fog?' Bucky interrupted with a hiccup. 'It's a high summer.' Solemnly: 'Must get our facts right.'

'All right, no fog ... When they spoke to us in murky, gas-lit alleyways, the walls dripping damp, unchanged since the days when Jack the Ripper and Fu Manchu plied their evil trades, et cetera, et cetera. Leave it to me. Sam will love it.'

'The pound notes paid to our informants won't do our expenses any harm,' said Bucky. 'But are you sure it'll work?' He felt in his pocket for the *Evening News* and registered astonishment when he saw that all that remained was half of a sports page. 'Don't you think we ought to have some names in it? What's the Chink equivalent of Smith and Jones?'

'Chang?'

'Lee?'

I laughed. 'I'll interview my Uncle Max. Max Lee.'

Bucky frowned. Clutching the bar for support: 'I knew you were a bloody oriental. But not a Chink. I thought you came from Palestine.'

This triggered a familiar, alcohol-inspired, exchange.

'You're the bloody foreigner,' I replied. 'I was born in England. You weren't. So here's an idea Bucky: why don't you go back to your own bloody country?' When I repeated 'bloody foreigner' Bucky screamed an obscenity and raised his fists. We were thrown out of the pub, I to catch a tube to Baker Street, Bucky to buy another evening paper to console him on the train journey to Epsom.

It wasn't just the fear of physical violence that made me support Stanley Buchanan in the aborting of our enquiries. It was the fear of such violence coupled to the absurdity of its invitation: the pursuit of a salvage operation for a palpably dubious story. A further consideration: Sam Campbell would have been furious if we'd returned to the office with genuine interviews that revealed ignorance or denial of the Monkey Brains Scandal. Sam wanted confirmation – any confirmation, anonymous or otherwise, no questions asked.

So I wrote the story much as I'd outlined it to Bucky (if rather less purplish and with the omission of Fu Manchu) and Sam did love it. But he didn't use it. He had a better idea. He arranged for Norman Dodd, the rent-a-quote MP for Dartford, to promise *People* readers that he would be raising the matter in the House of Commons, enabling Sam to parry further criticism and mockery with the reply: 'Since the matter is to be discussed in Parliament it would be inappropriate to make further comment at this stage.' Norman Dodd never did raise the subject in the House: it was a bit too rich for the blood of even that self-publicist. Not that it mattered. Such is the ephemeral quality of so much popular journalism, the Monkey Brains Scandal soon faded into saloon bar reminiscence.

Fear of violence and threats of violence are occasional journalistic hazards. I was assaulted only once, an incident shared with Robert J. (Bob) Edwards, at that time a young reporter who had newly joined *The People* from *Tribune* magazine.

The occasion was a story involving a Work at Home scheme operating from Great Yarmouth in Norfolk. Advertisements in provincial newspapers promised rich rewards to people who could transform shells (cockle, winkle, whelk) into brooches, necklaces and other jewellery by following the simple instructions contained with every £2 kit of shells (about £18 by today's standards). The rip-off was simple: nobody ever achieved the standards required by the Great Yarmouth conmen. The workers sent off their money, toiled to make the jewellery, paid for its postage to Norfolk, only to receive a mimeographed: 'Sorry, not good enough. Try again with another £2 kit.' What made the racket particularly nasty was its appeal to the old, the handicapped and other house-bound poor, anxious to supplement modest incomes.

I gathered the facts. Since the people at Great Yarmouth were known to be slippery, with matching lawyers, it was decided that when I confronted them I would have a witness to confirm the accuracy of what I later wrote. The witness was Bob, my choice influenced partly by the fact that he owned a motor car.

Progressively, various directors of the firms concerned were 'not available' for comment. Finally we were left with just one, whom we knew to be a local police officer. What we didn't know was that he was also the local heavyweight judo champion.

I rang the bell of his house. He opened the door. I said: 'We are from *The People* newspaper . . . ' and got no further. With a screamed obscenity he grabbed each of us by the collar and rushed us down the garden path and over the gate into the road.

'We must go to the police,' said Bob angrily, dusting himself down.

'We've just been to the bloody police,' I retorted, carefully testing my body for breakages. 'Want to go back and lodge a complaint? We've offered him the right of reply and you're a witness to what he said.'

'But all he said was "fucking bastards" which we can hardly put in the paper,' Bob protested.

'*Family* paper,' I corrected. 'Don't forget your mum in her little cottage in the country and those virgin-eared Sheffield bus drivers. Suits me fine if his reply is unprintable.'

We drove off, Bob unable to resist a two-finger salute before he accelerated round the corner.

Some months later I had the pleasure of being in court when the directors of the Work at Home scheme were sent to prison, the longest sentence – four years if memory serves me – going to the policeman. Bob soon left behind him the hazards of witnessing other people's stories: from graduating as a reporter and feature writer he went on to edit, among other publications, the *Daily Express*, the *People* and *Sunday Mirror* and climaxed his career as Senior Group Editor of Mirror Group Newspapers.

There was also an attempted assault. During the Messina Brothers investigations Tommy Webb, freelance photographer Bill Breeze and I went to Mayfair's Shepherd Market – Tommy to point out certain prostitutes, Bill to 'snatch' pictures of them, paparazzi style, while I was to keep a protective eye on Bill's plump and diminutive person. Once he had pointed out our objectives Tommy would stay in the car, its engine running – not, he repeatedly emphasized, for reasons of safety, but in case a quick escape was needed.

With the proper camera such pictures can be taken from inside a car at safe distance, but Bill's turned out to be a Zeiss Palmos, a great, heavy, pre-war German black box of a beast, its battered case held together with string, elastic bands and sticky brown paper. When Tommy stopped the car and pointed out a street corner at which the first woman he wanted photographed was standing among a group of other ladies, Bill climbed out of the car, set the light factor, then progressively adjusted the focal length as he walked towards her. Since one eye was fixed on the view finder and the other was closed, I had to guide him along the pavement – a paparazzi portrayed by an over-the-top Charlie Drake. Since everyone else in the street was staring at us, it didn't take long for the ladies at the corner to become aware of a tubby little man with an outsize box camera being propelled towards them.

A popular fashion accessory of the time was a long umbrella fitted with a ferrule like a 6-inch bayonet tapering to a wickedly sharp point. All the women at the street corner carried one and as we drew nearer, and as though by command, all were suddenly swung into a two-handed horizontal position ready for an order to charge.

'Have you taken the picture yet?' I stammered.

'Can't,' Bill replied. 'Got to get nearer. Haven't a long enough focal depth.'

I realized I was sweating. 'But . . . '

'No sodding buts,' Bill interrupted. 'And I'll never take it at all if your hand doesn't stop making my shoulder shake.'

When we were about 15 feet away, somebody did give an order. It was a truly terrifying moment, which can be fully understood only if you, too, have been the target of six obscenity-screaming whores in a bayonet charge.

As we turned to run Bill dropped his camera. Because of its make-and-mend repairs, it hit the pavement and disintegrated.

Tommy Webb was right: we did need a quick getaway, for while the women were slowed by long skirts and 6-inch stiletto heels, we were hampered by Bill's tiny legs. We won by seconds, umbrella ferrules hammering the car as we drove off . . . and then respectable citizens began to shout and gesticulate. Tommy drove the car to Park Lane where we discovered that not only was its side peppered with deep ferrule dents, but an umbrella was swaying in the panelling.

Bill Breeze received no compensation and little sympathy for his loss of camera. 'One of the hazards of being a freelance,' Sam explained, replaced Bill with Stan Janus, who owned a 35mm Leica.

During the Messina Brothers investigations Stanley Buchanan was instructed to pick up various whores to establish that they were operating from premises owned or leased by the Messinas. Having confirmed their occupancy, he should then have 'made an excuse and left'. Bucky invariably stayed: he hated to waste the firm's money.

*　　　*　　　*

From time to time I was able to offer Tony Helliwell items for his 'Follow Me Around' column. With a photographer I went to see Maurice Chevalier at the Mayfair Hotel on his first post-war visit to London. My intention was to get him to explain his collaboration with the Germans. But as soon as he saw the cameraman he started to gag. 'I take off my 'at. . . I throw it in ze air . . . I catch it . . . I wink . . .' The photographer snapped away. When he stopped to change the film, I asked a question on the lines of: 'Why did you perform for the occupying Nazis?' His reply was a puffed: 'I stick out ze lip . . . I raise ze leg . . . I come to London because every time I see Buckingham Palace I want to zing ze song. . . I smile and zay: "Ooh la la."' He reminded me of Gerald's description of Mrs Duncan's Jesus Christ – and was about as revealing.

Finally the photographer ran out of film, Maurice Chevalier ran out of breath, and I ran out of interest.

Back in the office I wrote a story on the lines of:

'Why was Chevalier silent? Why didn't he deny being a traitor who collaborated with the Germans? If he is a traitor why is he welcomed in Britain?' But since he was a Frog, and there was no sex or sadism or espionage to compensate, Sam Campbell didn't think that it mattered. (Not that Sam wasn't interested in famous show business personalities: he sent me to see Josie Collins, star of the First World War musical, *The Maid of the Mountains*. She couldn't remember anything.)

I offered the Chevalier story to Tony Helliwell. Since there was no way of presenting it except as a highly critical story of a star who had to be named, Tony didn't use it.

There was a night in the old Back Bar of the Café Royal when Peter Ustinov regaled us with tale after tale after tale. I had to assume they were droll: all were told in French. With the rest of the audience I listened with a fixed grin and from time to time a chortle.

That story wasn't used, either.

When Jack Hawkins was at the height of his popularity I interviewed him at the studio where he was making *The Fallen Idol*. I noticed that Hawkins had a hole in the heel of a sock. It was one of those bits of utter trivia for which fans have an insatiable appetite, since they demonstrate that even megastars can be human.

This story Tony did use. It began: 'Who is the famous film star?' . . . and told of the hole in the sock. But it didn't name the star.

I didn't even try to interview composer Richard Strauss when there was a press conference for him. (Johann would have had a hard time getting into *The People* even if Duncan Webb produced a dossier proving he'd stolen 'The Blue Danube' from Irving Berlin.) At least Richard Strauss, when pressed, was vocal in his denial of being a Nazi, or supporting Hitler, or of there being any fascist connotations in Nietzsche's *Thus Spake Zarathustra*. Indeed, he added for good measure, during the war some of his best musicians had been Jews.

SEVEN

El Vino Veritas

The El Vino wine bar in Fleet Street is shabby, draughty and otherwise uncomfortable. Despite these drawbacks (or maybe, via some guilt complex, because of them) it is much favoured by lawyers and journalists – and a grey concomitant hanging-on to the latter's expense accounts: shady informants, pachydermous public relations people and dubious literary agents clutching plastic document cases bulging with dog-eared manuscripts. Most embarrassing, old journalists who have forgotten the ephemeral quality of Fleet Street and return to El Vino hoping to be remembered and encouraged to refight battles for scoops now exclusive only to their own memories.

From time to time the establishment itself makes news: for refusing to serve men not wearing jackets and ties, or women who prefer to stand at the bar rather than sit at a table. It also has a reputation for barring customers, although the great days for this were during the autocratic reign of Frank Bower, a pompous, florid barrel of a man with a studied taste for gold-rimmed granny glasses, Edwardian-style suits, boutonnières, butterfly collars and floral waistcoats, who boasted of breakfasting on game pie and claret and lunching on tinned salmon. Frank's excommunications were arbitrary and whimsical. Thus, as Frank was large, Vicky the cartoonist was small. One day Vicky sneaked round the bar and put on Frank's bowler hat. It swallowed his entire head. Everyone laughed except Frank Bower, who barred him. That's how it was with Frank.

El Vino sells only wines and spirits and Frank relished

occasions when innocents came in and asked for a beer. 'Bier? Bier?' (as though rehearsing Lady Bracknell in the handbag scene). 'I'm not an undertaker' – and waved them out.

I was present when the then editor of *Illustrated*, Tony Clarkson, asked Bower what he was giving up for Lent. Was it, he ventured, short measure? Frank chose not to accept the remark as an attempt at gin-inspired badinage and Tony was barred.

I came close to being barred on two occasions. Once on a winter's day, with the draught knifing through the swing doors, I suggested that El Vino's was the only bar in London where the red wine had to be kept in the fridge to bring it to room temperature. (I was let off with a caution.) The second occasion was when I told Frank, who had a compulsive need to insinuate himself, that I didn't like my conversations interrupted by tradesmen. This was Bower-baiting on a grand scale and the effect was predictable. He went the colour of the claret that would drown his customers if, as seemed likely, he exploded, then went on to splutter that he was not a tradesman but a Vintner, a Freeman of the City of London, a Knight of St Colomba, and a man who lived on the North side of Clapham Common who took his daughters on an annual Christmas treat to view the cribs on display in the windows of West End and Knightsbridge department stores. When he'd recovered his breath: 'You're barred.'

I had a moment of inspiration. 'OK, but within 20 minutes the whole of Fleet Street will know that you barred me because you're anti-Semitic.'

Ever the shrewd anti-Semitic businessman, he told me two anti-Catholic jokes and gave me a glass of house red.

The one man whose very entry through the swing doors intimidated Frank Bower was the wonderfully eccentric former Lieutenant-Colonel of the Royal Dragoons, A. D. Wintle MC. During the First World War he had lost four fingers of one hand and the sight of an eye. He could see out of the other only with the aid of a blue-tinted, powerfully lensed monocle (although, with the connivance of an ophthalmic surgeon in the RAMC who had been a friend of his father, Wintle contrived to be passed fit for active service in the 1939–45 war). A monocled David Niven at his most suave, elegant and military and, like

67

Niven, a superb raconteur, Wintle was always polite and charming – except to Frank Bower whom he addressed in exclamation marks as though the Vintner and Freeman of the City of London was his batman.

'Bower! Dry sherry! Make sure the glass is clean!'

'Yes, Colonel.'

'Bower! Close the door!'

'Yes, Colonel. Right away, Colonel.'

I was having a drink with Wintle on the day that Frank, after much face-mopping with a polka-dot tablecloth of a handkerchief, found the courage to say to Wintle:

'Your initials are A. D. aren't they Colonel?'

A crisp: 'Yes.'

A deep breath. 'May I ask what they stand for?'

A brusque: 'You may not.'

'W-why not?' asked a flustered Bower.

'Why do you wish to know?'

'I . . . well, I'd like to call you . . . as I do other favoured clients. . .' Bower kneaded the handkerchief in the mottled parsnips that served as fingers. In a great falsetto rush: 'by your Christian name.'

Wintle frowned. 'Out of the question.'

'B-but why?'

'It would presume a degree of familiarity I am not prepared to accept.'

'I can't keep calling you Colonel,' Bower almost howled.

Wintle removed his monocle and stared at him. 'Thousands of men did,' he replied drily. As he screwed the monocle back in place: 'And how is your health?'

'My . . . health?' Bower spluttered, his face a short-fused aubergine. 'Why . . . why . . .' he swallowed. Suspiciously: 'Why are you interested in my health?'

'I was brought up always to be polite to my inferiors,' Wintle replied blandly.

Within 5 minutes the gallant Colonel had committed sufficient offences to have been banned for several lifetimes, but it was me that Bower could have happily strangled when Wintle said: 'Time for another drink, Cyril?' and I replied: 'I'd love one, Alfred.'

*   *   *

It was at El Vino that I made a witticism memorable only because at least fifty people thought it worth claiming as their own. It involved Rupert Denny, a journalist whose career took off (as I pieced it together via his fragmented admissions) in 1945 when he was a young reporter on the *Daily Telegraph*. Lord Camrose, then the paper's proprietor, telephoned the editor saying he wanted six cases of first-class champagne for a party. With the barrels of the artillery still warm, the Allies had greater priorities than the import of champagne, so where were half-a-dozen first-class cases of the stuff to come from? It did not take the editor long to arrive at an editor's solution: he rang the news editor. He, in turn, looked for his most expendable reporter and ordered Denny to find his lordship six cases of first-class champagne.

Enquiries among older members of the staff by a baffled Denny elicited the fact that the St James's area was the pre-war centre of the up-market wine trade. Denny went there, entered the first wine merchant's he found, and when he said that the champagne was for Lord Camrose, owner of the *Telegraph*, six pre-war cases soon emerged from the cellars.

Of such simplicity is brilliance made. Some days later his lordship telephoned the editor to ask: 'What's the name of the fellow who got me the champagne?'

'The name's just slipped my mind,' the editor lied.

'He knows his stuff. Great bubbly. Must know his wines, too. Is he our wine editor?'

'W-wine editor? Good lord, no. We don't have one.'

'Don't have one? The *Telegraph*? Why on earth not?'

'The war, sir. We hardly needed a wine editor during the war.'

A grudging: 'S'pose not.' Then an enthusiastic: 'But you'll need one now, eh? Soon the stuff will positively flow. So make what's-his-name your wine editor. As from today.'

'Well I'll be blowed,' said the editor later. 'Well I'll be damned,' said the news editor. 'Well I'll be buggered,' said Rupert Denny, who was happiest with a pint of bitter and large whisky. Yet, being an able reporter, it did not take him long, when the wine did flow, to use *pétillant*, *dégorgement* and *corsé* with the best of them – even if most of his material was cannibalized from the columns, books and publicity handouts of others. Even after several years in the job Denny was never quite sure of himself and was the only journalist in my experience to carry the cuttings of his columns in his breast pocket. 'This year's Mouton Rothschild? . . . There are so many wines, dear boy. Let me see what I wrote about it,' and the increasingly thick wad of cuttings would be produced and thumbed through until he found the relevant reference. Because of his lack of knowledge he could never bring himself to admit that he didn't know a certain wine and attempted to bluff his way (with a fair measure of success) through attempts to catch him out with obscure vineyards such as Migraine and Cadillac and even fictitious ones such as the claret I dreamed up one day – Chateau d'If or somesuch.

'Now what did I write about that, dear boy?' Out came the cuttings. (In later years he needed a briefcase to accommodate them.) 'Odd. I don't seem to have it here, but I remember it very well, dear boy. Are you referring to the red or the white? . . . The red? Yes, indeed. A rather big wine, clean and supple with a somewhat gravelly undertaste. Mind you, dear boy, for much the same money you could buy the Chateau Talbot, which I'm sure I wrote about. Let me see . . . Ah yes. It's a fourth year St Julien . . .'

He'd continue for what seemed hours, referring and cross-referring, unaware that his audience had often drifted away leaving him talking to himself. On one occasion in El Vino, however, he cut himself short with the exclamation: 'Must go, dear boy. I'm off to Bordeaux at 3 o'clock.'

'Who's Doe?' I enquired – and that, for what it's worth, is the witticism fifty others claimed as their own.

*　　*　　*

A man who knew a great deal about wine (if he didn't he put on an infinitely more effective front than Rupert Denny) was one-time Minister of Transport, Lord Marples. Since his millions were self-made (building) and he was a relentless self-publicist, he was a popular figure despite being responsible for the introduction of parking meters, traffic wardens and yellow lines. 'Do as I do,' he'd urge, peddling around London on his bicycle. He was also one of the Man in the Mask candidates during the Profumo scandal (although, in fairness, suspects were said to embrace every member of the Cabinet except for Lord Hailsham who was too old and Harold Macmillan who didn't know about it).

Ernest Marples' interest in wine became known to the public sometime in the sixties after he'd left the Ministry of Transport and began campaigning against the labelling of wine sold in Britain, complaining that anyone could put any description they liked on labels irrespective of the contents of the bottles. His particular hate was the abuse of the phrase *appellation contrôlée*, which should have been employed to describe only quality French wines of high standards defined by official French laws. It was, he argued, not only misleading but fraud on a grand scale since an international cocktail of near-rubbish could be passed off as great French wine at great French prices.

One of Ernie's chums was Sir Edward Pickering ('Pick'), then Editorial Director of Mirror Group Newspapers. Editor of the *Sunday Mirror* was Michael Christiansen. I was the paper's features editor. From time to time, nudged by Pick, Mike sent me to Marples' home in Belgravia to ghost impassioned stories castigating the government of the day and certain (anonymous) sections of the wine trade for failure to enforce the *appellation contrôlée* laws. I'm not convinced that it was a campaign calculated to send many *Sunday Mirror* readers to the barricades, but it gave the paper a touch of the up-market image it was seeking at the time. From my point of view the assignments were pleasant enough. Ernie and I would take the lift to the basement where he had two thermostatically controlled cellars, one for white the other for red. A couple of bottles would be selected and disposed of either on his roof garden or in his study. My only problem was that, since he always made me the same speech, it became progressively more difficult to write variations on the lines of: 'Unless the rogue firms put their houses in order, or the government acts, I shall be compelled to make exposures that will reverberate throughout the international wine trade.'

And then, as though all that had gone before had been a well-orchestrated hype, Marples announced that he was to set an example. He had bought a chateau, Les Laverts, in Fleurie, from which he would produce and export genuine, chateau-bottled *appellation contrôlée* wine, the name Marples writ large on the labels as the guarantee of the honest broker.

His flair for headlines assured him maximum publicity, but he couldn't resist taking his pitch to the heart of Fleet Street's wine drinking. A message was relayed to Frank Bower telling him that Lord Marples would appreciate his advice and guidance on a matter of some importance and that he would present himself at the wine bar at 12.30 pm.

Ernie arrived with an aide, was greeted with suitable obsequiousness and escorted to a table reserved at the rear of the premises. There Marples opened his briefcase, removed from it a bottle of what came to be known as Chateau Marples, and told Bower that he would enormously value the vintner's opinion, based as it would be on immaculate and unrivalled nose, eye, palate, judgement, experience, et cetera, et cetera. Not that Marples gave a tinker's damn for Bower's expertise: as the preening Frank solemnly opened, poured, examined, sniffed, raised his glass to the light, swished, sipped, gargled, swallowed and looked portentous, Marples' aide opened a suitcase laden with further, cork-loosened bottles of the stuff. With a nod, a wink and a five-pound note, Ernie obtained glasses from a barmaid, and before Frank realized what was happening samples were being passed around the bar together with leaflets detailing the wine's price and outlets of availability.

When a justifiably outraged Frank Bower did grasp what was taking place he promptly barred Marples and everyone else in sight who happened to be drinking red wine – including one of his nephews, a judge and two Queen's Council. . .

Then a story reached me from a sound source, well away from Fleet Street, which gave the entire business a Roald Dahl twist: that from its inception Marples' entire labelling and *appellation contrôlée* campaign had been a carefully and cunningly layered con trick to conceal the fact that his own wine was to be a fraud. The stuff sold in France was, of necessity, genuine; the British version was as mongrel and overpriced as any he denounced.

When I discussed the story with Mike Christiansen he agreed that we had either a sensational exposure on our hands or a million-pound libel action. The only way to prove or disprove the allegation was to buy cases of the French and British wines and have them tasted and analysed for variations. We decided to obtain a case of both, with six bottles from each case going for scientific analysis, the remainder being blind tasted by a panel formed of Masters of Wine, restaurateurs and the like (plus the obligatory TV personality). Mike set a date for a fortnight's time.

A case of the wine on sale over here was easy enough to purchase; to obtain a case of the French I sent Jonathan Perry to Calais. Perry was a swarthy Australian with a head like a multi-jowled pomegranate perched on a neckless and almost spheroid and legless body. He was a fine journalist with a marvellous gift for descriptive writing. He was also a very thorough operator, which no doubt accounted for the fact that he spent a week across the Channel before telephoning me to say that every wine merchant in Calais and its environs was so well stocked with alternative, old-established, wines they just did not have the room (or enthusiasm) for Lord Marples' brew. What should he do?

'Go to Fleurie,' I advised. 'To the vineyard. The chateau. They must sell the stuff there. The tasting is in a week's time. Remember?'

'But how will I get it back?'

'On the train.'

'A case of wine, cobber? All the way from Fleurie?'

'Hire porters. Like you'd do in Calais.'

'On expenses?'

'What else?'

This cheered him enormously. 'I'm on my way . . . Oh, and re expenses, do me a favour and forget that I transferred the charge of this call!'

For all his eccentricities, Michael Christiansen was a great tabloid editor with considerable technical skills and dazzling showmanship. He set new and boldly imaginative standards in popular Sunday journalism with his bravura projection of such series as *The Naked Ape* and *Chariots of the Gods*.

In fairness, his disasters could be equally spectacular. For example, despite the advice of his senior executives, and motivated to some extent by an impish desire to shock, he serialized *The Sacred Mushroom and the Cross* by John Allegro, which argued that Christianity had its origins in an erotic sect whose members worshipped an hallucinogenic mushroom the code name for which was Son of God since it contained God's sperm. Even nominal take-the-oath-in-court Christians thought this was a bit much, as they did the author's corollary that any reverence shown to a representation of the crucified Christ was really phallus worship. On the whole, however, Mike's judgments, if daring, were sound, and his enthusiasm ineffective. Working for the *Sunday Mirror* during Mike's regime wasn't well paid but it was fun.

Mike wound himself into a fine state of excitement for the Marples' story since it took him no time at all to convince himself that the former minister was guilty on all charges. Once we had the evidence it would make pages 1, 4 and 5, and the centre spread. To Mike's extreme annoyance, however, because of the legal perils involved in the investigation, he couldn't tell anyone else what was happening (including Ted Pickering) until we had that evidence and had given Marples the right to reply to it. So he nagged at me, every day and most nights, to know when Perry was due back with the wine. I wished I knew. There were no phone calls. Our man in Paris, Peter Stephens, couldn't find Perry, despite his unrivalled network of agents throughout France, and as I prevaricated Mike perversely grew more excited, even booking slots for a 60-second TV commercial, to the irritation of John Jenkinson of the Mirror Group's publicity department who was not given a clue to its contents although he was expected to produce it at 5 minutes' notice.

From Mike Christiansen's point of view the only thing that could be worse than Marples' innocence would be an absence of the evidence that would prove his guilt. But where was the evidence? Where was Jonathan Perry? For how long could I continue to cover for him?

He telephoned me just before lunch on the day before the tasting. From a call box. 'What the hell,' I began, to be interrupted by a beseeching: 'Please, Cy, *please*. Don't say a word. Just come. Now. *Please.*'

'Where are you?'

'I'll be in The Cock in Smithfield,' said Perry and rang off.

He greeted me with: 'I'll have a large scotch', followed by a flat: 'How are you?' then fell into staring, lip-pursed silence as

he awaited his drink and concentrated on a two-handed lift of
his glass from bar counter to mouth. He looked awful; crum-
pled and unshaven, bloodshot eyes flickering with panic. It took
much time and scotch to drag the story out of him. He'd been
to Fleurie (he had receipts for the rail fare and hotel to prove it).
He'd bought the wine (again he had the receipt). Cutting it short,
he had all manner of receipts from all over France. What he didn't
have was a case of wine.

'So where the hell is it?' I asked.

'I wish to Christ I knew,' he groaned.

'How can you lose a case of wine?'

'I must have put it down somewhere.'

He knew he had it at Lyon. He knew he had it the previous
morning when the train arrived at Paris. He was certain he had
it in the taxi when he went in search of a drink and possible (no
receipt) meal in Montmartre. He thought he had it when he went
to the Gare du Nord to catch the train to London. He may have
had it when he went to the buffet for a quick one. From then on
memory was obliterated by an alcoholic amnesia that was absolute until he awoke that morning to be assured by his wife that
when he tottered from the taxi in Streatham the previous night
he was in possession of neither a case of Fleurie nor any other
wine. 'I'm in the shit, aren't I?' he concluded, nodding his head
and so causing his chins to slap back and forth like a Newton's
cradle.

'More shit than a meths drinker's lavatory,' I assured him. It
was my turn to groan. 'You'll just have to come to the office this
afternoon and tell Mike. It's something I can't do for you.'

A few minutes later, hurrying to lunch, I visualized the scene
in the editor's office when Mike removed his spectacles and his
eyes went owl-blank to herald blue, bloody murder.

Jonathan Perry could well be fired. Or Mike's decision might
be to employ a familiar, Kafkaesque Fleet Street technique and
make him a non-person. From time to time one hears the saloon bar cry: 'Whatever happened to Wassisname?' when it is
realized that in the absence of news of his death the by-line of
a star has suddenly disappeared from a publication. Frequently
the answer proves to be that he (or she) has vanished into one
of Fleet Street's black holes. Most newspapers have them: part

of a floor containing a rabbit warren of virtually impossible to find offices in which no work is done except for the typing of expenses and the telephoning of wives, whores and bookmakers. Some occupants are old servants of the company tucked away (whether they like it or not) to await retirement. Others are the victims of self-inflicted, often 70° proof, wounds. And there are those non-persons Jonathan Perry could well join: people found guilty of unforgivable (if often forgotten) crimes but not fired for reasons of sentimentality or respect for their track records.

When, at 4.30, Jonathan was not back in the office I decided that at 5 I'd have to tell the editor what had happened.

Jonathan rang at 4.50. In a fine state of hiccuping excitement. 'Everything's all right, cobber. I've got the wine. It's arrived. Miracles still happen, *Deus vult.* Maybe it's holy wine. Candles must be lit. Prayers of thanksgiving. We. . .'

'I know you're pissed,' I interrupted, 'but what are you talking about?'

I finally dragged the fragments out of him and shuffled them into shape . . . After the taxi driver dropped Perry in Streatham he decided to call it a day. On his way home he remembered the case of wine a porter had placed in the cab but which his fare, as he recalled, had failed to remove. He stopped to check, and sure enough there it was in the back. He had no desire to return to Streatham, nor did he want to be bothered, next day, with the time-consuming bureaucracy of the Metropolitan Police Lost Property Office. It was a good excuse to take a day off to play golf, delivering the wine en route. After all (as he explained heavily to Grace Perry), he was saving her husband the trouble of going to the Lost Property Office in Lambeth, plus the fee they would charge. It would all add up to a lot of money. Oh dear, yes; a great deal of money. To say nothing of time. And time was also money, was it not? Plus the transport, because where do you park in that area? A bemused Grace gave him £10, much to her husband's fury (and no, I assured him, you can't claim it on expenses).

After I'd left Jonathan at lunchtime he'd phoned home for some reason – to be given the good news. He'd rushed back to Streatham to check that the bottles were intact, and they were.

It was all very hard to make out since his alcoholic incoherence was punctuated with the occasional *Te Deum laudamus*,

Dominus illuminatio and, presumably for my benefit, *Mazel tov*. But there it was, and by the time it was over I felt quite drained. 'Don't drink it,' I begged. 'Don't drop it. Just get it to the tasting.'

That event proved to be somewhat anti-climactic after the cardiac-threatening events of previous days. The experts argued about the wine's origins and quality (all suspiciously assuming they were in danger of being made fools of for some vulgar stunt) but when it came to comparing 1 to 6 with A to F they were in unanimous agreement: it was the same wine.

'Perhaps the analysis will show a difference,' I suggested to a morose Mike Christiansen when the results of the tasting reached the office.

Mike shook his head. 'I doubt it.' (He was proved right.) He pushed his spectacles up onto his forehead and said glumly: 'Mind you, it is a pity after all the time, money and effort. It would have made a great story. Had all the ingredients.' He sighed and then, in one of his characteristic, lightning changes of mood, took a deep breath, clapped his hands and beamed at me. 'What's done is done. What's dead is dead. Something else will come along tomorrow. You can't win 'em all.' He raised an arm above his head and wagged a forefinger. 'We must look forwards, not backwards. Let us make our way to the Stab for some gin and tonics and a game of chance. After all, it's not our fault that Marples is swine enough to be an honest broker, is it?'

I nodded. 'It's tragic when another good story is destroyed by the facts. . . Mind you, you could always do a Sam Campbell. In an updated style, of course. Salvage a couple of pages from the disaster.'

'How?' Mike asked suspiciously.

I pondered for a minute. 'In the *People* version it would have gone something like this (and probably still would).' Gravely: 'Despite the evil rumours circulating among the toffs in the wine-drinking circles of the so-called posh areas of London, we can prove that the much-loved Lord Ernie Marples is not a crook. . . The victim of evil gossip by society snobs jealous of the self-made millionaire . . . These Mayfair snobs dare to suggest that Lord Marples' wine, et cetera. . . Our independent tests, carried out by experts . . . Great expense, but worthwhile to clear an innocent man's name . . . Duncan Webb's full report begins on page five.'

Mike Christiansen clutched his stomach and made retching noises.

The following Tuesday the feature writers' expenses began to arrive for my signature. When I came to Jonathan Perry's it was a reflex action to reach for a magnifying glass to help me spot such ploys as lunch bill totals changed from £14 to £35 with a non-matching ball point, or a grey and dog-eared bill with virtually still-wet ink under the logo of a restaurant that had ceased trading years earlier. On this occasion there were, from his French caper, bills and receipts that were patently genuine, others that were so-so, some that I'd question him about, and then . . . And then, inadvertently tucked among them, a receipt that should have been destroyed – for a case of Chateau Marples purchased in London on the day of the miracle of the taxi driver.

If I told Mike Christiansen how he and the paper had been made fools of, Jonathan would be fired. There could be no alternative. In the circumstances, I would not feel particularly worried at being the agent of Jonathan's going, but I didn't want Mike to suffer the humiliation of knowing that he'd been conned. On the other hand, Jonathan Perry couldn't be allowed to suppose that he'd been ingenious enough to get away with it. I settled for giving Jonathan the most severe bollocking of his career and imposed my own punishment which, for Perry, was second only to dismissal: I fined him by refusing to sign either his French expenses or any others for a month. If he wanted to complain he knew where to find the editor's office. Finally, I made him swear, literally on a Bible (he was, from time to time, a practising Catholic), that he would never reveal the truth of the matter.

If Perry had reneged on his oath the story would have come back to me. And so, with Marples, Mike and Jonathan now dead (and may they rest in peace), this is the first time the truth about the Marples' wine tasting has been told.

*   *   *

While some business is carried out by design in pubs and bars, unsolicited stories, ideas and offers of services can be immensely annoying and self-destructive if the journalist to whom they are offered is trying to unwind for an hour. Hugh Cudlipp had to give up Fleet Street pubs because of such importuning but, since he liked the atmosphere of pubs, he turned a basement room of his home in Chelsea into a saloon bar (complete with parrot, Chelsea Pensioner (stuffed) and mahogany fittings bought cheaply when post-war brewers went on an idiot blitz of flock wallpaper and pink formica).

Later, and for much the same reason, he turned a cottage in the grounds of his riverside home into a private pub.

There is also the deal that occurs by accident.

One evening I was in El Vino with my brother and Bob Barmforth, then the *Daily Mirror*'s features editor. It developed, predictably, into a boozy evening and at some point Bob said: 'Gerald, we're coming up to Easter. Will you write us a short story?'

Gerald: 'How many words?'

Bob: 'Seven-fifty.'

Gerald: 'How much?'

Bob: 'Two hundred quid.'

Gerald: 'Three hundred.'

'Two hundred.'

'Three.'

'Two.'

'When do you want it by?'

'Tomorrow.'

'Then it's three-fifty.'

The argument continued in the Press Club where it punctuated insults, games of spoof, dirty stories and slanderous reminiscence until, as a new day raised a bloodshot eye over St Paul's, Gerald said to Bob: 'You want seven hundred and fifty words. Right?' Looking at his watch: 'Before lunch. Right?' He sank his teeth into the shoulder of Bob Barmforth's jacket, lifted him up and shook him from side to side. Releasing him he bellowed a triumphant: 'And it's for Easter! Right? In that case make it three-fifty and I promise to mention Jesus Christ!'

They shook hands on it.

If drinking is not altogether unknown in what is now only generically Fleet Street, there are reasons for it: the high level of occupational stress, accessibility, the frequent attempts at alcoholic bribery, boredom between assignments and the fact that much genuine business is conducted on licensed premises. Since, historically, most of the best editors drink, they are tolerant of the excuse Arthur Helliwell intended as the title of his never-written autobiography: 'I Was Pissed At The Time', although there are limits to tolerance, as Jonathan Perry nearly discovered.

*   *   *

Most Fleet Street teetotallers are drunks who gave up overnight, Hannen Swaffer among them. Before he went on the wagon there was the occasion during his editorship of the *Sunday Dispatch* when he was crawling up the back stairs on his hands and knees to be confronted on a landing by the proprietor, Lord Rothermere. 'Swaff,' he said angrily, 'there's too much drinking in this office.'

'I-I know,' Swaff replied with measured, drunken dignity. 'I-I'm going up to fire a c-couple of them now.'

It was after he gave up drinking that Swaff was in the *Dispatch* news room late one Saturday night with Rothermere when a big news story came over the tapes. 'I'll handle it,' said Swaff.

The proprietor fluttered a hand towards the sub-editors and reporters dozing at their desks. 'What about them?' he asked.

'Let lying dogs sleep,' said Swaff.

Percy Cudlipp, editor of the *Daily Herald*, told me of the days when a group of aspiring young journalists tried to imitate Swaff. They dressed like him – floppy trilby hat, starched upright collar with no wings (almost a stiff tube), stock instead of a tie, cigarette adhering to, and drooping from his lower lip – tried to write like him and occasionally attempted to stammer like him. With some contempt Swaffer called them 'my boy imitators'.

On one occasion Percy went to an opening night and met Swaff. As they entered the theatre they saw one of the boy imitators who was suffering from a large boil on his neck. 'I suppose', said Swaffer, 'he's breaking out with my indignation.'

EIGHT

The Tragedy Of Gerald Kersh

My brother Gerald had a remarkable talent, demonstrated by his twenty-three novels (many of them mini-masterpieces) and 3,000 short stories (some of them classics) until, towards the end of his life, creativity and energy were drained by sickness, the emotional (and financial) effects of a long and bitterly recriminatory divorce action, rising mountains of other debts, and alcohol.

In his prime, talent apart, he was a big and flamboyant man. Tall, with broad shoulders, a slim waist and a flat stomach, he was a very attractive man (so women told me), especially when he grew his beard, despite a large nose and small chin. He certainly had a powerful personality, was the best raconteur I have ever heard, and dressed boldly, but elegantly, and not as camply as it may sound: beautifully tailored suit, colourful shirt and tie, wide-brimmed trilby at a jaunty angle, gloves, a carnation in his buttonhole and one of his many walking sticks.

I once gave him a walking stick. Its head was carved into a clenched fist, on its back the words 'Fletcher Christian, Pitcairn Island'. One evening at the Café Royal Gerald saw a man with an identical stick and was able to say: 'Without looking closer I can tell you that your walking stick was carved by a descendant of Bounty mutineer, Fletcher Christian.'

'Good Lord! How do you know?'

'Eyes have they but see not,' Gerald replied – then realized that he was talking to Esmond Knight, actor and former naval officer who had been blinded serving aboard the *Prince of Wales* during the battle that resulted in the sinking of the *Bismark*.

Grovelling apologies were accepted, as were my brother's bottle of champagne and walking stick.

My first and last memories of Gerald are related to death – our father's and his. Father's because I have a residual memory of sitting in a room at Blandford Street in front of a narrow, Victorian, green-tiled fireplace as 18-year-old Gerald tried to explain to a 4-year-old boy that he'd never see his father again. (My mother was too grief-stricken to attempt the task, but at 4 one quickly forgets.)

Three years must have passed before I remember seeing Gerald again: when my mother, sister Sylvia and I stayed for a while with Aunty Esther and Uncle Max at Shepherd's Bush Green before moving to Westcliff.

He arrived out of the blue with a chess set and decided to teach me how to play. I was 7 years old. Soon realizing I was no boy genius, in the manner of Alekhine or Capablanca, he grew bored: there was no money to be made. Before leaving (for God knows where, since he was obsessively secret about his address), he said conspiratorially: 'Do me a favour, pal, and let me know what they're saying about me.' For months, with exercise book and pencil, I listened at keyholes, but didn't overhear a word. Nor did Gerald come to Pereira Mansions to discover what material I had for him.

He used to explain his refusal to give his address with vague and apologetic excuses that he was (yet again) in the process of moving house. There was no shortage of alternative reasons offered by members of the family: that he was living in sin with a Gentile; that he was ashamed of his impoverished circumstances; that he was dodging creditors; that he was terrififed of his mother knocking at the front door with food. Years later he told me that all of these speculations contained some measure of truth, and that his secrecy finally became an ingrained behavioural reflex.

I learned that he had been living in bedsitters in Bloomsbury and Camden Town, and worked variously as a Soho night club bouncer/manager, sausage salesman, cinema manager and all-in wrestler. Between times he sold a few short stories, married his first wife, Alice (a beautiful schoolmistress of whose existence the rest of us were unaware until after their divorce), wrote three novels – *Jews without Jehovah, Men Are So Ardent* and *Night and the City* – and a book of semi-fictional reminiscences, *I Got References*, and worked as a freelance feature writer for the *Daily Mirror*. He told me that in those days he was so hard up he wrote his first novel in some thirty days by sitting up at nights – and often all night – drinking threepenny cups of coffee in the Coventry Street Corner House, scribbling it down on paper stolen from their lavatory.

Jews without Jehovah was published in 1934 when Gerald was 23. It was wickedly comic, brilliantly observed and well reviewed, but my brother had been lazy: the book was too accurately observed, with little attempt to conceal the fact that it was a chronicle of family history and the absurdities of my uncles and certain cousins in their idiot fueds and business disasters – plus some descriptive character readings.

He might have got away with it were it not that the Millers were going through one of their bankruptcies and someone apprised Uncle Sam of the laws of libel. As word got around, the cousins joined in.

Sam always insisted that he didn't think the action would hurt Gerald: he had been assured that damages and costs would be paid by the publisher, and that all publishers were from wealthy families and for whom their profession was no more than a hobby. It is true that Gerald didn't have to pay any money – he didn't have any – but his publisher, Wishart, could hardly fight the case on the facts and, having to pay out some thousands of pounds in damages and costs, went bust. (Wishart then linked up with a man called Laurence to print the *Communist Manifesto* and similar publications.)

Years later the uncles, cousins and Gerald became friends again.

Gerald also worked for publisher Norman Kark, whose titles included *Courier* and *Shelf Appeal*, for which he wrote much of the editorial matter. He was rewarded with £2 a week, the occasional bonus, and permission to sleep on the editorial floor in Grand Buildings, Trafalgar Square. (Years later Kark told me how proud he was to have discovered a genius like Gerald Kersh, but didn't like it when I told him that I thought discovering a genius meant paying him a decent wage and setting him on his feet, not mill-owner exploitation.)

Gerald also had an amoral attitude towards other people's possessions: for instance a friend's typewriter that he borrowed, and our brother-in-law's concertina for which he said he had a purchaser. Neither were seen again.

None the less, despite all this activity, Gerald was not only eternally broke, but always in debt. The reason, to some degree, was that when he had money he went on Homeric benders that could last for a week at a time; it was also partly because, benders or not, he insisted, round after round, on paying for everyone's drinks; and partly because he was a compulsive giver-away of money. (I remember him, even after the war, borrowing a tenner and giving a fiver of it to a passing beggar. He was the master of the impulsive gesture.)

He was so full of ideas and such a quick writer the *Daily Mirror* used to call upon him when they had a last-minute feature space to fill. Tony Clarkson told me how, when features editor of the *Mirror*, he found himself in such a situation and sent envoys to the Fleet Street pubs just in case my brother was in the neighbourhood. Gerald was found, came back to the *Mirror* and said: 'Just leave it to me, pal. I'll write you something.'

And so he did, laughing to himself, causing Tony to say: 'It must be good if Kersh finds it funny.' But even he grew worried when phone calls from the composing room reminded him that the paper was due to go to press. A few minutes later Gerald handed in his copy. Beautifully typed, and exactly to length, it proved to be an 'Ode to Jane [heroine of the *Mirror* strip cartoon] from Her Nephew.' It began:

> I will not eat or drink again
> Until I fuck my Auntie Jane.

No one had realized that Gerald had started on a bender. The hole reserved for his piece was filled with whatever rubbish was to hand. He was forgiven: he always paid for Tony Clarkson's drinks.

During those pre-war years, Gerald would come to Westcliff from time to time and stay for a few days or weeks, depending upon his finances. Our mother would leave a ground-floor window open in case he arrived in the middle of the night, as he sometimes did. (In those days you could leave windows unlocked.)

If the rest of us had to sleep on armchairs or the floor, an attic room was always reserved for Gerald, even though, when he was there, my mother moaned that he didn't get up until noon, not realizing that he worked until 4 in the morning. He tried to help around the house, but preferred to go to a beach at nearby Chalkwell where he was part of a group of body-builders organized by the old wrestler, Walter Magnée. This led to another of Gerald's brilliant ideas: to make me the next world heavyweight boxing champion but four. Again I disappointed him: I didn't enjoy being hit.

Gerald wrote, drank and earned a few quid here and there (but not much from his books), and in 1939, probably to escape his creditors, volunteered for the Coldstream Guards. Somehow we came to know of this, but never heard from him except for one letter after my mother nagged me into writing to his Commanding Officer at Pirbright camp. The C.O. ordered Gerald to write to his mother. He did so – a furious attack on her for humiliating him. 'What can you do for the best?' my mother asked, and wept for days.

Then, based on a series he wrote for the *Daily Herald*, 'The Private Life of a Private', Gerald wrote and had published in 1941 his book about the Guards in training, *They Die with Their Boots Clean*. It was the right book – brilliantly clever in its flag-waving – at the right time, and earned Gerald a fortune.

He didn't stay long in the army after that: he was seconded to the Ministry of Information to write various forms of propaganda and then, when hostilities were over, was to go to Europe as a war correspondent (I'm damned if I know for whom). Anyway, after *They Die with Their Boots Clean*, book after book followed, all best-sellers, not only because he was famous but because they were brilliantly written. He wrote weekly for *The People* under his own name and as Piers England. He wrote a weekly piece for *John Bull* under the by-line Waldo Kellar. Plus one short story after another. Since it was not only quantity but quality, at this stage of his career he was probably the country's most talented, prolific and biggest-earning writer.

Although he never heard a gun fired in anger apart from London's anti-aircraft guns, he wrote cleverly about the war. His *Faces in a Dusty Picture*, set in the Western Desert, was so praised by the army's top brass he was asked to write a film script based on that campaign. He did: *Nine Men*. There was also a poem.

To quote from his book, *Clean, Bright and Slightly Oiled*: 'I was writing for *The People* then, under a pseudonym, Piers England. I wrote "A Soldier, His Prayer", put it on my page and said I didn't know who had written it. I could see nothing here to brag about.'

It began:

> Stay with me God. The night is dark.
> The night is cold: my little spark
> Of courage dims. The night is long.
> Be with me God, and make me strong.

In the book, at the end of the nine-verse poem, he wrote, 'I have seen bigger eggs hatched with less cackle.

'Almost before the paper was off the press a clergyman, a soldier, and several ladies claimed authorship of the verse. The clergyman said that he had written it, but wanted nothing – would we be so kind as to send a cheque to charity in his name? The soldier said that his natural modesty had kept him from signing his name, but now the murder was out would we pray forward money by return? The ladies were prepared to settle for sums ranging from half a guinea to five hundred pounds.

'We ignored these letters.

'In 1943 Harrap published a collection, *Poems from the Desert*. The Eighth Army's paper, *Crusader*, had run a poetry competition. My piece was a prizewinner.

'General Montgomery wrote: "The twenty-seventh poem has a unique history. Written on a scrap of paper, it fluttered into the hands of a soldier sheltering in a slit trench during the battle of El Agheila."

'I kept my mouth shut.

'A year or so later, a lady in Australia claimed authorship. Reuters gave out the claim as news. Harry Ainsworth, my editor, published a cool grey paragraph of incontrovertible negation.

'There the matter rests.'

During those Lucullan years he still didn't want to know his family, despite the letters sent to him at his new address: c/o Westminster Bank, Sloane Square. They were far from begging letters. On the contrary, my mother, convinced that he was starving to death in the absence of her *lokshen* soup, roast chicken and strudel, only wanted to feed him.

By a subterfuge, and via his then publisher, Heinemann, I discovered his address in a mews in Belgravia. I must have been 16 or 17 years old at the time. When I rang his doorbell Gerald opened it and nearly collapsed with shock. He dragged me for a walk round the block (despite a nasty air raid being in progress) and revealed that he'd told his current wife, Lee, that all his family had been killed in the blitz.

'But we weren't,' I pointed out unnecessarily.

He took me back to the mews cottage where he explained to Lee – a strikingly attractive Canadian – that he *thought* we'd all been annihilated by a German bomb, and told one of his superb improvizations in a tale about our escape from the jaws of death. It was, he revealed, the family next door that had been killed. From time to time I nodded: what else was there to do? Equally I don't know how much of it Lee believed.

Gerald bought a farm and then a penthouse in Dolphin Square overlooking the river. These were the great days of wine and roses. The Golden Boy could do no wrong. Except, perhaps, when he played poker. These games, I was told, were wild sessions, their irresponsibility influenced by the shrugged assumption that if they weren't blown up that night, there was always tomorrow. Gerald was the big loser. Apart from his reckless bidding, another reason was explained in a letter that American journalist, Harold Conrad, wrote to Bob Musel of United Press International. This was in 1952 when they were in Chicago for the Liston–Paterson fight, the last assignment on which Gerald was to be sent.

'Kersh, who used to be a wrestler, goes around bending dimes with his teeth. He's the No. 1 sucker in the nightly poker game. He has a big vein in the centre of his forehead and every time he tries to bluff his way through a big pot the vein sticks out like a neon sign. He's getting murdered and nobody will tip him off.'

His bank now sent my mother £4 a week (cash in a registered envelope), a goodly sum in those days. (As times grew bad it was to reduce to £2, then ceased.) When I was demobbed he bought me a pair of hand-made shoes from Harris in The Strand, and two made-to-measure suits from his tailor, Sandon of Stratton Street. Years later, when people began nagging me to settle Gerald's bills, he got to hear of it and wrote from America: 'In no circumstances pay any living soul one farthing on my behalf.' I certainly ignored a huge rent bill from Dolphin Square, but didn't tell him that I'd already paid off Sandon at a few pounds a month, feeling some sense of responsibility since the suits, although now worn out, had been for me.

He went to America for the first time in 1945, and in a letter to me in September of that year (address c/o his agent, who was always to change) he was, for the most part, bullish. 'America bought *Night and the City* for forty thousand dollars and I've cracked open *Colliers* and *Saturday Evening Post* for vast prices: $5,000 – five *thousand* dollars for a long short story.' Then the complaint that was to become, with his divorce and illnesses, the leitmotiv of the rest of his life: 'But all I have is an overdraft on account of tax.'

At about this time: 'As you know, Hollywood bought *Night and the City* for $40,000. This makes me the world's most highly paid writer: all they are using is the title. At $10,000 a word, had I written *War and Peace* I'd not only be immortal but own General Motors in the bargain. . . when they showed me the script I told them to have it suitably perforated and hang it in a tramp's lavatory . . .' The film was made on location in London, starring Richard Widmark as the central character, ponce Harry Fabian. Gerald was right: the film bore scant resemblance to the novel. Nor was it a good film.

Gerald seemed to be truly back on his feet now, for in 1947 he bought a house in Barbados, the existence of which his family learned about only when the newspapers reported that it had burned to the ground, and of Gerald and Lee's dramatic escape from death. I wrote him a letter of sympathy to which he replied on May 9:

'I saved all my papers, my clothes, and some books. I offered some of the local strong arm men rich rewards if they would save the most valuable articles of furniture – 18th Century four-poster beds etc. – which they proceeded to do by the primitive process of chopping them up and throwing them in pieces out of the window. It would have done your heart good to see a magnificent mahogany wardrobe, 12 feet long, exploding on the paved court. The entire province of St Peters turned up to help, and ran away in all directions with arms full of rare porcelain and solid silver cutlery. The coconut jigaboos of the locality are eating their paw-paws off monogrammed plate with silver spoons. Even a child of three was intercepted in the act of toddling off with my tortoiseshell and gold cigarette case. He was brought back with considerable eclat by Goodridge, my chauffeur – aided by Mascal, the strong man of the island.

'The fire engines arrived, naturally just too late. It was a most important event: the chief himself turned up. They had about two teacups-full of water in a tank which they proceeded to play upon the part of the building where it would do the least good, until I took the hose away from the leading fireman and did the job myself. And what an apparatus! As God is my judge I could pee higher.

'Oh well, I had a bargain. It was worth, easily, $100,000 and I got it for $20,000, lock, stock and barrel, by a series of the most subtle operations. It was practically uninsured. Yes, I had a bargain. I have had a bargain. And I am well and truly in the soup again. Kersh escapes? Don't you bloody well believe it.'

From time to time Gerald averred: 'My bones were made in England, and it is in England that I shall die.' In the hope of avoiding colossal tax debts, however, he (or Lee) decided that he would become an American citizen, but since that would take five years to achieve he became a Canadian resident to get on with, popping over the border from New York from time to time to re-establish his Maple Leaf loyalty.

Until the mid-fifties he continued to write some good novels, even if, when in England, he did have to stay from time to time in Tony Clarkson's basement bedroom and at a pub in East Sussex, The Rother Valley Hotel. Then there were flats in Hans Crescent off Knightsbridge, and in Lower Belgrave Street.

He had earned and he had spent – with no great worry about his debts. And so, what with one thing and another, he was broke again. How he paid his rents I never knew (assuming, of course, that he paid them). Nor were his illnesses confined to America. He consulted not-inexpensive doctors in Harley Street and once awoke in St Pancras hospital in North London from which he went to a convalescent home in Harrow. All more expense – or debt, since he was now beginning to write and sell less: his work becoming progressively less disciplined.

Drinking too much, he did some daft things at about this time: ordering visiting cards on which he described himself at *The People*'s Senior Feature Writer. I know: I was landed with the bill.

I was present at the BBC studios when he was part of a panel in a news quiz. Gerald distinguished himself by not answering one question, but spent the time hitting his fellow-contestants over the head with a pencil. The producer told me that before the show Gerald should never have been left alone in the hospitality room.

His letters from America began, invariably, with hilariously funny, shockingly libellous, scatological and probably apochryphal reminiscences of family and friends. Then to his bitterness about the machinations (real or imagined) of Lee as she screwed him into the ground with her alimony demands. He was always an enviably immaculate typist, but news about his illnesses was usually contained in handwritten postcripts.

On 1 December 1950, with a New York address, a letter from Florence (Flossie) Sochis, Gerald's secretary, who was to become the third Mrs Kersh:

'Firstly they [the University of Pennsylvania Hospital] established malaria unquestionably by a blood smear – which erases the canard that Kersh imagined his illness and was really an alcoholic. . . He has mysterious shadows in the lower left lung. These may be, at best, a malarial infection; at worst, one of the chest surgeons warned, a tumour or cancer.

'He's weak, sleeps a great deal, wonders if this Canadian residence notion is another of Lee's boners . . . I think it is, and believe he'd be better off staying in Sussex, reverting to British citizenship and working quietly.

'By promising some TV scripts by Kersh, if he's well enough to do them, I got another $1,000 this week. It will pay off some medical expenses, rent a little country house in hills somewhat reminiscent of Sussex . . . buy some food and fuel, and keep us awhile.'

On the same date a letter from Gerald: 'Professor Kirby prognoses cancer of the left lung . . . I am quite broke but Kersh is not dead until he stinks. Am establishing secretly a new pseudonym since Lee's lawyers have their hooks on every penny that comes my way now, so that I am sponging for board and lodging.'

Gerald, 17 December 1950: 'I am still of this world, although sick and in some pain where my left lung is sticking to my diaphragm.'

Gerald, 28 December 1950: 'As for my sickness, try and forget it. It's really malaria. I'm sorry I mentioned it.

'P.S. I am in hospital again.'

Cable from Flossie, 5 January 1951: OPERATION TODAY DISCLOSED LIVER ENTIRELY SPOTTED WILL FLASH VERDICT AFTER LABORATORY STUDIES DISEASED TISSUES MYSTIFYING MEDICOS.

There was no follow-up and my enquiries about his liver were unanswered. I can only guess – and it is a guess – that Flossie and Gerald were reluctant to admit anything that might have involved alcohol. On the same day as the cable, Gerald wrote to Harry Ainsworth (he sent me a copy of the letter) about his divorce from Lee. After asking H.A. to find him a lawyer he added: 'If, as well may be, the lawyer wants a few pounds as a retainer, be a good fellow and let him have them as from me.'

I don't think he got much joy: his next letter was filled with vituperative abuse about H.A.

February 1953, of the Inland Revenue: 'You know, I suppose, that I have earned many hundreds of pounds lately – of which I have never received a penny, and never will? Like Bill [William] Saroyan – he sold serial rights of a novel to the *Saturday Evening Post* for 50,000 dollars. The tax people were waiting *in the office* when he came for the cheque. He had to borrow 20 dollars to get home again to a broom cupboard in the Great Northern Hotel which he got on tick.

'I stay at the Great Northern when I go to New York: the Algonquin doesn't give credit any more. There's a certain something about the run-down old Great Northern now. Young unknowns

like to address their letters from there to delude their acquaint-
ances into the belief that they are good enough to have seen
better days.'

From Flossie: 'Several times what Kersh thought were com-
missions, H.A. regarded as "on spec." A hard offer might help
with our back taxes – if H.A. provides a bit for office expenses,
mailing, paper, typing . . .'

Poor H.A. To the end, Flossie and Gerald clung to the belief that
he was still in charge of the paper.

In the main his letters were still hilarious libels. When in England, although a bit puffy now, he continued to be a witty and
well-informed companion. He had a vast store of memorabilia
in the manner of why pubs are called the Goat and Compasses –
it's a corruption of the pilgrim inn name: God Encompasses. He
loved asking people questions about life's marginalia, especially
when they couldn't be expected to know the answers. He rarely
talked of his health or his financial problems; maybe out of embarrassment or, as a therapy, he preferred to write about them at a
distance. Yet, for all his smiles and plans, bright conversation and
muscle-flexing (he could still pick up 22 stone Willi Frischauer
by his shoulder padding with his teeth and shake him like a
rat), his eyes couldn't always hide the pain and bitterness and
frustration of a man who had once known greatness.

His divorce from Lee, heard in London, was messy and pub-
licized because he defended it, his losing in no way helped by
such exchanges as 'Why, on such-and-such a date, were you
found in bed with Mrs Sochis?' to which he replied: 'To keep
warm.'

At the end of 1955 he was again in America, this time never
to return to England. His homes were towns and hamlets in
the remoter areas of New York State: Pine Bush, Circleville
and Cragsmoor in the Shawangunk Mountains, from which he
could 'spot a creditor at ten miles'. On 18 February 1960 he wrote
from Circleville:

'I was taken to the hospital in Middletown. . . Suspicions of
abscesses in the colon. . . I lost about three stones, and Flossie
with virus pneumonia. Not one hour of peace in twelve years.
Well, I'm home again, neatly stitched and getting back to work,
being deep – oh, so deep! in hock.'

P.S. to a letter dated 3 February 1961: 'Just after I wrote the above I was rushed to an oxygen tent. Virus pneumonia and surgery involving the removal of a rib, et cetera . . . Re *The Implacable Hunter* [recently published in England] I never had a better crop of reviews. I asked Heinemann £1,000 advance. They said okay . . . The Inland Revenue took £900 of it. This is illegal!'

Then the dreadful letter of 2 June 1965:

'I am just out of the Presbyterian Hospital, having had cancer of the throat. They removed my larynx, which had two malignancies on it, thereby saving my life and preserving me (barring accidents) for some time to come. If anybody asks you, tell them from me that it's extremely horrible. I am totally dumb, of course – don't even breath through nose or mouth, but through a metal pipe let into my trachea. I must learn what they call "oesophageal speech" – i.e. a form of belching in the shape of words.

'A nice turn-up for the Old Raconteur: but I'll survive. Have finished a new novel which McGraw-Hill consider the greatest comic masterpiece of the century – 180,000 thousand words. I'll be surprised and hurt if it doesn't go over big.'

Then, by some irony of coincidence: 'Sorry you have sciatica. The worst thing about it nobody believes you have it.' The letter finished: 'What haunts me at the moment is a dread that a wasp might get into my breathing-pipe.'

13 December 1966: 'I went to be checked by my doctor and found I had got myself some more cancer – back of the tongue; which same tongue having split down the middle causes discomfort . . . I work on and am finishing another novel. The last, *The Angel and the Cuckoo*, is due out in England next month. Get hold of it. It ain't bad.'

I went to New York in 1967 and spent the night at Gerald's house at Cragsmoor. It was little more than a shack; quite isolated with sparse and not very good furniture, no television, one room piled with old newspapers, while a small mountain of beer cans dominated the back garden. On the living room table was a loaded revolver: protection, said Gerald, against the bears which, when hungry, would break in anywhere. The place was cold and shabby and I had the firm impression that Gerald and Flossie really were on the poverty line, particularly with his small earnings swallowed by horrendous medical costs.

Flossie, never slim, was now very fat, her once-black hair a frizzy grey pot-scourer. Gerald looked remarkably good, if very thin, and, to my astonishment, was able to conduct a normal conversation, even though the words came out as a sort of breathless, gravelly series of hiccups. We talked of the family and Fleet Street and old friends, his anecdotes having lost none of their wicked inventiveness. We stayed up late into the night talking, and next morning he took me to the bus stop to see me off to New York City. My last sight of him was as he waved and griiinned, no longer the upright and confident ex-Guardsman in elegant mufti, but a sad and tired man in a shabby mac.

24 January 1968: 'I turn up at the hospital and talk to people just out of anaesthetic and (as is usual) shocked, and tell filthy stories. Oddly enough, one doesn't need a larynx to say "Fuck", and "Shit", and I start my disciples off on these words.

'"To be or not to be" comes next . . .' This was sandwiched between chunks of other comic vulgarity and the letter ended: 'I got a tooth fixed that was missing when you came. They all ache but may not be removed – my jaws will be radioactive for years, and extractions from the bone may not heal. I'll survive . . . All the best to you both.'

That was his last letter. He died on 5 November 1969. He was 57 years old.

NINE

Another Shock Horror – The £10 Lunch

The Compasses in High Holborn stands opposite what used to be the Odhams Magazine building (*Woman*, *Illustrated*, *John Bull*, *Melody Maker*, *Picturegoer*, etc.) which, in turn, was next to Harrap the publishers. The pub was run by Harry Woodstock, who resembled a professional, if diminutive, tango dancer at a seaside dance hall: hair an advertisement for black Castrol; a three-piece, severely waisted, elaborately shouldered dark suit; stiff-collared white shirt with acorn-knotted burgundy silk tie, and a red carnation in his buttonhole. Odhams people used the Compasses, but few of the Harrap staff; if they could afford to drink they would follow their editorial director, Joe Gaute, to the Brown Bear which stood at the corner of Drury Lane. (Joe, a great patriot, regretted not having served in the war other than in the Home Guard, yet was inordinately proud of the reason: the Services could not supply boots wide enough to fit him since he had six toes on each foot, which he would demonstrate at the drop of a shoelace.) One of the eponymous Harraps did use the Compasses, however, because his working day went like this:

Arrive at the office at 11-ish. At 11.30, spot on what was opening time in those days, he would go across to the Compasses where, by rote and without a word being exchanged, a neat treble gin would await him. Ready in his hand was the cost, which he'd slap on the counter, then swallow the neat treble in one gulp, followed by a quick shudder which started at his ears and frissoned to his ankles. With this strengthener inside him – the entire operation took 30 seconds – he was off to the Holborn Restaurant at the corner of Kingsway for a more leisurely sequence of gins before he lunched, his meal washed down with a bottle of wine and several large brandies. Then it was back to the office for a few minutes before taking a taxi to Waterloo to catch the train to somewhere in Surrey where he had an arrangement with the Railway Tavern to serve him a couple before opening time on his way home. God alone knows how he spent his weekends.

It came to pass that one morning I was in my office at *Illustrated* with a hangover that screamed out for a bottle of Worthington. At 11.30 I was in the Compasses just as Harry, running a few minutes late, was putting on his jacket and taking his carnation from a glass of water on the bar. He served my Worthington and was pouring the obligatory treble gin when Harrap came in, slapped his money on the bar, raised the glass of water, swallowed its contents, shuddered from ears to ankles and walked out.

Since then I have never considered myself to be a truly heavy drinker.

Confirmation of this came some years later when I was features editor of the *Sunday Mirror*. Since early one morning Richard Burton had been in the Fleet Street area filming a scene for *The Spy Who Came in from the Cold*. Now it was 10 a.m. and Burton was thirsty. He came to the *Sunday Mirror* (I think to be interviewed by show business writer Jack Bentley) and asked Jack if he had a drink. He hadn't. In those days the only member of the staff with a drinks cabinet was editor Mike Christiansen, and soon after 10 was a bit early for his arrival.

Jack asked me what he should do. I told Mike's secretary to open the drinks cabinet. Burton accepted a very large vodka (or gin) with a phlegmy gasp which I took to be 'Thank you' and which was his sole contribution to the conversation as he swallowed two more big ones. Thus fortified, he braced his shoulders and left to face the day. (I'm not certain that Jack ever got his interview.)

Back to High Holborn . . .

When George Wensley (Tony) Clarkson was editor of *John Bull*, then editor of *Illustrated*, he was not among the Odham's journalists who used the Compasses. Rarely any other pub which involved buying a round, despite being a pubbable man. He had to count his pennies. Literally. He was on a fixed expense allowance which, at one time, he heavily overspent, causing his wife Pam, who had a laser beam of an eye for a missing ha'penny, to make him surrender his cheque book and replace it with a Diners Card, which kept him out of pubs for most of the time but allowed him a modest number of lunches for which Pam paid. He was given one cheque for emergencies (he'd produce it from time to time – a frail and grubby oblong which he dared not use and no self-respecting tradesman would accept), as well as pocket money for such needs as bus fares and haircuts, on which he made a small profit by walking halfway to work and allowing his hair to grow jacket-collar long. Tony also made a few secret pounds from his lunches. When he and I had lunch, for instance, it was invariably a matter of going Dutch with Tony collecting my share in cash. Assuming he did this with some of his other eating partners, what he did with his secret cash accumulations – apart from buying the occasional drink – must have been part of an exotic side to his life with which few were familiar, or he saved it to purchase surprise gifts for his family.

Other economies included wearing only crepe-soled suede shoes (obviating the need for shoe polish or repairs), a coin-operated telephone at home and the purchase of wine at auction: absolutely filthy job lots of obscurities for which no one else would bid.

So Tony's expenditure reached an acceptable level, meaning that the balance of his expense allowance (like almost everyone else's) contributed in some measure to the family budget. Then, because they were fixed expenses, the day came when Her Majesty's Commissioners required to know how they were accounted for, any unspent balance being regarded as income for tax purposes. If this worried Tony, he told me that it drove his wife to something approaching a nervous breakdown: what if their enquiries spread to her income which, although paid in her maiden (professional) name of Pamela Mink for such disparate enterprises as working as a film extra, appearing in swimming galas and selling junk from a stall in Portobello Road market, was still presumably traceable if the Inland Revenue put their minds to it?

It would be best, the Clarkson accountant advised Tony, to tell the tax people that the balance of his expense allowance – nay, far more than the balance – was spent at home on crucial business dinners, Sunday luncheons and vital Bucks Fizz and caviare receptions.

'Of course, sir,' said the tax man. 'May I see the receipts?'

'I didn't know I had to keep them,' said Tony.

'Of course not,' said the inspector sympathetically. 'Come back in two years with the relevant receipts for those years. Starting from today.' He smiled and made an entry in his five-year diary.

As Tony told me the story, they went on an orgy of receipted expenditure in Harrods food hall on a scale to provide dozens of luxury tinned meals with vintage wines for more than double the Inland Revenue's time requirement. The trouble was that the Clarksons were so conditioned to feeding their guests from the local market they couldn't bring themselves to offer them the joys of Harrods. Instead they kept these gastronomic extravaganzas for really special occasions: romantic meals for just the two of them at their house in Chelsea's Anderson Street.

Unlike Tony Clarkson, most journalists face the problem of justifying their expenses to their heads of department on a weekly basis, after which they are further countersigned, then sent to cashiers who fine-tooth-comb them, resentful that certain expense sheets are in excess of their own weekly salaries. This rancour is understandable when, from familiarity and observation, they know that a journalist eats only in the staff canteen, is office bound, yet puts in generous claims for lunches and mileage. When editor of *Reveille* I had an executive who, judging from the receipts accompanying his expenses, managed to persuade all his luncheon guest to travel by bus from central London to a restaurant near his home in Barking, in the glummer reaches of the Thames Estuary, to share a chicken vindaloo. Bernard McElwaine of the *Sunday Mirror* seldom ate, so made up his expenses with large amounts of mileage, although he couldn't drive. *Show Business* writer, Jack Bentley, could drive – and drive like Jehu – he was so keen an operator he would often manage Glasgow and back in a day, twice a week, without a pause for a hotel bed or to buy the people he was interviewing lunch or dinner.

Not that one resented patently inflated expenses if they included a profit justified by a splendid exclusive of a story, and involved some wit and wisdom. A favourite example of the latter goes back to *The People* where, one Saturday night, I was running the News Desk when a flash came over the tapes of a murder in Paddington. I sent Trevor Handoll, who was doing a shift for us, to cover it. His expenses the following Tuesday included, under the heading COVERAGE OF PROSTITUTE'S MURDER IN SUSSEX GARDENS, the item: 'Gratuity for information to brothel keeper who wanted £1 . . . Ten shillings.' No one, in all decency, could query such an item: Trevor deserved the 10 shillings for sheer inventive flair.

At a differently daft end of the spectrum were Stanley Buchanan's expenses after I sent him to cover the 1953 Canvey Island flood disaster. They included the item: 'Hospitality to heads of armed services in charge of Operation Canvey: Major–General So-and-so, Rear-Admiral Such-and-such and Air Vice–Marshal Whatsit . . . 3s 6d.' By today's standards allow for inflation and make it £2.50. I called him to my desk and asked: 'How in God's name can you entertain three heads of the armed services for three-and-sixpence?'

'Ah,' said Bucky, tearing a corner off a piece of copy paper and chewing it. 'I'll tell you what happened. I phoned in my story and thought I'd have a drink. It was just about opening time so I was the only one in the pub when all this top brass walked in. Thinking there might be a story I said: "Gentleman, would you care to have a drink with *The People*?" And they did. They each had half a pint of bitter.'

'Bucky,' I sighed, 'You entertained a major-general, a rear-admiral and an air vice-marshal for *three and fucking sixpence*?' A longer 'Aah' from Bucky as he tore off more paper. 'You're thinking that four halves of bitter don't come to three-and-sixpence.' He looked around. Then, conspiratorially: 'To tell you the truth, Cyril – and this is just between the two of us – I had a pint.'

Dear Stanley Buchanan. The announcement of Princess Elizabeth's engagement to Lieutenant Philip Mountbatten was made in July 1947 after the Princess returned from a tour of South Africa with her parents and sister, the journey there and back aboard the battleship *Vanguard*. Bucky was sent to Portsmouth in search of 'a real womb trembler of a story' and found a steward who, for a few pounds, showed him the Princess's cabin and told him of the framed, tears-of-happiness-stained pictures of the handsome lieutenant that had been on the bedside table. If these were not riches enough, he then showed Bucky a bundle of letters from Philip to Elizabeth which had somehow come into his possession and which he was prepared to sell for £25. It seemed a snip, only Bucky didn't have the amount of money with him. He telephoned the then news and features editor, Harry Ashbrook.

'We must have it,' Harry cried. 'It's the scoop of the century! I'll wire you the money at the main Portsmouth post office.'

'And a couple of quid to buy the man a drink.'

'And a couple of quid. Just phone me before you catch the train back to town. To make certain everything's OK.'

In those days *The People's* petty cash float totalled £20, was kept in a tin box in the news editor's desk, and invariably contained less money than IOUs. Harry found about a fiver in the float, chipped in a couple of pounds, borrowed the balance from various members of the staff and the manager of the Freemason's Arms, and so was able to wire £30 to Stanley Buchanan in Portsmouth. This done, he went to tell Sam Campbell of the scoop of the century.

According to Harry Ashbrook, as Sam listened he grew progressively more sallow and began to shiver. 'Are you all right?' Harry enquired at the end.

Teeth chattering now, Sam replied: 'Of c-c-course I'm not all b-b-bloody right,' as he searched in some desperation on his table for appropriate pills and tablets. Having swallowed a selection and checked his pulse, he continued in the theatricality of near-hysteria: 'Have you all gone completely mad? Some hairy-arsed matelot has stolen letters written to the future Queen of England by her fiancé. That ape Buchanan has bought them. I'm supposed to publish them. Do you realize what's happened? What *will* happen? The sailor will be hanged. Buchanan will go to the Tower. You'll join him as an accomplice for supplying the money. (Defect to the Russians, while there's still time, if you want

100

to save your skin.) And I – I, as editor of this newspaper – I will probably be publicly flogged on Tower Hill before joining you. . . Princess Elizabeth's private correspondence stolen and fenced by *The People* . . .' Rummaging again on his table of medicaments: 'No cyanide, but there must be an overdose of something. I might as well get it over with. Don't fancy going to Moscow . . .'

'Bucky will be phoning in before he leaves for London,' said Harry with a gulp.

Some of the cocktail of pills and potions must have had a calming effect. Chest heaving, Sam said flatly: 'Sit by that bloody telephone until he does. And remember that this conversation never took place. The entire incident hasn't happened. Understand that? . . . Good. And make sure Buchanan understands it.' A disconcerting attempt at a laugh. 'Tell him MI5's after him.'

Stanley Buchanan rang from Portsmouth station minutes before his train left for Waterloo. 'MI5' did the trick: he leapt aboard in a state of absolute terror and spent the entire journey locked in a lavatory where, he told us, he tore the letters to fragments before flushing them, spreading the task as long as he could in order to scatter them as thinly as possible along the line. Knowing how Bucky reacted under stress, I'll wager that at least some of Prince Philip's *tendresses* disappeared via the Scot's digestive system.

Come to think of it, I never did get back the £2 I contributed to the purchase of the scoop of the century.

One of the cheekiest expense account fiddles was perpetrated by the diminutive, large-moustached Harry Ashbrook, and involved advances for expenses (the tin box being intended only for emergencies). He'd type out: 'Please advance Harry Ashbrook £5/£10/£20' and sign them H.A. Since he copied the schoolboy-square initials Harry Ainsworth used and sent them direct to the cashiers, it was hardly his fault, he argued, if the latter assumed they were authorized by the editor. (*The People* editorial offices were in Long Acre, the cashiers at 222, Strand, opposite the Law Courts, half a mile away, where the lift was operated by aged gentlemen using a rope with which to raise and lower the sideless contraption. It took Odhams Press some years to join the post-war world, such as ceasing to refer to cinemas as kinemas.) Anyway, Harry Ashbrook would then H.A. an authorization to his expenses to more than cover his advances, and since the simplicity of such robbery encourages greed, the time came when the chief accountant was emboldened to ask Harry Ainsworth and Sam Campbell if it was all right for the expenses of the news and features editor of *The People* to exceed the combined total of the Odhams board.

The following day the news and features editor of *The People* was Charles Rowe.

It was *The People* that employed a man whose expenses, unique in my experience, had to be increased whether he liked it or not. This was Ken Bailey who, when he joined to write about radio and television, was said to be a practising Quaker, which meant among other things that he never told a lie. Certainly his expenses proved to be limited to bus and tube fares and the cost of cups of tea and bath buns in the BBC canteen. By today's standards they totalled two or three pounds a week – less than the price of a round of drinks on his colleagues' expense sheets. Sam Campbell, who had as much respect for the firm's money as Harry Ainsworth, was enormously pleased, until the accountants hinted that everybody, but everybody, should follow the splendid example set by this paragon, whereupon Sam gave Ken a fixed expense allowance and told him to sort it out between his conscience and the Inland Revenue.

Usually expenses – or what is left of them after advances – are collected on Fridays. At Odhams, High Holborn, it was on Thursdays, which meant that in the evening the Compasses was relatively busy for that fag-end day of the publican's week. Quick to become aware of this was one of life's more amiable, if unsuccessful, conmen, Maytum White.

I first met him when, after serving time for some newsprint fraud, he sold his Wandsworth (or Wormwood Scrubs) memoirs to Sam Campbell, which I ghosted. Conmen, of whom I met my share in Fleet Street, either when we exposed them or when they sold their 'shameful confessions', fell into various categories. Maytum White filled the *People's* 'cad' description: tall, good looking, elegantly dressed, well spoken and arrogant, thus giving the impression of being a real toff (i.e. gentleman). The story he sold us was an excoriating attack on the brutishness of certain warders in the prison concerned, earned him some money, but did him no good at all when he went back inside a few months later.

The trouble with Maytum was that while in prison he would devise some grand, foolproof confidence trick for which, on his release, he needed a chauffeur-driven Rolls, a Savile Row/Jermyn Street wardrobe, a suite at the Ritz (and so forth) with which to create a suitable background ready for a kill that never came: along the line he'd be arrested on false pretences charges for the acquiring of his props.

His sentences were never for very long periods, but in the end, tired and dispirited, he came to the conclusion that he was not destined to become a master criminal. For a while he tried his hand as a petty one, and it was during this period that I met him in the York Minster in Soho after a gap of about ten years. Red-veined and watery eyes blinked from what was now a magenta loofah of face, his dated clothes were frayed and grubby and several sizes too large, although he still managed to wear his greasy James Lock homburg at a defiantly jaunty angle. He was in the area looking for old chums in the hope that one would cash him a cheque for £10 'to save me the trouble of going to East Ham'. Why that remote and bleak suburb? 'The cheque is made out to me, opened to "pay cash" but means I have to go to Barclays in East Ham to cash it . . . I'm between bank accounts at the moment.' With a touch of his old stylishness: 'Actually, to save me time and trouble, you can have it for a fiver.' I understood his generosity when I read the signature on the cheque, which Maytum insisted upon showing me as an added assurance that it wouldn't bounce: Aristotle Socrates Onassis.

I bought him a scotch, for which he thanked me with a nod before looking for other old chums. Having established that I now worked for *Illustrated*, it did not take him long to find the Compasses, or to discover that Thursday was a popular day there. This led him to trying his hand at journalism, which involved hanging around El Vino, The Wig and Pen Club and various pubs in order to establish contacts and sell them ideas and diary items. In the end he did quite well at it.

Indeed, it was the end that provided the best reason for mentioning the tragi-comic Maytum White. He collapsed in the street one evening, recognized a heart attack and said to the passer-by who came to his aid: 'We are in Fulham, are we not?'

'Yes, but . . .'

'Fulham!' Maytum White gasped. 'S.W.6! I can just see the obituary in *The Times*: "Maytum White dies in Fulham." No, no, no, it won't do at all. I can't possible die here! Be a good fellow and drag me across the road to S.W.7.'

The bemused man did so, whereupon Maytum White uttered a grateful sigh as he expired in South Kensington.

★   ★   ★

It was an item on my expenses – ironically absolutely genuine, not a penn'orth of profit – that caused me to leave *The People* and join *Illustrated*. This was in 1954 with Sam Campbell now in undisputed control of the paper, Harry Ainsworth sharing his time between attempts to save the ailing *Daily Herald* ('What about free insurance?') and rolling up a trouser leg behind the locked door of his office at meetings with fellow Freemasons. Tony Clarkson had asked me a number of times to join *Illustrated* to negotiate the purchase of series, but I couldn't decide until my mind was made up for me as the result of a lunch which began with Sam calling me to his office where he sat beaming and rubbing his hands. 'It's going to be a corker, chum,' he greeted me.

'What is?'

'Orson Welles.' (The actor was in London playing Othello in a generally badly received production at the St James's Theatre.) 'He's finished in Hollywood. They won't have him back. He's washed-up. Burned-out by drink and women. Hated. Finished. Done for. Up to his eyes in debt. So get him to do a series for us: "The Evil Men of Hollywood. The Sordid Facts by Orson Welles." He'll give us the dirt, chum; he must hate them as much as they hate him. All the sex and the vice. All the big names like . . . er . . . Clark Gable and Edward G. Robinson, Madeleine Carrol . . . um . . . Laurel and Hardy. Rin-Tin-Tin.'

'A *dog*?'

'A dog,' Sam echoed bleakly, then, recovering quickly: 'Animal cruelty, chum! Great womb-trembling stuff. It's going to be a corker. Offer him 150 quid for a three-part series. I'm told he's so broke he'll jump at it. On the breadline, but wants to live posh. Soften him up with a lunch. He must be starving.'

'Aren't they paying him at the St James's?'

'Peanuts,' said Sam with an airy wave of his hand. 'I'm told it's all taken at source for alimony. The play's going to fold any minute, anyway. So hurry.'

Because he needed to be at the theatre in the morning, Orson Welles opted to lunch locally at Wilton's in Bury Street. It was only when I arrived there that I remembered hearing that Wilton's was arguably the most expensive seafood restaurant in London. Those were the days before credit cards were widely used, and I had no cheque book, but it was Friday, so I had a week's salary in my pocket, plus the balance of my expenses – a total of about £10. This may not sound very much, but was the equivalent of £100 today. So I wasn't worried. To begin with.

I think it was the way the big man's eyes sparkled and he seemed to salivate as he read the menu that cautioned prudence, so while he ordered a large vodka and tonic, then another, I stretched out a half-pint of lager. Welles continued with a dozen Number One oysters. I chose the potted shrimps. Since the oysters were delicious (he assured me), he had another dozen. I settled for the toast that had accompanied the potted shrimps. We (mostly he) washed down our hors d'oeuvres with a bottle of Chablis. Another bottle accompanied 'a really nice big lobster, waiter. Plain grilled with butter, and a salad on the side.' Since the price of lobsters was determined by size, I hadn't the faintest idea what Welles was letting me in for, so I told him I was a potted shrimp freak and ordered another portion as my main course, hanging on to the toast in case he wanted cheese or pudding. He did. Both. Followed by coffee and two large brandies.

Then thank the Lord, he had to hurry off for a meeting (doubtless early tea at the Ritz), assuring me that he'd be happy to provide a three-part series on Hollywood, and no, he didn't need a ghost since he was not a complete illiterate having written a few bits and pieces in his time, including the film script for *Citizen Kane*. 'Mind you,' he warned me, 'it might not be as lurid as your editor expects.' Interestingly for a man on the breadline, he didn't mention money, and when I diffidently volunteered

£150, he shrugged an indifferent: 'Sure. Whatever you say. It'll be fun to do.'

When the bill came the management did not have to call the police, although I earned filthy looks for badly undertipping and for the silver and pennies that helped make up the total. In my panic I forgot to retain a few coppers for a bus fare and had to walk back to the office.

As I walked I realized that, while Orson Welles had been a delightful companion, full of great stories, I'd been so worried about being able to pay the bill I'd only half listened to him. But I do recall asking him what his next film was going to be about, and his very slow and very solemn reply: 'It's going to be about a circus . . . The hero is a clown . . . But underneath his smiling face . . . He's really a very happy man . . .'

Orson Welles' material arrived just two days later: great stuff, consisting of a string of very witty Hollywood anecdotes. Unfortunately, the humour was much too clever for *The People*, and in any case Sam Campbell was expecting powerful exposures, as he wasted no time pointing out as he went through it. 'What's it all about?' he groaned from time to time. 'What does it all mean? . . . No wonder he's all washed up.' With a cry of triumph he came across one of his anathema words: psychiatrist. 'I suppose he means mind doctor. So why doesn't he say so? Look, chum, think of your Sheffield bus driver reading *The People*. Does he know what psychiatrist means? Course not! If he did he'd buy the *Observer* or *Sunday Times*. Are we supposed to run a panel with each instalment translating all his intellectual lah-de-dah into English? . . . Psychiatrist! I suppose the clown went to university.' (Another of Sam's great hates.)

He continued reading, his face a set sneer, his silence punctuated by *pshaws* of contempt and catarrh-noisy sniffs at his Benzedrine inhaler. When he reached the end of the second instalment he signed heavily and uttered one of his most damning criticisms: 'It's bloody *magaziney*, chum. Look, it's all very posh with long words no one can understand. Your highbrow toffs on the *Spectator* and *Times Literary Supplement* will lap it up. *But what's the point of it all*? Where's the dirt? Where's the filth? The bitterness?' After swallowing some rhetoric-calming tablets: 'I suppose I'd better finish it.' And so he came to the anecdote about

Spyros Skouras, the penniless Greek immigrant who fulfilled the American dream by becoming millionaire president of Twentieth Century-Fox. It went something like this:

On their twenty-fifth wedding anniversary Skouras asked his wife what she would like as a present. She smiled and with a shy giggle said that in romantic remembrance of old times when they were poor and shabby she'd like to go back to the hotel at Niagara Falls where they had spent their penny-pinching weekend of a honeymoon. Skouras did better than just go back there: as President of Twentieth Century-Fox it needed no more than a snap of the fingers and a cheque book to obtain the same room, refurnished and redecorated in the manner of twenty-five years earlier; to instruct everyone present in the hotel that weekend to dress in the clothes of the period; to ensure that the band confined its music to the year concerned; and for the hotel to dig out and reproduce the relevant menus.

So they went to Niagara Falls, and in the bedroom at the end to the first day, Skouras asked his wife: 'How's it so far, honey?' She assured him that so far it was all right, adding: 'And now if you remember, beloved, I went to the bathroom first, then you.'

'Of course, my darling,' said Skouras indulgently.

When he came from the bathroom the lights in the bedroom were dimmed, but not sufficiently to conceal the expression on his wife's face as she sat in bed, looking him up and down. 'What is it honey?' Skouras inquired.

'I was just thinking,' she replied.

'Thinking what, honey?'

'Twenty-five years ago you were a Greek God... Now you're just a goddam Greek.'

When Sam Campbell reached the end of the story, which also completed the series, he asked: 'Where's the rest of it?'

'Rest of what?'

'The instalment.'

'That is the end.'

'You mean Greek God, goddam Greek is *it*? You mean that's funny? A joke? When she reads it, your old mum in her cottage will be rolling on the floor screaming with hysterical laughter?' Sam nodded. 'That's great. Wonderful.' He beamed. 'Now explain it to me.' He leaned back in his chair, put his feet on his desk, hooked his thumbs into the armholes of his waistcoat and cocked his head to one side. 'Go ahead.'

I had no intention of allowing Sam to enjoy half-an-hour of Kersh baiting. 'I don't understand it either,' I said. 'I'm merely showing you what Orson Welles wrote.'

'Sure,' said Sam, all sweet reason. 'Just go back and ask him what it means. Explain to him that neither of us can make head nor bloody tail of it, so what's it all about?'

'Shall I take him to lunch again?' I asked innocently, then remembered that I hadn't had time to put in my Wilton's expenses.

'Ah, the lunch. How did it go?'

'Fine. But you were right when you said he's starving.'

'How's that?'

I told him. By the time I'd finished Sam's feet were off the desk and firmly on the ground, while his thumbs were out of his waistcoat and helping his fingers in their agitated rummage among the pills and potions. 'Y . . . You . . . *YOU* . . .' After much deep breathing and the use of a throat spray, an incredulous: '*You spent £10 on a lunch?!*'

'It wasn't my bloody fault,' I protested. 'I'll show you the bill. All I'm down for is ten bobsworth: half of lager, two portions of potted shrimps and a glass-and-a-half of Chablis.'

'*Ten bloody quid!*' Sam howled. 'In future, if you want to spend more than £2 on a lunch, get my permission first.' This wasn't a wild, forget-it-in-the-morning outburst of fury: in the morning he sent a memo confirming the edict.

I tried to visualize the Over £2 law in action. Suppose my guest and I ordered our meals, and I worked out that with a tip the total cost would be £1 17s 6d. Then my guest says: 'I wouldn't mind some cheese with another glass of wine (small port) if that's all right with you.' Realizing that this would take the cost to £2 2s, do I say: 'Hold on a minute while I make a quick phone call?' And if I did, would I be certain of knowing where Sam Campbell was lunching that day? If not, or for some other reason I cannot raise him, do I say to my guest: 'I'm afraid it's not all right. *The People* doesn't run to cheese and an extra glass of wine (small port) . . . Oh, and here's the ticket for your hat and coat. Pay at the cloakroom, there's a good chap.'

When I caught Sam in a suitably amiable mood, I pointed out the impracticabilities attending the £2 rule. He sighed his why-am-I-surrounded-by-idiots? sigh. 'You've got it the wrong way round, chum.'

'How?'

'More than £2 is going to be the exception, not the rule. There's far too much money spent on lunches. Work it out for yourself. People whose stories we buy get paid, so there's no need to buy them lunch, is there? People who want to get in the paper should buy *us* lunch. People we expose don't deserve lunch, do they? I know there are in-between situations, so you buy them egg on toast at Lyons, or sausage and mash and half of bitter at the pub.'

'You're worse than H.A.,' I said, appalled.

Sam grinned with genuine pleasure at the compliment (even at his most sincere he made one think of Chaucer's smyler with the knyf under the cloke.) 'Of course,' he conceded, 'there are times when you need to do something more posh, like this fiasco with Orson Welles, and . . .'

'At your suggestion,' I interrupted.

'But I didn't suggest twenty quidsworth of champagne and caviare in Mayfair!' Sam countered. 'What I'm saying is that when you think you need to buy one of those Flash Harry lunches, see me first and I'll tell you whether it's worth more than two quid and if so where to go. Otherwise take 'em to Lyons. You'll be amazed at how many eggs on toast you can get for two quid.'

I felt my stomach moving slowly towards my throat at the thought of a future dominated by endless egg and toast lunches. As soon as I could I left Sam's office, telephoned Tony Clarkson and a fortnight later joined *Illustrated*.

TEN

The Man Who Cut Stalin

When Tony Clarkson – tall, broad, strikingly handsome – arrived from New Zealand, his first job was as a sub-editor on the *Daily Worker* (now the *Morning Star*). Not long after his appointment he was sent for by the editor whom he found flanked by the paper's editorial committee. All were glum-faced and with restless eyes (the sort of communists who, having avoided being purged, look apprehensively about them in case threatened with an enema) and without a greeting between them, unless you count the editor's: 'You're fired . . . er . . . um . . . Comrade Clarkson.'

'But why?' asked a flabbergasted Tony.

'You're fired,' the editor repeated.

Again: 'But why?'

'It is better you do not ask, comrade,' said the editor.

Since the editor and committee now remained inexorably stony-faced and silent, Tony went, the lack of explanation matched by lack of compensation. It proved to be no great hardship financially (his salary, the union minimum, was reduced by the need to pay back a percentage as a voluntary contribution to party funds), and his search for a job took him to the *Daily Mirror* where he became features editor, before volunteering for the Royal Navy and then joining *John Bull*, followed by *Illustrated* and *Reveille* after the war. For years the 'But why?' of his dismissal from the *Worker* teased him: what had been his sin of omission or commission? Tony discovered the answer when, at some reception, he met Palme Dutt.

'But why?' Tony asked him.

'We're going back a few years, aren't we?' said the ageing Bolshevik. 'But I remember the occasion well, comrade. How could I forget it? God, you nearly gave us all heart attacks. You had to go. There was nothing else for it.'

'Heart attacks? Me? How?' Tony squeaked. He squeaked with some frequency during moments of surprise, elation and ecstasy.

'Remember Stalin's speech?'

'Which one?' asked Tony.

'The one before you were fired. The one you subbed into the paper.'

Tony remembered with a falsetto: 'Yeah! Sure!' It was one of those Soviet speeches that went on for hours. Tony's task, as the sub-editor concerned, had been to fit it into the paper. 'Yeah,' he repeated. 'I was very pleased with it. I remember it well. Thousands and thousands of words, and what a problem to get them to fit in the space! In the end I had to cut only a couple of hundred, nibbling away here and there. Fiddle, fiddle, fiddle. I reckon I did a good job on that.'

'That's why you were fired.'

'For doing a good job?'

'For cutting two hundred words, comrade.'

'Out of all the thousands? Who could have noticed? It wasn't even one or two solid chunks. Nibble, nibble, nibble. Christ, no one *could* have noticed.'

'My dear comrade, you could have thrown out the advertisements (assuming we had any), omit the daily appeal for funds, kill the sport and any other trivia of the day, but you do not commit your unforgivable crime. The screams from Moscow about revisionism, recidivism, bourgeois Trotskyism . . . Because of you – doubtless pleased with yourself for playing the role of a professional journalist – we thought we were all facing expulsion from the party. Moscow checked every word in the *Worker* against the speech. Now do you see why you had to be fired and are doubtless on a Kremlin list to this day? Why you are lucky not to have had an assassin stick an ice pick into your neck, comrade?

'*You're the man who cut Stalin!*'

*   *   *

My bloomer with a Communist Leader came when I actually met one. This was in 1956 when I was on *Illustrated* magazine and Connery Chappell was its editor. (This was after Tony Clarkson had edited it – all part of the Fleet Street carousel, as will be explained.)

Marshall Tito, fabled wartime partisan leader, then president of Yugoslavia, favoured his own brand of communism: a policy for non-alignment with the rest of the Soviet bloc. Accused, as a result, of deviation from orthodox doctrine, he withdrew his country from the Cominform, and was regarded in the West as something of a hero: David defying the Stalin Goliath.

He would be eminently worth an interview, and so I wrote saying so – only in more effusive circumlocution – to the Yugoslav ambassador in London. This resulted in a visit from the press attaché, a Mr Pasic. Why did I want to interview President Tito? I gave a sort of 'Because he is there' reply. Was I a communist? No. Had I connections with the partisan-turned-traitor Mikhailovich? No. Or the so-called King and the rest of Yugoslavia's gang of royal traitors? No. And so it went on. Goodness knows what answers he was expecting.

There were more meetings with Pasic, who proved to be an amusing companion on the occasions he relaxed from his role of interrogator. After a nine-month period of gestation, word came from Belgrade that *Illustrated* could send to Yugoslavia to interview and photograph the President.

When I told Connery Chappell, he twanged his braces a couple of times before he said, baritone-serious: 'I think this is one which, as editor, I should go on myself.' He changed his mind overnight, realizing he had more important things to do. 'You go,' he advised. I left for Yugoslavia with photographer, Peter Waugh .

We stayed the first night in Belgrade and were astonished at the rude reception we were given by the hotel staff. It took so long for our luggage to be brought to our rooms we went to the foyer and carried it up ourselves. Requests for a drink were ignored. We asked for a taxi to take us on a tour of the city: nothing happened. Then someone on the staff realized we were English and advised us: 'They think you're German, so always carry your passports in your hand and make certainly people can see that you are British.'

The Yugoslavs were still filled with hate because of the atrocities committed during the German occupation. Now the Germans were back as tourists: rude, aggressive, selfish, and generally looking for another war to lose. Accompanied by wives and children, they toured the city in search of the street corners where they had shot people and used them as backgrounds for happy family snaps. No, they were not popular.

So we carried our passports like banners and found the Yugoslavs to be utterly charming.

We went on to the island of Brioni on the Istrian coast where Tito had a villa. Apart from that (certainly in 1956), it boasted little more than two five-star type hotels. Visiting Brioni was by invitation only, such invitations limited generally to party intellectuals who formed the post-revolution aristocracy.

Tito also had half his zoo at Brioni; the other half was on his private island, Vanga, which held another villa and his personally tended vineyard. The first day was spent on Vanga, where I did my interview as pheasants paraded the footpaths and does peered at us from the bushes. Our interpreter was Dr Joza Vilfan, Tito's general secretary, although I suspected that the President knew more English than he'd admit.

During a break Tito demonstrated his extraordinary charm: he was the most charismatic man I have known. His was true, natural charm. It could not be quantified, or modified by political attitudes: it was inherent in the man. Tito's wife, Madam Broz (she never adopted his *nom-de-guerre*), had fought alongside him with the partisans, was Junoesque in her attraction, and was also charming, if lacking her husband's touch of magic.

Tito cut watermelon, made coffee and poured superb 1892 and 1896 Slovenian wines selected from what he whimsically referred to as his 'library'. We drunk from crystal glasses shaped like decorated boots, and Tito smiled as he filled them. His wife looked on expectantly. The reason was soon apparent: unless you knew the correct way to hold the glass, wine poured over your shirt from 'invisible' holes.

That night Peter and I and Dr Vilfan ate at the hotel on Brioni. Sometime during the evening I was hit by an agonizing attack of gastroenteritis. Fortunately I was offered the services of Tito's private doctor who was accompanying the President. The ailment must have been common in the area: he had his cure to hand. This consisted of a glass of herbal tea, a small bottle of opium drops to be taken with sugar, and a sulfa-something tablets. The concoction worked – but at what cost! I spent the entire night on the lavatory, my head over the bidet. The treatment was severe, maybe crude – but efficacious – although in the morning i was utterly drained, desperately tired and kitten-weak.

We were to take pictures on Brioni, including shots of Tito in sparkling white uniform ('For the ladies,' he smiled), piloting his naval launch and at the second half of his zoo, which included a leopard, a camel and ostriches, all of which came when called and ate out of his hand. When we met at his villa the doctor was there and asked me how I was.

'It's a diabolical liberty,' I replied, stomach-clutching and without thinking. 'I come to this Communist country and the first thing you do is purge me!' As I said it I groaned and wondered what constituted the Yugoslav equivalent of salt mines. But it must have lost something in translation for Tito roared with laughter and poured us all bumper glasses of 100° proof plum brandy – slivovitz – which traditionally must be swallowed in one gulp, even at 9 in the morning.

Or maybe it lost nothing in translation, but was Tito's Revenge: having guessed how I'd suffered during the night, and was aware that you need a fully operational galvanized gut to drink slivovitz at 9 in the morning. One thing is certain: he got the better of the exchange. Having swallowed the stuff my stomach was so raw I could neither eat solids nor drink alcohol for a week.

But the story and pictures made ten pages in *Illustrated*.

*   *   *

Back to Tony Clarkson whom I came to respect for, among other things, his mastery of the ploys involved in restaurant drinking.

As I have said, Pamela Clarkson taught him the virtues of good husbandry. There was the occasion when, needing to stay overnight in Paris in order to attend my wedding, she'd argued that it was foolish to seek a hotel on the main tourist drag and would have slept in the car had she not been eight months pregnant with her second son, Wensley (himself now a noted journalist). So Pam drove around the back streets of Paris (although he had an office Jaguar, Tony could not drive) until she found a very reasonably priced room. The surprise expressed by the receptionist at Pam's condition and the baggage brought in by Tony was equalled – nay exceeded – by that of the Clarksons when the receptionist telephoned to say that their hour was up and unless they wanted to renew their hire of the room for a further hour another lady and her friend were waiting to use it. By having to pay for the room on an hourly basis for the rest of the night it would have been infinitely less expensive for them to have booked a suite at the Crillon. It certainly guaranteed that the Clarksons were up and about very early the following morning.

As for good restaurant drinking, Tony Clarkson taught me rules I have remembered but seldom have had the courage to follow. For example:

In a restaurant, Tony counselled, beware the host who arrives before you, does not wait at the bar, but goes straight to the table. 'Now, there's a mean one!' he assured me. 'If you spot him, sneak into the bar, order a couple of quick doubles, charge them to Mr Thing, and ask if that gentleman has booked a table. *"He's arrived?"* Suitably astonished and contrite, go to the table.'

Beware even more, Tony advised, the host who asks: 'Do you like rosé?' for here indeed is a nasty piece of work who probably wears home-knitted socks. If you reply, politely, that you are inordinately fond of rosé, he will almost certainly say: 'Splendid! Let's have a glass of rosé. We can always have another glass later if we want it.' Somehow, however, Tony warned me (and rightly) you always go on to a black coffee. No brandy.

Tony gave me the only proper reply to the 'Do you like rosé?' gambit. It is simply: 'Yes, a bottle of rosé would be fine.'

Tony was convinced, with some truth, that the most embarrassing of hosts is the man who orders a half-bottle. If the glass-at-a-time man is ignorant, the half-bottle man is mean and sadistic, since halves are usually limited to the diarrhoeal ambiguities of house carafes which defy tasting or analysis. Tony's answer to the half-bottle (carafe) man was: 'Aren't you drinking?'

On the obverse side Tony taught me how to get away with ordering the least expensive wine if your guest is also in possession of a list or is looking over your shoulder. You cry: 'Chateau St Pancras at only £3 a bottle!' Lowering your voice to a whisper: 'By God, they've underpriced this one.'

It was difficult to overlook the wine list when lunching with Tony: because of deafness in his left (I think) ear you had to sit next to and close to his right ear. The problem, he confessed, was when he lunched with Hugh (now Lord) Cudlipp, who had the same problem in the same ear. As Tony's *capo di tutti capi*, he decided who sat where, which meant that he could hear Tony but Tony couldn't hear him. Tony assured me that, after a couple of bottles of wine, Hugh's 'Are you fucking deaf?' could be heard by the hard of hearing in the outer suburbs.

As for the selecting of wine, Hugh Mackay (brother of Ian, Fleet Street's finest essayist) once worked for the J. Walter Thompson advertising and public relations agency where he was put in charge of an intriguing investigation into why most people choose the third wine in any section of a wine list (be is white, red, claret, Burgundy, Loire, and so on). The agency had been given the assignment by a hotel and restaurant group who could not understand why the first and second on their lists of colours and regions did not sell, even when they were reasonably respectable products. Psychologists were hired by Hugh to probe and analyse. Their answer was fascinating in that it had nothing to do with the wine. Generally the host thought the first on the list must be too inexpensive (i.e. cheap and nasty). The second was too near the first. After the third the prices became too high. Bingo! They settled for the third. If the problem was psychological, so was the solution: a three-card trick of a shuffle was played with the numbers and prices at the top of each category and everyone was happy.

Tony confided to me at the end of a reminiscent and gin-lachrymose evening that, despite their years of friendship, he found it difficult to forgive Hugh Cudlipp for talking him into buying Hugh's boat, *Tetta.* It was an ugly and clumsy clinker-built beast, having been converted by a declining Dali of a shipwright from a lifeboat off an old liner.

At the end of his first season of ownership, Tony enquired of a boatyard on the Thames about lifting *Tetta* ashore for the winter for a bottom scrape, re-caulking and painting. The experts examined the boat, exchanged sighs, teeth-clickings, head-shakings and what used to be called meaningful glances before their leader announced that if they took the boat from the water it would have to be at the owner's risk: sometime during the winter a noise like a manic, atonal xylophone would echo along and across the Thames Valley as *Tetta* fell to pieces, the boat being held together only by the swelling caused by the water in her timbers.

Painting the boat proved to be a problem. Confined as it was to the area above water that the Clarksons and their guests could reach by leaning over the side, the waterline was an eccentric zig-zag, while Pam and Tony, terrified of what might happen if they attempted to scrape or burn away the paintwork on the superstructure, restricted themselves to applying successive coats of Woolworth's finest, so adding to *Tetta*'s considerable weight and progressively reducing the light admitted by the portholes to smudge-edged dots.

Moored on the Thames, it never left the river (or even the stretch between Henley and Walton). It was forever breaking down. I was aboard the day when Tony suffered the ignominy of being towed to shore by a small boy in a diminutive rubber dinghy to whom Tony shrieked in panic for assistance.

In *Tetta*'s cockpit stood a great oblong wooden casing from which a metal pole projected. This was the gear lever, with a simple, no clutch, method of operation: push it forward and the boat went forward; pull it backwards and the boat went into reverse; put it in the middle and the engine was in neutral. The only other mechanical challenges (apart from the engine) were the wheel, the hand throttle, the fuel and temperature gauges and speedometer, their presence academic since apart from the wheel none worked and *Tetta* seemed to decide upon her own speed – usually a maximum of 3 knots given the right tide and a following wind.

So piloting may seem to have been simple enough, but since Tony couldn't drive a car he wasn't very good at handling *Tetta*, especially when you add a couple of bottles of wine and a few Thames locks. Pam, although an excellent driver, wisely wanted nothing to do with *Tetta*'s problems. So as a general rule Tony invited guests who could drive and park a motor car and, as a bonus, examine the boat's engine when it expired like a weary and asthmatic soda-water syphon, and could do so without giving a shrill scream before going below in search of a secret (i.e. non job lot) glass of wine.

During one breakdown – I think *Tetta* ran out of fuel – I said with a sort of a kind of a cliché of a light laugh: 'You were a lieutenant-commander in the Royal Navy during the war, so surely a battle-scarred hero of the East Indies Fleet can nurse this noble vessel to shore? Remember that film with John Mills or Richard Attenborough [it had to be one or both of them]? And as the ship limped in how all the cheering crowd on the quayside sang Rule Britannia?'

Tony jumped up and down (literally) and falsettoed: 'If you n't behave I'll put you off the boat!' If aquatic disaster was not humiliation enough, Tony didn't like being reminded that his service had not contained much seamanship but was mostly concerned with the production of newspapers and magazines for the armed forces.

The day came when I enquired about *Tetta* and Tony told me, after much squeaking and prevarication and gin, that he no longer had her. His evasiveness was such that I was sure that he had scuttled her for the insurance money. The truth, when it emerged, was even more improbable: he had sold *Tetta* to an innocent who believed her to be the one surviving lifeboat of the *Titanic*.

*   *   *

It's ironic, at this stage of the game, to recall how Sam Campbell, the scourge of conmen, was himself a bit of a villain. He lived at Farnham, Surrey at Stella Cottage, once the home of Dean Swift's eponymous girl friend. It was, I remember, a beautiful place with a duck pond, riparian rights and half a share in a farm across the road. I went there just the once: to buy and bring back to London a collapsing Alvis motor car he conned me into buying. Fool that I was, I couldn't even drive at the time, and a teeth-flashing Bob

Edwards kindly travelled with me to Farnham in order to help me and my L-plates drive the doomed cow back to town.

(What happened, I wonder, to Sam's daughter whom he, like so many well-off alleged socialists, was to send to Roedean, but who was then about 5 years old and kept kicking me. 'What a great game!' cried the child-besotted father. 'Let's all kick Cyril!' And they did: I have corrugated shinbones to prove it. Bob being an obliging fellow, would have joined in had I not wagged a warning finger at him.)

Living where he did, and owing half a farm, Sam reckoned he was a good countryman. An arcane gem of bucolic law he passed on to me was: 'If you're ever lost in a wood or a forest chum, look for the moss on the trees. It always grows on the north side. So you always know where north is and can find your way home . . . What? . . . Oh yes! Let's kick Cyril again . . .'

Some days later, limping through Regent's Park, I looked at the trees. The first one I saw had moss on its east side. A day or so later I had occasion to tell Sam of my discovery. His eyes widened, and with no more pause than it takes for a short and sad sigh he replied, eye to eye: 'The silly buggers planted it the wrong way round.'

*   *   *

Tony Clarkson may have cut Stalin, but it was the cutting of circulation that caused him to lose the editorship of *Illustrated*. Great journalist though he was, the days of huge magazine sales were coming to an end as television began to replace reading and appropriate advertising revenues. As a picture magazine, *Illustrated* was particularly vulnerable, with TV offering the added dimensions of immediacy, sound and movement, and although various options were open to its proprietors other than closing it (that came later) all but one involved investing money. Inevitably Odhams Press took the one: removed the editor and engaged a replacement at a lower salary. For some months Tony suffered a long dark night of the soul in the Odhams Magazine Unit – a one-desk cupboard of meaninglessness towards the rear of the building, itself a badly converted wool warehouse in High Holborn where finding even the offices of the magazines was a Hampton Court maze of a challenge.

His gloom was deep enough to cause mutterings of resignation. 'Never resign until you see the whites of their fivers,' I advised. Nor did he, the fivers being produced by Hugh Cudlipp for taking over the editorship of *Reveille*, which Tony ran with enormous sureness of touch from 1957 to 1970.

Tony's replacement on *Illustrated* was Connery Chappell, who came up a floor from editing *Picturegoer*. On the day after his arrival he summoned me to his office and said: 'Take a seat, Cyril.' As I did so he picked up the receiver of one of the three telephones on his desk and asked his secretary to get him Leonard Coulter in New York. These were the days before direct dialling, so there was time to pick up the second phone to ask for Henry Khan in Paris. He scratched his chin as he contemplated the third phone, then with an 'Ah-ha!' of inspiration asked his secretary to ring his wife. This call came through quickly. 'Hello,' he boomed (he was a great boomer, believing it made him sound like Jack Hawkins). 'How are you? . . . No, just checking that you're OK. . . . No I'm not drunk . . . Can't stop. Got calls booked to Paris and Little Ole Noo York. 'Bye, darling.' When Paris came on the line it was: 'Henry *mon ami! Comment-vous portez vous*? . . . Just checking that everything's marching well . . . Can't stop. Got a call coming that I booked to New York. *Au revoir, mon ami.*' The call to Coulter was a similar non-event. When it was over, Connery said to me: 'Was there anything else?'

'N-no. Nothing.'

'Fine. See you soon.' He stuck his thumbs under his braces and twanged them. (He always wore braces and constantly twanged them, having been told that Alfred Hitchcock did so.)

I discovered that Connery repeated the telephone charade that day with his deputy, Harry White, photographers Joe Waldorf and Jack Esten, writer Robert Jackson and others. The reason for this odd behaviour emerged when, in the lavatory, my secretary overheard Connery's secretary telling another secretary in strictest cross-your-heart-and-hope-to-die confidence that Connery had been overwhelmed to discover that his desk held three telephones all of which were connected to the switchboard, and with which he could contact people across the world, and as editor of a picture magazine with an international coverage was actively encouraged so to do. But what was the point of having three telephones if he could not impress people with the fact?

So Harry White, Joe Waldorf, Jack Esten, Robert Jackson and myself, among others, were called in to witness and marvel at something we knew, from previous editorships, had long existed. What was never learned, in the ladies' lavatory or elsewhere, were the reactions that day of Coulter, Kahn and Mrs Chappell.

Quite apart from telephones and twanging braces, Connery was forever being impressed. As editor of *Picturegoer* he was impressed by film stars and directors and press agents. Thus he wore herringbone-patterned suits because Ralph Richardson was said to favour them. He grew a moustache in the manner of Don Ameche whom he had sat next to at a dinner. He took to lunching at the Dorchester because Leslie Banks was said to do so. Troubled at never seeing him, Connery wondered if he was using the wrong restaurant at the hotel until Harry White gave me the task of telling him, *en passant*, that it was tragic that they didn't make 'em like Leslie Banks any more, today being the tenth (or whatever) anniversary of the actor's death.

For some weeks Connery was in a lunchtime quandary until he heard that Laurence Olivier often ate the L'Ecu de France. So he went to that establishment, which he alternated with The Ivy, The Caprice, and Grosvenor House Hotel and other places where great names were said to congregate. Yet I have a feeling that if they were ever coincidentally present, they failed to recognize him.

Dear Connery. He often wondered why people in France had to struggle to keep straight faces when he was introduced to them. Who was I to tell him that, pronounced in the French fashion, his Christian name was a very, very vulgar version of stupidity.

Tony Clarkson had engaged me on *Illustrated* as features adviser. For the most part this meant negotiating with publishers and literary agents for books suitable for serialization or as one-off features, then adapting them for publication.

It could be a frustrating task. A number of people – particularly the newer and more awkward agents – didn't want to sell me things, despite being offered generous sums of money. I had to buy large lunches and much strong drink just in the hope of squeezing from them information about the goods they had on offer. After a while I discovered part of the reason for this reluctance – a sense of shame about the quality of the books on their lists, even if it was the stuff that would sell. An added dimension with agents: although much of their income came from the 10 per cent cut they received from selling serializations of their client's works, they truly hated doing business. So when a publisher gave me materials and added: 'If you're interested, Exe, Wye, and Zed are the agents,' I'd telephone, make an offer, and could sometimes hear the groans at the other end of the line.

These accompanied the thought: 'Oh God! This means having to haggle over the price and then cope with a contract. Then they'll send me a cheque which I'll have to pay into the bank and then calculate my 10 per cent cut and send a cheque to the author for the balance. Then again, can I get more money elsewhere? Since I have no idea of a fair price I'd better put it up for auction.' Having been told by well-wishers that being an agent was a doddle, they were now bitter at not having Agatha Christie and Somerset Maugham and war hero authors whose material sold itself. There were noble exceptions, such as my own agent, Jim Reynolds, but he used to be a publisher. Generally speaking, give me publishers any time, even if some are slow payers.

All this is by the way. My career on *Illustrated* progressed when I was made features editor and found myself in charge of a dozen writers and a similar number of photographers.

The latter were masters of the art of writing expenses. Their totals were enormous, but could rarely be faulted: apart from taxis, no one item cost more than a trifling half-a-crown (say 50 pence today). Hire of deckchair for model to sit on . . . Ice creams for model to lick for photography . . . Cloakroom fee for model to change (plus tip) . . . Sunburn lotion for model . . . Gratuity to small boy for holding cameras (to avoid sand getting in them) . . . Ice Cream for ditto . . . Car park fee . . . There was no trick unknown or unused, and most didn't need receipts.

Mallindine (whose first name I forget at this distance since he was always known as Mally) had a splendid answer when *Illustrated* was caught up in an Odham's economy drive and photographers were told they could save money by using a bus or the Underground instead of taking taxis. Mally did his research, went to Holborn station, demanded to see the Station-master and said: 'Either order me out of the station or have me arrested.'

After many 'Ehs?' and 'Whats?' and much blinking by the Stationmaster, Mally said: 'According to by-law so-and-so [he quoted it in its entirety, including sub-sections, minor clauses and paragraph numbers], 'it is an offence to carry inflammatory substances on London Underground. I have twelve highly inflammable films in this case. Will you please do me the courtesy of ordering me to leave.'

'Bugger off,' said the stationmaster, convinced he was dealing with a drunk or a lunatic.

A delighted Mallindine did so, and returned to the office with the information that he'd been barred from using the Underground because his inflammable films constituted a fire hazard. He quoted the by-law and smiled broadly when I told him he'd better stick to taxis. So Mally, and all the other photographers, continued to use the Underground and charge taxis.

Another bit of sauce came from writer Allen Andrews whose expenses regularly carried the item: 'Hospitality cigarettes – non cigarette smoker myself.' This was true in that he didn't smoke cigarettes: the money helped to pay for his pipe tobacco.

Driving with photographer Eric Auerbach made me think he was unbalanced – until he explained that his fits of manic giggling were due to most sets of letters on UK number plates being filthy words in Czech.

Ken Russell, the film maker, worked for me as a freelance on *Illustrated* in the fifties, wearing a pyjama top instead of a shirt and taking marvellously imaginative pictures. A classic was a beautiful study in light and shade of a row of 'city gents' – bowler hats, black jackets and striped trousers, umbrellas and brief cases – crossing Hyde Park on pogo sticks. (As a favour to me, he took the photographs at the christening in 1956 of Tony Clarkson's younger son, Wensley.)

At about this time *Illustrated* ran a series on Baron, then the most fashionable of society photographers. It involved publishing selections of his pictures of famous sitters – Dame Margot Fonteyn, Mae West, Dame Edith Sitwell, Alfred Hitchcock,

George Bernard Shaw, and so on – to which he added his captions. The magazine needed photographs of the photographer, so somewhere in the files of whoever now owns the Odham's Picture Library are photographs of Baron arriving at Victoria or Waterloo railway station accompanied by a young assistant festooned with the great man's cameras: Anthony Armstrong-Jones, now Lord Snowdon. (When he did set up on his own the young Armstrong-Jones came to see me with pictures to sell. I don't recall ever buying any.)

The finest story I know involving a photographer is of *Illustrated*'s Russell Westwood's derring-do during the Suez fiasco. I sent out something of a blanket coverage with Britain's sea and airborne troops, the French and the Israelis. Russell landed with the British. At some point during our advance he walked forward into No Man's Land, calmly snapping away. Colleagues, from all sorts of nationalities, and in a Babel of tongues, shouted at him: *'Come back! Come back! That's a minefield! A MINEFIELD! Come back!'*

Doggedly Russell plodded on, clicking away until, film exhausted, he turned back – to a hero's welcome. His outstanding bravery was explained when he sent me a cable requesting batteries, which proved to be not for his flash gun, but his deaf aid.

*   *   *

One day a group of staff, led by writer Chiquita Sandilands, burst into my office to say: 'The editor! He's screaming out for Harry White' [his deputy], 'but since Harry's on holiday, could you go?'

I listened at the wall that separated my office from Connery's, but could hear nothing. 'No,' said Chiquita, 'he's in the lavatory and wants a pair of scissors.'

As an editor Connery was entitled to his private lavatory. It was situated, like a corner cupboard, on a landing between *Illustrated* and *Woman* on the floor below. His cries had been heard only because these journalists had used the stairs rather than Odham's eccentric lift service.

Me, flatly: 'A pair of scissors.'

'Yes,' said Chiquita as the others nodded. 'And please hurry. He sounds on the verge of hysterics.'

Utterly baffled, I picked up my scissors, which had slim, sharply pointed, 8-inch blades and were used mostly for cutting up page proofs, and trotted down to Connery's lavatory. After I knocked at the door and introduced myself: 'What's up?'

A gasped: 'Scissors. Under the door.'

'Are you sure you're all right?'

Pleading now: 'Under the door. *Please.*'

I tried, but the scissors were too thick. 'You'll have to open the door,' I told him.

A groan, then the door opened an inch, Connery's finger-ends curled around it. 'So what's the matter?' I asked, holding back the scissors from the bits of fingers on display.

After much persuasion and prevarication it transpired that the scissors were not for some dramatic self-immolation because Laurence Olivier hadn't recognized him at the Ritz, but to cut his pubic hairs free from his zip.

I passed him the scissors.

In many ways Connery Chappell did appear to be a bit of a braces-twanging clown, but he was a good journalist with the political wit to keep one option open: on *Picturegoer* and *Illustrated* no one was allowed to attack the Rank Organization or its films. So when his tenure at *Illustrated* came to an end (the rumour was a nervous breakdown inspired by Anna Neagle coming up to him at the Mirabelle and saying 'Hello') he had a bolthole: Rank's boss, John Davis, offered him a directorship at Pinewood Studios where he was put in charge of producing the firm's initial, tentative and generally dreadful excursions into television series.

(Harry White wept when he announced that the great man was leaving *Illustrated*: a hypnotically disconcerting sight since tears poured for both eyes, despite the fact that one was a glass replacement of the victim of Dunkirk.)

Those early Rank ventures into TV are remembered now with hilarity at their awfulness by curio collectors, and with affection only by a lunatic fringe of self-flagellants. Connery's brief was to make them as inexpensive as possible and sell them here and in the United States for vast sums of money. Forgotten or unknown actors from Hollywood B-films were brought over to star in them. British supporting actors were required to adopt mid-Atlantic accents (metaphorically where the exports were to sink).

They really were appalling cheapo abominations. Closed venetian blinds hid the absence of even a painted canvas backcloth of an outside set, while 'Let's go!' cutting to where they were next supposed to be, saved money in terms of scriptwriters having to think up (i.e. use another scene for) a visual exit from a block of flats or wherever. Outside locations came from film libraries to be used for back projections, and all music was out of copyright. And so it went on. (Even the Pinewood tea boys and canteen waitresses were said to be so ashamed that they used *noms-de-plume* and pretended to work elsewhere.)

Somewhere at Pinewood Connery discovered the set for a St James's Palace scene from some Regency romance, and a blackcloth showing St Paul's Cathedral in the nineteenth century. What a way to save money: create a TV series around them! The pilot had the bewigged and powdered Prince Regent at St James's Palace stamping a foot and saying 'Aw ma, I don't wanna get married,' before being seen, to the accompaniment of Chopin's wedding march, outside St Paul's with its background of smoke-belching Industrial Revolution chimneys. When someone pointed out that the Prince Regent didn't live at St James's Palace and (quite apart from the smoking chimneys and Chopin) didn't marry at St Paul's, Connery twanged his braces and boomed: 'Let him sue.'

Connery enjoyed it enormously while it lasted. At one stage he telephoned me and arranged, very conspiratorially, a meeting in the bar of a hotel somewhere in that grey area where Bloomsbury abandons faded gentility for soot- and squalor-patinated St Pancras. I know I probably didn't rate the Savoy, and that he made the meeting sound very hush-hush, but why the masochistic exercise in damp and decay? I never did discover the answer, although I toyed with the idea that Connery was fantasizing the role of one of Pinewood's current TV heroes, a New York cop on loan to Scotland Yard as an undercover operator. Thank God – and assuming my theory to be correct – Connery didn't attempt to imitate the actor's habit of speaking through the almost closed lips of an expressionless face as if advised that even the slightest display of emotion would crack the Polyfilla hiding the wrinkles of the oldest policeman in living memory apart from Dixon of Dock Green.

The next mystery came when Connery arrived. I had ready for him the large Gordon's and tonic with ice and lemon that had been his immutable pre-meal or saloon bar drink for as long as I'd known him, but he said with a frown and some disapproval: 'No, no, no. Not gin. Scotch. Teacher's. No ice.'

I was going to ask him why the change from gin, but he began telling me, in his amusing – if lengthy and extravagant – manner, anecdotes about Pinewood, of new restaurants and wines he had discovered, and so on. While drink followed drink, reminding me of his conversion to scotch, I didn't manage to squeeze in a question about the whisky distillery he'd encountered on his road to Damascus.

He went on to tell me why he wanted to see me: to write the pilot for a TV series about Dick Turpin, preferably one that didn't involve many locations or too much riding, swordplay or other swash and buckle, both for reasons of economy and because the actor they wanted to play the highwayman wasn't so agile these days, being arthritic, haemorrhoidal and a bit of a drinker. Snapping his fingers to order another round, Connery went on: 'And don't make the language too obscure. Lay off the "Prithee" and "Have at you" and "Lawks-a-mercy" and "Zounds" and things. The Yanks have got to understand the dialogue.'

'A sort of West Country western,' I suggested.

'Exactly!'

'Eh me hearties, let's mosey down to the pen at Noogate and spring Dead-eyed Dick before they lasso him for a necktie party at Tyburn. We'll bushwhack 'em in the Strand.'

Connery considered this and replied: 'You can have *some* English in it. Just don't overdo it.'

He changed the subject back to himself and the point came when he said: 'John Davis. We call him The Big Fellow. He comes to Pinewood every Thursday. Has an office there. And do you know Cyril, every Thursday afternoon he calls me to his office. Without fail. *Every Thursday afternoon.*' Connery's voice was now truly filled with awesome respect. 'He then takes out his keys and opens his drinks cupboard – and he doesn't do that for any Tom, Dick or Harry I can tell you – and with his own hands pours two large, neat Teacher's. Despises gin.'

Which is how I learned why Connery Chappell gave up Gordon's and tonic.

I did the Dick Turpin pilot in collaboration with writer Peter Baker, but Connery left Pinewood before he could do anything about it.

One of the people who most impressed Connery was Odham's man in Paris, Henry Kahn: a short, squat, yet solid man who always looked in need of a shave and whose black hair was cropped to his broad, flat skull long before skinheads were thought of. Equally odd to the memory because it, too, had yet to be invented, was his Sony Walkman: in fact a primitive hearing aid. (At the time of the Fall of France Henry went to the abandoned Galeries Lafayette in Paris, stole a bicycle and pedalled towards the coast and freedom – on the way being deafened by the bombs dropped by the Germans on fleeing civilians.)

He returned to France after the war to continue his journalistic career, and was married two or three times. When I first knew him he was living with a lady and when I asked him why he didn't make her wife number three (or four) he replied: 'Because I don't want to lose her.' This may sound simplistic, but the logic was unarguable: like so many multi-married men Henry had a death wish in that he always married a clone of the women who had caused him so much initial grief. (Ironically, although he did not marry this last lady it did not prevent her from robbing him blind and running away with a teenage burglar.)

Henry impressed Connery (and also the knowledgeable) because he was not only a great *amateur* of food and wine, but a good cook. He knew what it was all about without Sunday supplement or TV cookery feature whimsicality and/or pretentiousness and/or patronizing to help him turn a kitchen into a full colour gastronomic Utopia. His affectations were private and I discovered them by accident.

For one, he had a sort of Visitors' Book in which he entered the names and dates of his guests, noted lunch or dinner, listed what he'd cooked and added his comments: 'Mushrooms could have done with another quarter of a minute' sort of thing. For another, he spent much of his life going through the 900-plus pages of *Le Guide Culinaire* by the great Escoffier, with its 6,000 plus combinations and permutations of recipes, just for the fun of testing them and adding his comments and criticisms. (Generally a placid guest, the one thing that depressed him was when he came to London and people said: 'You must be so looking forward to something English for a change,' and he'd find himself eating steak and kidney pie/pudding, limp cabbage and collapsing boiled potatoes up to a dozen times in a fortnight.)

One night, with my wife Suzanne (a lovely French lady and herself no mean cook) I went to dinner at Henry's flat in Montmartre. His other guests (names forgotten) were the *maire-adjoint* and his wife from Besançon in the Jura. The deputy mayor was an expert on France's hundreds of cheeses, particularly Gruyère, which his family had been making for some 500 years, give or take a generation.

Henry cooked a superb meal of sole followed by duck and things, but his *pièce de résistance*, for the benefit of the deputy mayor, was a huge area of olive wood which Henry could barely carry in from the kitchen so laden was it with cheeses, in the middle (needless to say) a vast slab of Gruyère. 'Tell me what you think', invited a beaming Henry, who had spent a fortune buying the cheeses from Fauchon, probably the most expensive specialist shop of its kind in Paris.

The *maire-adjoint*, finger pointing, toured the board – Camembert, Brie, Pont-L'Évêque, Munster, Versailles, Forêt du Nord, Reblochon, and so on and so on, each rewarded with a frown, a move, a murmur of pleasure, a little groan or a nod. Finally Henry could contain himself no longer. 'The Gruyère!' he cried. 'What about the Gruyère?'

The deputy mayor turned his attention to the centrepiece whereupon his frown became its deepest and his mouth its most glum before he shook his head and gave a sort of a bark. He pulled himself together to say with a mixture of reproof and apology: 'Too many holes.'

It transpired that this wasn't a joke: experts do judge Gruyère by the number (and size) of its holes.

ELEVEN

Play Up, Play Up And Pass The Scotch

The Rome Olympics in 1960 inaugurated the dramatic emergence of black African athletes when Abebe Bikila of Ethiopia won the marathon. At conference, Reg Payne, then editor of the *Sunday Mirror*, asked sports editor George Casey: 'How is it that this nigger wins a gold medal? Here are we in the West, with all the training facilities and tech-fucking-nology and diets and gyms and drugs and what have you, yet this coon comes out of the jungle and beats us. You're supposed to the fucking sports editor, so tell us how he did it.'

George – a memorably big, broad, strong-as-an-ox cockney – didn't need time to consider the question. 'Look, Skip [all editors were diminutives of Skipper], if your only training was a hundred yards start on a starving fucking lion you'd also break the marathon record.'

At the other end of the intellectual sports spectrum of the Mirror Group was Peter Wilson (father of TV's Julian), an anachronism among Fleet Street's ragamuffins of the day. Harrow-educated, moustache-twirling and elegant in his double-breasted Glen Urquhart checks (he was said to favour a monocle at weekends and his cane was reputed to be a swordstick), he entertained guests at the Derby with champagne and oysters served from the boot of his car; the epitome of much-envied upper-class charm and style.

Yet, as 'The Man They Can't Gag', he created a genre of sports reporting – particularly boxing – that was, from its inception, an utter parody. This sort of thing, and I do not exaggerate, except to economize on paragraph marks:

Tonight I am proud to be British. (With an introduction like that you knew our chap lost.) *As he stood there, in the loneliest square in the world, his mouth an unzipped red purse, only a heart as big as his body kept Thingummy going on rubber legs as Whatsit thundered cruelly clinical straight rights into his pathetic and bloody mask of a face with the pitiless remorselessness of a steamhammer. But our hero did not flinch during the twenty seconds of that first round before he was clubbed, with callous cruelty, into unconsciousness. My pounding heart testifies to his bravery. Make him boxing's first knight. TODAY! I demand it! It is not for nothing that I am called The Man They Can't Gag!*

Peter Wilson could make those 20 seconds of pugilistic disaster last for three pages in the *Mirror* followed by 2,000–word instalments in endless series: 'My Greatest Fights' . . . 'Great British Champs' . . . 'Ringside Witness' . . . even when the time came for short *aide-mémoire* biographies of the fighters to preface the stories for the benefit of all but the most aged boxing fans with total recall.

*　　*　　*

When Michael Christiansen edited the *Sunday Mirror* and hired a sportsman to write (or put his name to) a column or series, he made certain that the sportsman's contract included a Clause Thirteen. Even if the contract was made up of only eight clauses one of them was numbered thirteen. This stated that the person undertook to play for a *Sunday Mirror* team one game of football/cricket/golf/snooker – the choice to be that of the editor, at his absolute discretion – each season for the duration of his contract. Mike assumed, generally correctly, that racing drivers, high jumpers, tennis players and boxers could have a go at one of these (and other) sports, and even if they were not their own would still prove to be world beaters when compared to the overall ragtag and bobtail of the native *Sunday Mirror* players. It didn't always work (why should Mary Rand be able to play darts or Henry Cooper set a new altitude record for flying a kite in Kensington Gardens?), but Mike had his triumphs when his cricket team took on village sides whose morale was destroyed by the appearance of former England cricket captain, Ted Dexter, and similar names from a formidable list of other champions.

Which is how I can say that from time to time I played in the same side as Ted Dexter, my greatest triumph being in a game against the *Sunday Express* when I scored three runs (all, somehow, off the back of the bat) before being bowled by Dennis Compton.

Mike was the true Corinthian in that he played his cricket, golf, football, darts, cribbage, dice games and poker for the sheer love of so doing. As a player he had no silver-plated eggcups to celebrate success at these sports and pastimes, although one of his exploits did make news of a sort.

This occurred when Mike called me to his office to show me a new golf club he'd bought. Why he chose me I will never know since I have never played, or wanted to play, golf, and its terminology has always been as obscure to me as the imperfect in Albanian grammar. I nodded, smiled and, dredging P. G. Wodehouse memories, said that it was a jolly good niblick or mashie.

Mike groaned and made cone shapes with his fingers and placed them on top of his head, a familiar gesture when he was angry. 'It's a driver!' he cried. 'Look, I'll show you.' He crossed to his desk on which stood, for some reason, a bag of pears. 'Just lie on the carpet.'

I did so. He placed a pear on my head. Although I, too, had had a couple of drinks that lunchtime I expected a symbolic tap as he knocked it off. Instead he posed, aimed a powerful drive at the pear but, being the lousy golfer that he was, missed it and thumped the driver into my temple.

I don't remember much of the next hour or so. It transpired that as a result of my screams Mike's secretary, Mary Webber, rushed in. Her howls, before she fainted alongside me on the carpet, brought another secretary, who testified that Mike was kneeling by my body, tears rolling down his cheeks as he moaned: 'I've killed him. My God, I've killed him.' This secretary had to wit to telephone the Medical Department. By chance the Mirror Group's medical consultant, the excellent Dr Bernard Berman, was there.

Examinations proved that there was no concussion or more serious injury, after which Bernie gave Mike the mother and father of bollockings.

The story was to find its way into *Private Eye* and the *Sunday Express* diary (complete with cartoon illustration). In the meantime, Mike gave me large scotches and made the most generous gesture of contribution to a non-golfer that he could think of: 'If you like, I'll let you caddy for me at Walton Heath on Sunday.'

The expectancies of Mike's Sunday cricket and golf teams suffered from the inclusion of members who, being executives of the paper's editorial staff, had stayed in the office until at least 3.30 that morning, drinking and playing poker. (If the gaming and alcohol were optional, the long night wasn't: although the areas of distribution shrank towards the London and Manchester printing centres as the hours passed, it was still possible to make changes if anything newsworthy took place. Not only for central London and Manchester, but aeroplanes, vans and coaches would be hired to deliver copies containing late news over fairly wide areas.)

So most of Mike's Sunday sportsmen had been in the office since 9 or 10 o'clock on Saturday morning. Although Mike could have left early on Saturday nights, handing over to his deputy, Joe Grizzard, he argued that it was the editor's duty to be in charge until the week's work was done.

The poker began at about 11, soon after the pubs shut, and as the players grew more tired and inebriated, the sessions grew progressively more acrimonious, even if from time to time a drop-out was revealed by a snore that had been assumed to be eye-closed concentration.

The real problem was not the booze or the tiredness, but both when combined with a house rule that said that at certain points the dealer of the moment was entitled to nominate his personal, unorthodox, version of the game. By about 1 o'clock these options became increasingly surreal: three kings or better to open, with all deuces and the ace of spades wild . . . Red deuces and black tens wild, a full house needed to open. Other variations had references to the nicknames of their inventors. Hotlips Misère, or Hotlips Misère with deuces wild, for instance, meant that the winner was the player with the worst hand, so everyone discarded court and wild cards and hoped not to have them replaced by 'worse' cards. Mo's Special was an absurdity which ruled that after a discard everyone passed their hands to the left. This was repeated twice, then back again, after which betting began in earnest. Other revisions were so complicated as to be beyond recall.

Small wonder that the players would grow confused about what was going on and what was supposed to happen next, and this bewilderment, plus tiredness and alcohol, let to truculence and near-hysterical arguments, the knocking over of glasses and a general shambles. Yet, surprisingly, never to blows. (Not so surprising, perhaps: at this stage the players had hardly the strength to raise a card, far less a fist.) Messengers, bringing copy, telexes and other material, were so terrified of entering the bedlam of Mike's office they had their union's official approval to push material under the door after midnight on Saturdays.

Mike himself rarely joined in the arguments: he persisted silently over the chaos rather in the manner of an intoxicated owl.

Remarkably, if anything newsworthy did occur, it had the effect of immediately sobering everyone in the office.

Finally the OK would be given for the paper to shut shop. So, too, did the poker. Most of the players lived outside London and would arrive home with little more time than to have a bath and a shave before driving across country to attempt to focus on a cricket or a golf ball, the team's rendezvous a local pub selected because the landlord didn't mind opening the back door a bit early.

We deserved those Saturday nights, having worked bloody hard during the week to produce, as a consistency, the best issues the *Sunday Mirror* has known; daringly intelligent for a popular tabloid, boldly designed and cheeky.

An instance of the latter: the picture showing the back view of a woman, skirt lifted, using a stall in a men's lavatory. This shock horror was explained by the caption: the 'woman' was, in fact a drag artist – but I can still hear the screams of outrage from both inside and outside the Mirror building.

Then, to make fun of the papers that published nudes, Mike ran a picture showing some 200 of them, male and female, jogging across the Californian sand dunes. Since the picture had to be taken from a distance to get them all in, and the print was from a colour transparency, the sex of most of them was not clearly distinguishable even though the photograph occupied all the centre spread. The real point was the MORE NUDES THAN OTHER PAPERS WOULD DARE PUBLISH IN A MONTH – sort of joky headline. It still brought protests, including those from the eagle-eyed who disputed the number of people we said were in the picture. Nobody could be bothered to check.

*   *   *

The most absurd game of poker I witnessed took place away from Fleet Street, above my uncles' bakery in Shepherd's Bush. On Saturday nights, when the shop and bakehouse in Askew Road had been cleared and cleaned, the week's takings counted and the unsold cakes, and bread reassuring Uncle Sam of the non-existence of God, Uncle Dave would have his weekly shave and change into a cream silk evening shirt with a ruched front, black patent leather shoes, a brown suit and blue silk tie. Then, a dog-end behind his ear, he would stand outside the shop for an hour or more, grimacing to himself as he processed various thoughts, from time to time consulting the gold half-hunter chained to his waistcoat. Finally he would go back inside and lock himself in his cupboard for the night.

When I asked my mother why Uncle Dave behaved in this manner, she shrugged and said: 'He's got his funny ways . . . Anyway, it's none of your business, Nosey Parker!'

My sister Sylvia, at that time a passionate reader of *Red Letter*, *The Oracle* and similar romantic magazines, assured me that she knew the reason. 'It's a deep and tragic secret,' she breathed. 'Uncle Dave has never married because he fell in love with a beautiful princess [presumably Jewish] and they had arranged to meet outside the shop when it closed one Saturday night. But her father was a cruel despot and wouldn't let her marry a lowly baker, and keeps her locked away in his castle. Or perhaps she's been carried off by gypsies. Uncle Dave doesn't know which. It is shrouded in a tragic mystery even Madame Estelle's crystal ball can't unravel. So every Saturday he keeps a vigil outside the shop, nursing a broken heart, faithful to her memory, knowing in his innermost being that one day love will find a way and she'll step off the tram and they'll live happily ever after.'

It sounded wonderful, but the truth, as I learned years later, would never have made *Red Letter* or *The Oracle*.

When he closed the shop door behind him on Saturday nights, Uncle Dave had every intention of going to the theatre or cinema. But which? And where? There was more choice in the West End, of course, but by the time the show finished it would mean a taxi home. So why not locally: the Lyric Hammersmith, the Commodore, or the variety show at the Kings? Then again, if he went to the Shepherd's Bush Empire he'd be able to get a supper of fried halibut at The Mikado in Holland Park Avenue. On the other hand there were good restaurants up West. The kosher ones would be closed, but there were others like the Corner Houses. But which one? Strand, Coventry Street, Marble Arch or Oxford Street? That depended on the theatre of course. But would he get in on a Saturday night? The Palladium and Stoll and Holborn Empires might be packed out. But wasn't that also true locally? He could try the Walham Green or Chiswick Empires, or was he more in the mood for a good film? And what did he really want to eat? Perhaps the best thing would be to decide where to eat and then pick a show or a film that was most handy . . . The turmoil continued until a final look at his watch caused Uncle Dave to realize that it was too late to go anywhere.

While this ritual was being observed outside the front door, another was taking place upstairs: a vast fish supper followed by a game of poker that lasted until 5 o'clock on Sunday morning. Uncle Sam and Uncle Lew would be joined by another brother, Aaron, who had a bakery in Camden Town, and Teddy Ruda, one of a famous family of East End fishmongers. Teddy, who resembled a young George Raft, was my grandmother's nephew, had married her daughter Hetty, and so was also her son-in-law. Others joined the poker school on an occasional basis, but these were the regulars.

The trouble with Lew and Sam was that although they were keen poker players they couldn't play poker. They knew the composition and progression of hands and the bidding, but the game demands other elements: the proverbial luck of the draw, a degree of awareness of your opponent's psychological approach, combined with a capacity to bluff. While they could do nothing about the first, they had no capacity for the second, and their bluffing was in the classic mould of imbecility. Sam would whistle with what was meant to be nonchalance when he held a bad hand, to deceive opponents into thinking it was good, and groaned when he held a reasonable one; while Lew revealed the quality of his hands by scowling at anybody who bid against a good one and feigning twitching impatience at players slow to bid against a bad one.

It followed that since Uncle Teddy was a competent player he was the most consistent winner. This was bad enough. Adding to Sam and Lew's irascibility was Teddy's utter lack of sounds or gestures. He played with the cliché poker face as he chain-smoked Kensitas, his only emotion a thin sharp smile with all the warmth of a gelding knife when he won a hand. Another complication was that, while Sam and Lew were passionately concerned with winning, Uncle Aaron preferred to lose. He felt guilty when he won. A short, neckless barrel of a man with glasses too small for his face and a smudge of a moustache, he would insist on putting in everyone's ante, bet recklessly, and on the occasions when he won a pot was visibly distressed and tried to make amends by even more outrageous betting in subsequent hands.

Sam and Lew managed to contain their frustration and irritability until Teddy left for home. Then came the explosion of fermented rage.

Sam: 'And some people say there's a God. You want more bloody proof, eh? What a gambler! What a dirty rotten gambler. He comes round for a friendly game of cards and plays like he was a stranger.'

Lew: 'What do you expect from a common fishmonger?'

Sam: 'May I never move from here if I lie, but that lousy gambling-mad fishmonger's never coming here to play again.'

Aaron, with an elaborate yawn: 'Until next Saturday.'

137

Sam, thumping the table: 'What does that mean, eh?'

Aaron: 'Why the shouting? You'll wake Mother. Anyway, is to lose a few shillings the end of the world?'

Sam: 'It's the principle of the thing. And anyway you played like a *shmok*.'

Aaron: 'It's only a game.'

Lew: 'Go tell the fishmonger. It runs in the family. Remember when the brother, I forget which one, was given the money to buy fish at Billingsgate? Remember? And how he lost it all – hundreds! – on the dogs at White City?'

'At least he had the decency to lose,' Sam retorted.

And so it continued until, exhausted and enervated, Sam climbed the stairs to bed while Lew walked to his house in neighbouring Wendell Road and Aaron went in search of a taxi.

Teddy's winnings? Seldom more than £2.

One day I went into Sam's office where he was sitting in his swivel chair, dressed as usual in a white cotton coat and trousers, every inch Your Friendly Neighbourhood Baker, even though he was utterly baffled by the creative workings of the bakehouse. He was thumbing through a boys' magazine that had been left behind in the shop – *Hotspur*, *Adventure* or *Wizard* – when he uttered a great 'Aaaah!' of delight. I looked over his shoulder and saw a page of mail order advertisements for the japes and wheezes Sam found so irresistible. He read through them, giggling, then came a mighty intake of breath. 'Look at this!' he gasped, pointing with a trembling carrot of a finger.

I looked. Tucked between a new, improved, even more comical itching powder and a packet of six rubber bedbugs guaranteed to provide hours of harmless hilarity, was an advertisement headlined: BAFFLE YOUR FRIENDS WITH AMAZING CARD TRICKS! It went on to describe packs of playing cards aimed at the young magician: once you had mastered the simple code hidden in the design on the backs of the cards you knew their suits and face values.

'We'll have what they call a joke, eh?' Sam whispered. 'Teach that bloody gambler a lesson he won't forget in a hurry. But not a word, eh? Not to Lew, Aaron, nobody. Like I said, it's what they call a lark. A surprise. You follow?' He rubbed his hands together. 'I'll show 'em how to play cards. Just the once. I'll write off today for a pack, and while I'm at it I'll send for stink bombs. I'm nearly out. If I tot up, will you get the postal order?'

'Sure. But you'd be better off with two packs. One to practise with, the other to open new for the game.'

'You may be right,' Sam admitted. Then a laugh. 'We'll have some fun, eh? But mum's the word.'

The cards arrived and Sam practised whenever he could find time and temporary privacy: the office, his bedroom, even the lavatory, to the bewilderment of other members of the family whose doorknob rattling evoked the response: 'Eight of hearts. That'll teach the bastard.' Finally he assured me that he was ready to take on the poker school.

Sam was in high humour that night: an explosive cigar for Teddy and a finger ring connected to a rubber bulb so that Aaron was squirted with water when he shook hands. Then he produced the cards, and to comments that they weren't the usual ones from the Penny Bazaar Sam replied that they were a gift from the man from whom he bought yeast. 'Maybe they'll be lucky,' he added with an elaborate wink in my direction.

During Uncle Sam's practice sessions it had become obvious to him that he could read the backs of the cards only when he was the dealer, and that he could not memorize all the hands (plus replacements for discards) that he dealt. 'So I'll concentrate on the bloody fishmonger,' he told me. 'It's him I'm after.' Even so, reality proved more problematic than rehearsal. The backs of the cards were of a blue and white floral pattern, their secret code contained in a tiny clock design in the petals which varied only fractionally in revelation of suits and values. To read them with any semblance of speed and accuracy needed the qualities of a computer-programmed hawk.

Sam dealt the first cards of his first hand normally to Lew and Aaron and Gussie Jay the tailor, who was a guest that evening, but when it came to Uncle Teddy he had to bring the card close to his face for some seconds in squinting concentration as he silently mouthed what it was.

'So all right,' said Teddy, 'it's the jack of spades. Are you going to deal it or eat it?'

'W-what?' Sam screeched and dropped the pack on the table. As his shaking fingers scrambled them together, Gussie Jay shouted with evident relief: 'Misdeal!' and tossed his cards into the centre of the table. Sam ignored him. In a near-falsetto to Teddy: 'H-how did you know?'

'You held it high enough for everyone at the table to read,' his brother-in-law replied drily.

An 'Aaah' of relief from Uncle Sam.

'But why hold it up?' Lew asked. 'Something wrong with your eyes?'

'Eyes,' Uncle Sam echoed. In a grateful croak: 'Yes ... Yes, that's it. Eyes. I need new glasses. Eyes. I must get new glasses.'

'It dangerous to neglect the eyes,' said Uncle Aaron. 'They're very useful for seeing. Remember with Yossel Ginsburg's boy? The one with one leg? That was due to the eyes. You recall?'

'How can a leg be due to the eyes?' asked Gussie Jay.

'He was short-sighted and fell down a hole in the road,' said Lew.

'Tragic,' said Aaron. 'Mind you, it kept him out of the army.'

'Yes, you've got to look on the bright side,' Gussie Jay agreed.

Teddy took another cigarette from his packet. As he tapped down the tobacco he asked, an edge to his voice: 'So what's this Yossel falling down a hole got to do with playing poker?'

'Not Yossel,' said Aaron, 'the son. The one with the fancy name. Martin or something. But Teddy's right: let's get on with the game.'

Sam shuffled the cards, now adopting the hunchback pose of a Talmudic scholar, which enabled him to hold the pack close to his eyes yet face down to the table. To avoid confusion he kept his eyes closed except when dealing to Teddy.

At the end of the game Sam's eyes matched the bloodshot dawn. As people went home, I curled up on the sofa for a few hours' sleep as he went to bolt the front door. I heard him climb the stairs, but instead of continuing to his bedroom on the next floor he came into the front room. 'How did he end up winning, eh?' he demanded, beating the table with the edge of his hand. 'Tell me. How did he do it, eh? Ooh, what a hooligan. The dirty fishmonger must've cheated. How else could he have won, eh?'

'You mean that he, too, could read the backs of the cards?'

'What else? ...' Sam froze and his face purpled. 'Y-you 'sinuating I also cheated, you toerag? For me it was what they call a joke. A bit of a giggle. A lark. But with him it must have been deliberate. You follow? Yet you're comparing?' His two teeth reflected his quivering anger.

'All I'm saying is that Uncle Teddy is a fly East Ender and he could have been aware of those packs of cards. So perhaps he, too, read the backs . . . No, he couldn't have.'

'Why not?'

'You know how quickly he shuffles and deals . . .'

'Like a proper card sharp,' Sam interrupted.

'. . . he just wouldn't have had time to read the patterns.'

'All I know', said Sam angrily, 'was that all I wanted was a joke he wouldn't forget in a hurry, and that all I get out of it is that Lew is going to tell Katie, who'll open her big mouth to Gertie, and I'll have to go to Feitelson to get my eyes bloody tested.' Miserably: 'So how did he bamboozle me?'

The answer seemed simple enough: Sam might have been able to read Teddy's hand, but Teddy had a shrewd idea of the quality of Sam's from his brother-in-law's pattern of play.

God must have tossed a coin to determine the Chosen People and the loser paid. (As my mother used to say, echoing the pain and bewilderment of the centuries: 'What was the bargain? For what were we chosen? The Cossacks? Pogroms? Hitler?') Perhaps this Jehovistic caprice accounts for so many Jews being gamblers, as though striving to find compensation on earth for the impossible odds of God's two-headed celestial penny. But how explain to Uncle Sam why he was such a bad gambler, why he was almost always a loser and Teddy a winner, without upsetting him too much?

The question was saved an answer as Sam with a brief 'G'night' shuffled from the room and laboriously climbed the stairs. The following Saturday it was back to playing cards from the Penny Bazaar, albeit with new glasses with which to read them.

TWELVE

Some Of My Best Friends Are Jewish

The swarthy Peter Stursberg, with his Canadian accent and beak of a nose, was the butt of much heavy humour, particularly as closing time approached and his journalist colleagues were running out of jokes and gossip. The exchange would go something like this:

'New trouble in Israel, eh Peter? You must know all about it. What does it mean?'

Stursberg: 'How should I know? How many times must I tell you that I'm not Jewish?' (To his credit he never added that some of his best friends were.)

'Don't talk rubbish! With that face? That name? Who do you think you're kidding?'

After a long sigh: 'I've told you a thousand times: my complexion and my nose are because I'm partly Red Indian.'

'But a name like Stursberg? Come off it. Your parents must have been German or Austrian refugees.'

'It's an old Canadian name that goes back centuries. From a town in Ontario.'

'Rubbish!'

'No it isn't.'

'Of course it is.'

And so on until the day Percy Cudlipp said: 'Of course he's Red Indian. And of course he's Jewish. He's the last of the Ikey Mohicans.'

Since no one could top that, Peter was left in peace (although the truth of the matter was never established).

Philip Zec, certainly a Jew, was one of the half-dozen of Fleet Street's great political cartoonists. When he was made editor of the *Sunday Pictorial*, Frank Bower of El Vino asked waggishly: 'How will you be able to work on Saturdays?'

'I'll keep my hat on,' Phil replied drily, and walked out of El Vino never to return.

Stanley Jackson was a journalist and author of whom it was said that when he was asked to write a biography of the (most famous) Aga Khan he prepared himself by being weighed on jockey scales against a similar poundage of the Aga's press cuttings. Stanley, who had the sort of face my mother would have described as 'a map of Jerusalem', said to me one day: 'I did enjoy your novel about Minnie Ashe,' adding in his gravelly voice: 'I know so many Jewish people.'

'Including your parents?' I enquired. He refused to speak to me until, weeks later, we met over writer Willi Frischauer's gefilte fish. When Willi went on a crash diet he could reduce to 18 stone. Going on the wagon meant giving up brandy for champagne, on which he insisted it was impossible for him to be drunk even if he was mostly responsible for three empty Louis Roederer bottles. A lovable, well-informed man, Willi was also a dreadfully bad writer in English – as distinct, as an Austrian, from his native German. He acknowledged this, and was furious when something appeared in print more or less as he'd written it, complaining bitterly that it should have been completely rewritten; for what else were sub-editors employed?

For Willi, however, journalism was one thing, authorship another. He wrote a number of books and insisted that he, and he alone, wrote them: not a word was cut or altered, nor a paragraph mark changed. (If you read his books you know this to be true.) An early one, however, was written with Robert Jackson, *The Navy's Here*, about the German prison ship, *Altmark*, which was laden with the crews of merchantmen sunk by German surface raiders. Altmark was captured by the destroyer *Cossack*, the leader of its boarding party leaping aboard *Altmark* with the cry: 'The Navy's here!' Research into the story was necessary in Germany as well as Britain, so the book was published with a joint Frischauer–Jackson credit for authorship. When Bob Jackson said that he had rewritten the English version of Willi's contribution, and had knitted the entire manuscript together, Frischauer didn't forgive him for as long as he lived.

Later Willi was to write a number of stilted and bland biographies, including those of Onassis and the apparently irresistible Aga Khan.

Then came his book on Otto Preminger, about whom he did know something since they'd been to school together in Vienna and had remained fairly friendly. One evening Willi telephoned, virtually begging me to go to his flat in St John's Wood to read his opening Preminger chapters.

I did so. It seemed to be the usual harmless pap and corruption of the language, but since I hadn't been invited as a literary critic I could only say: 'So?'

'Don't you see?' Willi cried. 'It is the most devastatingly critical work I have ever written. Preminger will never forgive me for this! He'll never speak to me after this revelation!'

'But what is it?'

'Don't you see?' Willi repeated with a howl. 'I reveal for the first time that . . . that . . . *that he's half-Jewish!*'

I was baffled by Willi's concern. Why should it matter if Preminger was half-Jewish? If there was any reaction from Preminger it must have been of shrugged indifference, since no bellows of rage were reported, even by Willi.

When one got to know Willi well one came to appreciate what amounts to a familiar cliché: that his extrovert exuberance, emphasized by his Bunterish size and appetite for good food, and his earnest demands that 'Fee British must stick togezzer', concealed sensitive introspection.

Willi adored his wife Nikki. When she died he wrote to me saying that life was no longer worth the living and he'd soon be joining her. I learned that he'd written or spoken to a few other intimates along the same lines, and I shared the view that Willi was one of those people who, because they keep talking about suicide, seldom carry out their threats or promises.

One day Willi decided that the time had come to drive to Beachy Head and throw himself onto the rocks below. When he arrived he found the grassland at the top of the cliffs carpeted with picnicking families. Since he thought that it would be in the worst possible taste to frighten the children or make an exhibition of himself on such an occasion, he decided to find a good restaurant, have a decent dinner accompanied by champagne and brandy, then return late at night when Beachy Head would be empty apart from courting couples too self-absorbed to take notice of his presence (and sudden disappearance).

He had a splendid dinner, and it created such a feeling of euphoria he opted to postpone Beachy Head and return to London.

Willi told the story well, but after a few weeks the heartache and loneliness of life without his beloved Nikki overwhelmed him. He took an overdose.

*   *   *

All this business of being Jewish or non-Jewish or part-Jewish! Journalist Paul Callan once told me that he is half-Jewish. He also claims that he went to Eton. One night in the Salisbury in St Martin's Lane when we were young reporters on *The People*, Bob Edwards told me that he was half-Jewish. He was doubtless being polite and anxious to put me at my ease (although I was perfectly comfortable) and for the same kindly motive has probably been, variously, half Christian Scientist, Zoroastrian, Roman Catholic, atheist, gymnosophist, Methodist, Sikh, Presbyterian and mornings-only Seventh-Day Adventist.

Harry Ainsworth was said to have flirted with anti-Semitism until it was pointed out that his employer, Lord Southwood, formerly Julius Elias, was said to be Jewish, and that Freemasonry had strong links with the Old Testament, including King Solomon's Temple and Tubalcain, whereupon he joined Hannen Swaffer in his detestation of the Catholic Church which was said to disfavour both Freemasonry and spiritualism.

A regular user of fleet Street pubs and bars, where he drank Homeric quantities of whisky, was the Russian journalist, Maurice Podeschwa of Tass; plump, amiably gregarious, permanently smiling, invariably dressed in a dark blue, double-breasted suit with red tie on a white shirt the collar points of which appeared to have been starched in Carmen rollers. It is simplistic to say Russians have no sense of humour. It is just that there is a cabbalistic quality peculiar to the Soviet faculty for laughter. Jokes that had other drinkers registering some sort of response on the Richter scale of grin to gaffaw left Podeschwa stony faced, while his: 'Harold Wilson smoke pipe, but pipe not Harold Wilson' had him doubled up in scotch-splashing laughter at the brilliance of his wit.

Perhaps, once again, something was lost in translation.

I discovered that Maurice lodged a couple of doors from my mother in St John's Wood together with other communist journalists. Their landlord, the extremely aged Mr Wheat, who claimed to have been a founder member of the Bulgarian Communist Party, told my mother during an evening of sad nostalgia how a number of old communists like himself had been able to equate their politics with their Jewishness: who but the Reds were to fight against the Tsar's, and later Hitler's, pogroms? (Equally, he admitted, who was to foresee the anti-Semitism of Soviet fascism? But this, he insisted, was a hiccup; one day the Marxist truth would be realized.)

Maurice Podeschwa, Mr Wheat said affectionately, reminded him of the old Jewish Bolsheviki: every morning, on his way to the lavatory, he heard Maurice whispering his morning prayers.

When, mischievously, I asked Maurice about his prayers he paled, then laughed loudly and unconvincingly before saying (I won't attempt to write the accent): 'You must have made mistake, Kiril. There are still Jews in Soviet Union. But not me. I cannot be Jew. As good communist I am atheist.'

This had a sort of a familiar ring. 'My Uncle Sam is also an atheist,' I replied, 'But my mother has always said that Hitler would never believe him.'

'B-but Hitler dead . . .' Then, by way of what was probably the KGB's Lesson Six in Instant Verbal Recovery, Maurice said: 'What are your views on dichotomy of reactionary Anglo-American Alliance vis-à-vis fundamentalism of Soviet-Sino inter-Leninist dialectics of Marxist counter-capitalism?' (Or words to that effect.)

At such moments a protective shutter snaps down on the thinking area of the brain, switching it into neutral, allowing the tongue to tick over with inanities.

Maurice once asked me something about the H-bomb; a question so complicated and convoluted I soon lost track of its meaning and purpose and so said, with a wink and a smile: 'I suppose the best thing would be for the West to bomb the Kremlin before you bomb us.'

Podeschwa's jowl collapsed into a fair imitation of an anaemic bloodhound's. After several gasps of horror he managed a squeaked, but intensely serious: 'Tell me, Kiril, are you anti-Soviet?'

'Of course not,' I replied, but I don't think he was ever to believe me.

Maurice's literalism and lack of any semblance of a Western sense of humour made him the victim of much heavy baiting. Bernard McElwaine of the *Sunday Mirror* was among his most active teasers. Remarks like: 'Bare Russian not Russian bear' had Bernie and his cronies positively baying with hiccups of vodka-and-tonic in El Vino. Podeschwa took it all with an amiable (if non-comprehending) smile.

If Podeschwa claimed to have a personal enemy it was Eric ('Call me Buffo, old boy, everyone does') Chapman. Buffo's background was vague: was he a reduced gentleman, or the former servant of gentlefolk who had acquired manorial accent and postures? No one could be certain since Buffo Chapman answered all questions about his background and work by tapping the side of his nose with his riding crop and a stammered: 'Official Secrets Act, old boy.' For Buffo, shabby-elegant in jodhpurs, riding boots, boldly checked hacking jacket and cap and a vaguely regimental tie on a Tattersall-check shirt, admitted no more than that he was in Royal employ at Buckingham Palace.

The elderly Buffo, with his hypnotic sequence of facial tics, did nothing to discourage Podeschwa's vision of him going to the Palace every morning and changing into the full dress uniform of an officer of Hussars before escorting the monarch with drawn sabre while singing snatches from decadent operettas.

Fascinated by journalism, Buffo spent much of his off-duty time in Fleet Street. When we met he'd look around, possibly recognize a few faces, then whisper: 'Anyone else famous here today, old boy?' If, perchance, a well-known name was present, Buffo's eyes would positively gleam and he'd bite at his lower lip to control his excitement. And so he met, if only at raised elbow distance, such stars as Nigel Dempster, Robert H. Wilson, Jak, Dennis Compton, Derek Jameson, Kingsley Amis, Michael Parkinson and Maurice Podeschwa.

Buffo and Maurice usually bumped into each other at the Devereaux. They'd start off politely enough with the usual nonsenses: weather, prices, the awfulness of London Transport, television and football, and why so-called independent radio had sponsors for so many of its programmes. Then, after a few drinks, they'd turn to East–West politics, discussions that rapidly descended into bellicose posturing as dialectics dissolved into abuse on the level of 'Bolshevist cad' . . . 'Imperialist lickspittle' . . . 'Commie hooligan' . . . 'Bourgeois swine' . . .

Under it all there had to have been some fondness, otherwise why would both continue to go to the Devereaux except as an improbable double exercise in masochism?

From time to time many of the journalists who knew Buffo wondered about him. Was Eric real or (unlike the usual run of money-hungry conmen who haunt Fleet Street) merely one of life's fantasists whose deceptions are limited to public house ego inflation? Thus an ex-RAF corporal becomes a former fighter pilot, and the porter at a block of flats hints that he owns it. We have all met men with grubby fingernails claiming to be surgeons or consultants: medicine is a great favourite among pub hallucinators since they assume they won't meet any real medical men in the establishments they frequent, and reckon that a little knowledge, spread thin, goes a long way.

If, perchance, they are caught out, they change pubs via 'Excuse me, I must go to the loo' (or something similar) as did Harry Davis, a pathologist whom an off-duty policeman recognized as a southwark mortuary attendant . . . Mark Devlin, a plastic surgeon who proved to be a male nurse in the VD clinic at St Mary's Hospital, Paddington . . . Vernon Watney, the brain surgeon who was a porter at Barts – and so on. Some are well-known but unexposed Walter Mittys since those aware of their charades listen, shrug into their beer and say nothing. Why bother?

Like others who knew Buffo I wasn't sufficiently interested in the truth about his job until the day he came to mind when I was talking to a *Sunday Mirror* writer who had contacts at

Buckingham Palace. 'Does Eric Chapman really exist?' I asked. 'Does he work at the Palace. If so, what does he do?'

It was doubtless inevitable, in the very nature of such Believe It Or Not events, that the journalist concerned should come into the Devereaux at lunchtime during one of my visits there, to say breathlessly: 'I though I might catch you here. I've just come from the Palace . . .' As will have been guessed, Chapman and Podeschwa were standing there. I grimaced and little gestures, but she misinterpreted me and said: 'No, it's all right. I'm quite calm. Just a bit breathless. I've got to go and see a contact in a minute if I'm not interrupting . . .'

'You are,' I assured her.

'. . . I've time for half a bitter. Anyway, I can't stop. Just thought I'd let you know about Eric Chapman. He does work at the Palace . . .' More agonized expressions and gestures resulted in: 'Are you all right? Anyway, Chapman works as a groom, mucking out the stables in the Royal Mews . . .'

Her voice trailed away as she saw Buffo tremble, his eyes bulge, and tics agitate his face as though they were a subcutaneous nest of maddened ants. I am sure he would have fled had he not been paralysed by shock (as Podeschwa and I were by surprise) and then by the Russian's great bear hug as Maurice said emotionally: 'Why didn't you tell me you not capitalist lickspittle but lumpenproletariat?'

'Eh?' Buffo managed.

'Serf.' After another 'Eh?' from Buffo: 'Slave, dearly beloved comrade.'

Chapman recovered sufficiently to say with some semblance of dignity: 'Don't you dare call me a slave. This is a free country. And don't you "dearly beloved" me either, you . . . you pervert.' But it was apparent that his heart wasn't in it.

'I'll buy large scotches for celebration,' Podeschwa roared. As he released Buffo and turned towards the bar the hapless Royal groom fled. The *Sunday Mirror* reporter stood bemused for a few seconds then remembered her appointment.

'Why he run away?' asked a frowning Podeschwa.

'He felt humiliated.' I attempted to explain that there are people who like to indulge in harmless self-aggrandisement, hence Chapman's hints that his association with the Royal Family was

149

on a somewhat more intimate level than that of a groom clearing away manure-pebbled straw. 'Does it matter?' I asked. 'Indeed, who can blame him? But he was caught out.'

Podeschwa nodded and breathed a long, sad sigh. 'Such decadence. In Soviet Union no shame in work we do. No one humble. All equal.' Again he nodded, but his pity for Buffo turned to what sounded like muted truculence in muttered Russian. Then, reflectively, as though continuing the same thought sequence in English: 'These Royal lackeys all same as in days of Tsars. Scratch skin and find anti-Semitism.'

'But what has that to do with you?' I asked. 'You keep assuring me that you're not a Jew.'

Maurice Podeschwa seemed to blink himself awake, 'What?'

'You said you thought Buffo was anti-Semitic and I thought you were making a personal point. Otherwise why mention anti-Semitism?'

Maurice's face went grey and his chins trembled as he reached for a handkerchief with which to mop his face and wipe the palms of his hands. He licked his lips and looked furtively about him. He tried to speak, but all that emerged was a sort of phlegm-heavy gurgle. Still twitching, he cleared his throat, blinked a few times and tried again. 'Unfortunate . . . er . . . what you call it?'

'Freudian slip?'

He frowned. 'No. Is problem speaking English. Difficult language. What I meant to say was maybe he *thinks* I am Jew. People say my face has certain Hebraic aspects. In certain lights. And lights here . . .' He gave up with a hands thrown in the air gesture, looked at his watch, said that he had to rush back to the office, and hurried away with a rictal caricature of a smile.

Thanks to the catalysis of the *Sunday Mirror* reporter it had proved to be a memorable lunchtime and I had the whimsical thought that Maurice scampered off, not to work, but for an afternoon of chastening flagellation in the basement of his embassy. More seriously I've considered from time to time the agonies he must have suffered attempting to balance the official atheism of the good communist with secret Judaism.

I never saw Buffo or Maurice again. Chapman just vanished, while Podeschwa was occasionally sighted by others at press conferences until, some months later, I was told that his tour of duty had come to an end and he'd returned to Moscow.

*   *   *

I went for lunch in the City with fellow journalists James Pettigrew and John Knight.

'I'll pay for the cab,' I said, then discovered that apart from a few copper coins I had no money smaller than a £10 note. I apologized and asked if one of the others would pay.

'Mean Jew,' said Jimmy.

Inside the restaurant I said, by way of contrition: 'Let me buy the drinks.'

'Flash Jew,' said John.

There are times when it is impossible to win.

Which brings to mind . . .

As happens in business organizations, certain members of the *Sunday Mirror* staff occasionally lunched together, paid their own corners, then either tossed up for the receipted bill or took it in turns to pocket it and present it on expenses as 'Lunch with X'. (There is a distinguished Fleet Street photographer who has never bought anyone anything in his life. Humping his equipment, he hitch-hikes to and from assignments even in central London, and his expenses are made up entirely of fictional taxis and mileage and 'Hospitality to . . .', plus nudges and winks to waiters: 'If you give me a few undated bills – blank ones will do – I'll take your picture and send you a couple of prints.' He assured me that it's a ploy that seldom fails.)

The tubby Bernard McElwaine and I used to lunch together on a fairly regular basis. We'd share the cost and take the bill in turns. There were no confusions: Bernie was a meticulous diary-enterer of anything involving money owed. Then one day we went to Sheekey's and I paid for the taxi there, Bernie to pay for the one back to the office, as was practice. When the bill came, instead of the normal, split down the middle, Bernie said: 'Ah, but you had smoked salmon to start and I had jellied eels. Then you had the turbot and I only had the smoked haddock.' Taking out an office ballpoint and memo pad he worked it out to the penny including proportion of the tip. Opening and closing his mouth like a gaping carp, he finally managed: 'So my share of the bill is 50 pence less than yours.'

As I stared at him utterly confounded, he pocketed the bill (although it should have been mine) and seemed to fall asleep in the cab back to the office, thus preventing me from raising the matter with him.

As soon as we arrived at the *Mirror* building however, and before I could give him a shake, Bernie jumped out (so far as his bulk allowed him to jump), handed me about ninepence towards the fare and did his impression of a disabled seal as he executed a hurried wobble in the general direction of the Press Club. (At the time he was the *Sunday Mirror's* literary editor and it showed: from the rear you could see that his right arm was several inches longer than his left as a result of carrying suitcases laden with review copies to a local bookseller.)

A couple of weeks later Bernie asked me when next we'd lunch. 'Never,' I replied, 'unless you tell me what happened last time.'

Bernie's jowl quivered as he chewed at his cheeks for some seconds then said: 'What?' After I'd reminded him, he had another chew, did his gasping carp bit and said: 'What you must remember, Cy, is that I'm retiring in seven years' time and must start to watch my pennies.'

Coming from a penny-watcher beside whom Harry Ainsworth was a profligate (Bernie always arrived late at the office in order to qualify for a cheap day return on the tube and, when he retired, used his bus pass to come to the *Mirror* building in order to slip his post into the mail Out tray), I could only utter a tiny 'Eh?' followed by a meant to be funny: 'You've proved, Bernie, that despite what people say there is somebody worse than a mean Jew.'

'What's that?' he asked suspiciously.

'A mean Gentile.'

I'd forgotten that, although Bernard McElwaine was a noted wit and raconteur, he was utterly humourless where money and religion were concerned. So we never did have lunch together again – the reason, as it was relayed to me, my outrageous anti-Christianism.

*   *   *

Among the libel actions with which I was involved while on *The People*, one was brought by a former German who claimed to be a doctor of something or other and had discovered THE panacea, its curative powers embracing even cancer.

Although most laws protecting the public from nostrums are fairly recent, alleged cures for cancer have been proscribed for many a long year. So I obtained a bottle of this elixir and sent its brown and evil-smelling contents for analysis. It proved to be humus: liquid compost complete with traces of leaf, twig, animal and bird droppings, fragments of carcasses and anything else dug up at random in a wood or forest.

I then went to the West Country to see Dr Marian (I'm pretty sure that was his name) and confronted him with the analyst's findings. He regarded me as though I was insane. 'Of course it's compost!' he cried. 'What did you think it was?' He went on to explain that since compost made fruit and veg grow better and healthier, why shouldn't it do the same for human beings? 'After all,' he argued, 'we are all living creatures.'

After an hour in his company I decided that Dr Marian wasn't a villain but a nut. A misguided fanatic. Dangerous? I suppose so in terms of claiming a cure for cancer. (When I asked him about this he readily gave me the names and addresses of two sisters who had been cured of the disease – one breast, one bowel – by drinking his magical liquid. When I visited them the two aged ladies sang their soprano praises of the doctor and the efficacy of his humus. Great stuff, until they gave me the name of their GP who assured me that neither lady had ever suffered from any form of cancer for Dr Marian to have cured.)

Dr Marian said that he didn't know about the laws governing claims for cancer cures, and would reword his advertisements. I believed him and wrote a story on the lines of Dr Marian being a well-meaning but misguided clown, and that right-minded people should just ignore him.

This wasn't good enough for Sam Campbell, of course. Where was the headline? 'ARREST THIS WICKED "DOCTOR" . . . The Conman who cruelly deceives cancer victims by selling them manure!' *That* was a headline, and so Sam rewrote my story to justify it.

Dr Marian sued. I learned later that his solicitor advised him against it, if only because of his cancer cure claim, but how can you argue with a man who *knows*? Whose faith is absolute? So the case did come to court, and *The People* had ready a massive and formidable army of witnesses, who included a royal doctor (Lord Horder), a distinguished cancer professor/consultant, and the director of the Ministry of Agriculture's soil bureau at Rothamsted in Hertfordshire.

And me.

On the morning when I was to give evidence about my interview, I went to see Sam Campbell. He took one look at me and rolled his eyes towards the ceiling as he groped among the medications on his side table.

'Something wrong?' I asked.

'Wrong? *Wrong*?' He swallowed. 'That bloody waistcoat, for a start.'

I was wearing a dark burgundy waistcoat loaned by my brother, since Gerald had assured me that it would create an impression of the Bohemian academic which could not fail to impress a jury. 'I know it doesn't fit very well,' I said, 'But Gerald has a 48-inch chest and I'm only 40.'

After blindly swallowing various tablets and sticking a Benzedrine inhaler into a nostril, Sam croaked: 'Fit? *Fit*?! I'm the one who's going to have a fucking fit if you don't take off that bloody waistcoat! . . . Jurors! They all pay rates and own their houses and buy the *Telegraph*. With a waistcoat like that they'll think you're a bloody Commie bumboy. *Take it off*!'

'Aren't you a ratepayer?' I asked.

'I don't buy the *Telegraph*,' he retorted.

In order to remove the waistcoat I had to place my hat (broadbrimmed and black and again borrowed from my brother) on Sam's desk. He pointed at it with a finger that quivered. 'And . . . what's that?'

'A hat.'

'I can see it's a bloody hat, but since when have you worn a hat?'

'To take the oath.'

'What bloody oath?'

'Witnesses have to take the oath,' I explained.

'I know that . . .'

'. . . and since I'll take it on the Old Testament I'll need to do so with my head covered. Wear a hat.'

Sam Campbell stared at me, frozen with horror. After about 30 seconds he blinked and said weakly: 'A hat . . . Oath . . . Old Testament.' I nodded, and there was another silence until Sam erupted with a scream, then lowered his head as his fists hammered at his desk. This was sufficiently calming for him to be able to say in only a slightly cracked voice: 'I . . . I told you about juries . . . Conservatives . . . I see them every day on the train from Farnham. Carry the *Daily Telegraph*. Never open it,' he added reflectively. 'At least not on the train. Too busy talking to one another. They're all bloody fascists. I know. I listen to them.' After a further bang on his desk he said vehemently: 'So don't you see, you ape? Those jurors are all bloody anti-Semitic and you want to wear a hat and take the oath on the Old-fucking-Testament in Yiddish! Are you completely insane?'

'What should I do? Affirm?'

Sam frowned at me. 'Eh?'

'Not swear, but affirm. Say I'm an atheist.'

Sam groaned. A shudder went through him as he clutched his head in his hands. Looking at me through his fingers: 'Atheism! I thought you had at least some bloody common sense. Atheism! That's almost as bad as being a Jew, for God's sake!' He lowered his hands and took several deep, calming breaths as he scanned his medicine table. Then, wearily: 'I'm tired. I'm getting old. I have a paper to edit. So go to court, accept whatever bloody Bible they offer, take the oath and tell the truth as we rehearsed it yesterday.' He waved a hand weakly in dismissal.

I left my hat with the waistcoat and walked down Bow Street to the Royal Courts of Justice in the Strand, feeling nervous since I had never before been called as a witness, and a bit apprehensive about Sam Campbell's advice. But, I told myself, he is the most seasoned of campaigners and must know what he's doing. Worry turned to near-panic when the time came for me to take the oath, and as I did so, bareheaded and swearing on the combined testaments, I half-expected, in the Law Courts' forbidding cold discomfort, a Gustave Doré-style zig-zag of Jehovistic displeasure to smite me between the eyes.

When the Odham's lawyer, Hugh Davidson, who was the defence junior, took me through my evidence, the epitome of avuncular gentleness, I began to relax.

Then Mr Godfrey (later Judge) Russell Vick stood up to cross-examine. He had a friendly smile on his plumpish face and his voice was soft and kindly as he said: 'I noticed, Mr Kersh, that you took the oath on the Bible.'

'Yes, sir,' I replied, the sweat beginning to percolate.

'You didn't ask for an Old Testament or wear a hat?' He made it sound more of an observation to the jury than a question.

'No, sir.'

'So you are a Christian?'

Somehow I couldn't bring myself to utter what everyone in court would immediately recognize as a palpable lie. I said: 'Well . . . sort of,' and remember thinking: 'Why did I let Sam Campbell con me? I'm cornered.' I looked with some hope at the judge, Mr Justice (later Lord) Devlin, but he sat impassive except for a twitch at one corner of his mouth. I looked at the jury. They were grinning.

Russell Vick's voice went thundery. 'Sort of? *Sort of*?! Just tell the court, Mr Kersh; *Are you a Christian*?'

I managed a weak, desperate and (to me) very Jewish sounding: 'Not necessarily.'

The rest of the cross-examination was of no consequence: it was evident that nobody was to believe a word I said.

I was seething when I left the court, a rage due in no small part to the humiliation I had suffered because of taking Sam Campbell's absurd advice. When I arrived back in Long Acre I marched straight into his office, and when I'd finished my introductory remarks – edited of adjectival colour and free character reading, it was along the lines that he shouldn't have messed about with my story in the first place and that I was stark raving mad to have allowed him to influence me with his demented jabber about the anti-Semites of Farnham – he was staring at me with a sort of near-respect: I doubt if any member of any of his staffs had ever addressed him in such a manner. I then told him of the start of the cross-examination and the court's reaction to it.

'I should have remembered my mother's wise words,' I said bitterly. 'When I was bullied by anti-Semites at Marylebone Central Infants School, she told me that there was nothing to be ashamed of in being a Jew and taught me to shout, over and over: "I am a Jew and proud of it too!"'

'I'm not sure it would have gone down all that well in Number Two Court,' Sam mused, 'But don't worry, chum. You're evidence doesn't matter a tinker's cuss. Wait 'til that idiot jury hears the experts. Including the royal doctor, eh? He'll set their wombs trembling.'

He didn't. Nor did the other expert witnesses. After hours of deliberation the jury couldn't come to the unanimous verdict that was necessary in those days, and so the case would have to be re-heard if Dr Marian wanted to bring it again. He didn't, but I shared the bewilderment of Sam Campbell – and the lawyers on both sides – as to why there had not been a quick verdict in favour of *The People*.

Some months later I met a woman I half recognized, just as she couldn't quite place me. It turned out that she had been a member of that jury. 'What happened?' I asked.

She agreed that I had not been the most impressive of witnesses. More important, she was a former nurse who knew quite well not only that it was illegal to claim a cure for cancer, but that the miracle breakthrough, when it came, would not be found among the mephitic decay at the bottom of Dr Marian's garden – especially as no two bottles of his cure-all could have the same content. This had also been explained by the experts, but the other members of the jury couldn't understand a word of their jargon, and they didn't think much of Lord Horder either, since a proper royal doctor would wear a frock coat and carry a top hat, and since Dr Marian was a foreigner why not give him the benefit of the doubt? After all, they were sure that he meant well. Only by sheer chance was there this ex-nurse on the jury who refused to budge from her belief of what was right.

When I told Sam Campbell he whistled and shook his head with incredulity then, after a short silence, nodded and chuckled. 'That explains it.'

'Explains what?'

'Why they never open their *Telegraphs*. It's like those rolled-as-thin-as-a-pencil umbrellas Guards officers carry when they're in civvies. They can't be opened. They're sewn up. It's all show. And so those apes never open their *Telegraphs*. Like the *Observer*: far more widely carried than read. They're all bloody secret readers of *Comic Cuts*, the bloody clowns. They're just pig ignorant snobs.' He waved a finger towards me. 'Never get called as a witness again, chum.'

'If I do I'll wear a hat.'

'That reminds me,' said Sam. 'I meant to ask you, but it went out of my mind. That chant your old mum taught you. How did it go?'

'I am a Jew and proud of it too.'

'And when you shouted it at the school bullies, did it work? What happened?'

I had to admit that they'd half-murdered me.

THIRTEEN

The Queen's Bed
And Tuxedo Junction

When Arthur Christiansen (father of Mike) edited the *Daily Express* he issued to his staff lively analytical bulletins about the paper's editorial performance, plus his hopes and philosophical observations. Cyril Morton, sometime editor of the old *Daily Sketch*, attempted to emulate Christiansen with memos pinned to the editorial notice board. One stated: *The perfect news story will contain four ingredients – religion, royalty, sex and mystery.* Beneath it some wag wrote: *Example: 'My God,' said Princess Margaret, 'I'm pregnant. Whodunnit?'*

Cyril could have added two more ingredients: show business and astrology. During the days of the bitterest, yet most knockabout, rivalry between the *Sunday Pictorial* and *The People* (i.e. before they were under joint ownership), the *Sunday Pictorial* was streets ahead with its show business coverage. They even had a show business writer who died of drink, Dick Richards, while *The People* had no one specifically covering that area unless you count their film and theatre critic, former short story writer S. Rossiter Shepherd, a dignified, spade-bearded old gentleman who carried a monocle in one waistcoat pocket and an ivory and silver toothpick in another, and who burst into tears (I was there) when Sam Campbell 'modernized' his by-line to Ross Shepherd.

During the war when a skeleton staff mucked in to do what had to be done to produce the paper, Shep (as he was known to his colleagues) asked Harry Ainsworth: 'Is it all right if I call myself features editor?' Typically, H.A. replied: 'Call yourself what you bloody like as long as you don't want more money.' It must be said that Shep's talents were somewhat limited: as features editor the nearest he came to typographic design was to send headlines to the composing room marked: 'Please set in some nice type.'

But while the *Pic* made no fuss of their astrologer, Constance Sharp, *The People* gave much space and build-up to their Edward Lyndoe. Mine you, it was Lyndoe who announced 'There will be no war' in the issue of 3 September, 1939. But he recovered quickly. The following week he wrote: 'Hitler must lose! The madman who defies the stars!' (Equally the *Sunday Express*'s astrologer of the day insisted: 'I see no reason why they [Hitler and Stalin] should cease to remain anything but the best of friends' – the front page announcing Hitler's invasion of Russia.) A dedicated follower of Lyndoe was the socialist politician, Ernest Bevin. During the war, when he was Minister of Labour, the prediction for his star sign had to be written after his wife secretly told Harry Ainsworth what Ernie hoped would happen during the following seven days.

If the *Sunday Pictorial* led *The People* in the area of show business, the measurement was essentially one of quantity since that of quality was a metaphysical abstract, most of the printed material consisting of oleaginous pap – rewritten versions of the semi-literate press releases issued by film and theatre companies, the latter running the still-flourishing variety theatres. The *Pic* also had the advantage of being infinitely more picture conscious, which somehow more than balanced the occasional references by Hannen Swaffer in *The People* to Sophie Tucker, George Robey and Mary Pickford.

Away from show business and the stars and other regular features, *The People* under Sam Campbell exposed and thundered with puritanic zeal, sex being all right if he could make it sound dirty or, if he was in a facetious mood, saucy – by way of a poke in the ribs like a battering ram, for Sam had no real lightness of touch and little sense of fun (as far as journalism was concerned) away from his pleasure in the discomfort or misfortunes of others. (Mind you, great cackles of laughter came from Sam's office as he added his Cromwellian adornments to stories.) Sam was therefore astonished to the point of head-shaking incomprehension by the chutzpah of *Sunday Pictorial* editors under the impish orchestration of editorial director Hugh Cudlipp. (Chutzpah is translated from Yiddish as 'cheek', but like so many words from other languages it defies literal translation. It needs example, the definitive being the story of the man who murdered his parents then asked the court for clemency because he was an orphan. That was chutzpah.)

'Arrest this evil man!' Sam would cry, and so was open-mouthed at the *Pic*'s treatment of the cleric who assaulted small boys and whose protest about harassment they demolished under the absolute chutzpah of a headline: 'Go Unfrock Yourself, Father Ingram!' (Later was to come 'Sir Vivian Fuchs Off To The Antarctic.')

There was the *Pic*'s search for a new, authenticated, Virgin Birth. Somehow there was a winner with (as an added miracle) a Harley Street consultant to authenticate the event (although the Pic didn't make too much of this since the chutzpah of the idea was patently better than the dubiety of the actuality).

Another great was 'Lady Chatterley's Lover – The Expurgated Version.' Completely misunderstanding 'expurgated', the punters queued to buy the *Sunday Pictorial*, and the series was so successful the paper got someone to write a sequel: 'Lady Chatterley's Daughter'.

Despite the Messinas and 'I Took A Lorry Ride To Shame' and similar successful exposures and purchases, Sam's sureness of touch sometimes slipped, as when he bought for a considerable sum the memoirs of Franz von Papen. Chancellor in 1932, von Papen paved the way for Hitler's takeover and served as the Führer's deputy from 1933 to 1934. As ambassador to Vienna his intrigues smoothed the coming of the *Anschluss*, and he was later ambassador to Ankara. Given eight years by a German de-Nazification court after the war, he served two. His memoirs, apart from being the inevitable apologia, revealed little but an over-weening self-importance. If von Papen's memoirs were distinguished it was for being the most boring political reminiscences ever.

Why did Sam buy them? Why purchase material which, had anyone on the staff suggested it, would have resulted in the culprit's castration? It was hardly 'witty, humble and human,' nor could Sam attempt to put it across on the line of: 'I am telling my story as a warning to other Reich Chancellors who might be tempted . . .' Sam would never reveal his reason for buying it, and when asked about it there was no pitying, head-shaking: 'Don't you recognize a real corker?' and in no way could he assure his questioners that it was a real womb trembler that old mums in cottages couldn't wait to read when *The People* was brought home by their bus-driving sons in Sheffield. The most anyone got out of him was a defensive: 'Did you have anything better to offer me?'

Sam also serialized books by Lord Russell of Liverpool, which (particularly when Sam had finished with them) detailed in drooling near-obscenity the German atrocities in such places as Auschwitz. Behind Sam's spurious moralizing justifications to the readers for running the material, there lurked infinitely more than the token degree of sadism needed by all good editors. Why else buy the stuff – and make each serialization last for months? I'm obliged to Bob Edwards, in his excellent autobiography, *Goodbye Fleet Street*, for recalling: 'Cyril Kersh's joke in the office was that when Sam had wrung every sickening word out of each book he would keep it going for another week or two by starting again at the beginning.' (Thinking back, I'm not certain that I was joking.)

Another of Sam's less happy – fortunately more comical – decisions was to attempt to boost the circulation in Wales by taking on Keidrych Rhys as a columnist for the Welsh edition, Keidrych having been sold to him as the most controversial, aggressive, maverick, iconoclastic (etc., etc.) writer in the Principality.

Keidrych said he wanted to write the column in Welsh, and Sam thought this an absolute corker of a witty idea. It was to cost *The People* a small fortune every week in overtime since the Long Acre compositors needed to copy the material a letter at a time rather than rattle through sentences. Keidrych had to make his own corrections, write his headlines, and effect any cuts to fit the column to the available space. Lawyers were unable to read the material for libel. Keidrych also worded the posters for the newsagents and paper sellers. Never have I known such control over material by a non-proprietor: even editors invite select members of the staff to have an advance read of their leaders or other contributions (although, generally, they are in search not of frank and fearless opinions – to which they do not take kindly – but of gasped gratitude for being chosen for the privilege of a preview).

Sam, while approving the Welshman's corker of an idea, but not having thought it through, wriggled out of the resultant dilemma of not knowing what was going into the paper by the simple expedient of delegation. As he explained in his office, he'd leave supervision of Keidrych's material to me. Helping himself to a large pink tablet from a tin: 'Want one? . . . No? They're very good for . . .' He peered at the label. 'Wind.' He frowned. 'Wrong one.' He turned from his medicine table and decided to polish his spectacles. Then, feet on desk and trying to sound winning: 'You're an old hand here, Cyril. He won't be able to con you, will he chum?' I realized with some astonishment, that Sam was actually embarrassed.

'In Welsh?' I protested.

'It's probably a bit like Yiddish.'

'I don't speak Yiddish, far less read it.'

'Really?' Sam sounded quite surprised. Replacing his glasses and tugging at the points of his waistcoat: 'Shout, chum. That's the answer with the Welsh. Just shout and Taffy . . .'

'Keidrych Rhys.'

'. . . will understand you. Sounds daft, but it works with Hugh Cudlipp. He's Welsh. If you don't shout, he doesn't understand a word you're saying.'

'Hugh's deaf in one ear, for God's sake. Anyway, it's not a matter of shouting. Keidrych speaks perfect English.'

'Well, there you are then,' said Sam, embarrassment dissolving into irritability. Forehead furrowed, he began another examination of his medicaments. 'You'll soon shout it out of Taffy Bach.' He managed a smile. 'Oh indeed to fucking goodness you will and we'll double the circulation in Wales.' He dismissed me with a wave of a tube of Preparation H suppositories.

Since decibels were not going to serve as a lie detector, I had to take Keidrych's solemn word (sworn in both English and Welsh) that he was writing about the greed of capitalist Welsh landowners and the inhumanity of the tied cottage system, or the justice of the cause of the striking dockers at Milford Haven, or how the miners deserved better compensation for their pneumoconiosis – and so on. All good stuff guaranteed to have 'em shouting for more.

The truth was revealed in a letter from a Labour MP for one of the Welsh constituencies. Run of the mill letters to the editor were handled at the time by Chief Sub-Editor Walter Morley, who was inclined to feed them to reporters to deal with, or throw them away (especially if they arrived after lunch). Those threatening, or activating, legal action, or addressed to the editor by name, were processed by Sam's secretary, Kate Wadleigh (who at one stage also ghosted Gilbert Harding's column for *The People*).

This letter only Sam could deal with. It began with the familiar cliché that since *The People* was owned by Odhams Press which also owned the *Daily Herald* it should be more positive in its support of the Labour Party. (Sam had a simple answer to this complaint: *The People* was an independent paper, and although owned by Odhams Press, so were *Debrett's Peerage* and *Mickey Mouse Weekly*.) The letter went on to say that Keidrych's column had been perfectly acceptable until the previous Sunday's.

In it, not only did the evil Keidrych make fun of his fellow Welshmen, attacking what he called their sexual and religious hypocrisy, but he also lampooned Welsh socialism, rugby, miners' choirs, the Royal National Eisteddfod and other sacred Welsh rituals, which (according to Keidrych) included incest and a reluctance to take baths. (Apparently this last item was in rhyme and, in loose translation, began: 'All your jests and all your tears Won't make a Welshman wash his ears . . .')

Normally Sam Campbell would have thought this a bit of a giggle, even if he was attempting to raise circulation in the Principality. What took the smile off his face was the information contained in the letter that, while Keidrych indeed had a reputation as the most controversial, aggressive, maverick, iconoclastic (etc., etc.) writer in Wales, it was not in the manner Sam Campbell supposed.

Keidrych Rhys was an intellectual.

In his magazine, *Wales*, Keidrych published excerpts from Robert Graves' 'The White Goddess', 'a historical grammar of poetic myth', and works by Dylan Thomas and Caradoc Evans, whose biting satires of Welsh sophistry caused riots among his countrymen.

As I read the letter over his shoulder and helped hold it steady, his own hand trembling vigorously even after his eighth or ninth perusal of it, Sam Campbell stammered: 'The man's one of those egg things' (it transpired he meant the rebarbative egghead). 'I . . . I thought you were keeping an eye on him.'

'In Welsh?' I released my hold on the letter and raised my hand in palm outward defensiveness. 'Yes Sam, I did tell you I don't know any Yiddish, and yes Sam, I did shout at him, and yes Sam, I was going to run a check on him, but you sent me to Stafford to buy up next week's shameful confessions.'

'Are you trying to be funny?' Sam frowned, since he was a man who took shameful confessions very seriously.

'Certainly not,' I said, trying to sound aggrieved. 'You know – the blind beggar who drives a Rover and will agree in the paper to stop conning the public when we pay him £100 for his story.'

Sam nodded, gave a long and noisy exhalation and shrugged. Too expert and confident an editor to jump up and down and then alibi himself with the board of directors, he soon calmed down (more or less). Confirming that the allegations were true, and since there was no second chance for intellectuals, Sam wrote to Keidrych Rhys firing him. Kate Wadleigh then hurried to Amos Jones, the corner chemist, to replace two exhausted Benzedrine inhalers and renew Sam's stock of Valium.

*　　*　　*

Odhams bought Hulton Press in 1958, the package including two once truly great magazines, *Picture Post* and *Lilliput* (both well past their best), as well as the comics *Eagle*, *Swift* and *Robin*. *Picture Post* was soon to be absorbed into *Illustrated*; *Lilliput* hung on until it was merged with *Men Only*.

Then the Mirror Group bought Amalgamated Press, its titles ranging from *Woman's Journal* and *Women's Illustrated* to the cosily evangelic *Sunday Companion* and *The Children's Newspaper*, the best-ever publication for youngsters: again, in its day. Odham's response, as it were, was to take over the Newnes magazine empire, which included *Woman's Own*, *Tit Bits*, *Men*

165

Only and *Country Life*, and, on its book side, the *William* series by Richmal Crompton.

Mirror newspapers had now grown into the International Publishing Corporation (IPC). Its chairman, Cecil Harmsworth King, was reputed to have asked: 'Why battle with Odhams?' and supplied the answer: after a bitter fight, IPC took it over. (Wags at the time said the furniture in King's office did not contain chairs for his visitors but prayer mats.) IPC also bought Paul Hamlyn's publishing firm for £2,500,000 and made him a board member: a long way from selling books on windowsills in Charing Cross Road.

The enormity of the International Publishing Corporation would have seemed to make it immune from attack. No way. Costs rose, particularly on the newspapers. Apart from increases in the price of newsprint, IPC suffered from outrageous wage demands by the print unions (plus payment to these unions' non-existent members whose fictional names appeared on the pay sheets), as well as gross overmanning and eccentric management. Mind you, when I was an executive on the *Sunday Mirror* I didn't complain: we enjoyed wonderful perks, including membership of BUPA, motor cars (including tax, petrol and servicing), free newspapers plus newspaper allowances, telephone rental and most calls, plus the occasional invitation to the firm's boxes at the races and the Festival Hall. Money was spent as though it carried a sell-by (or give-away-by) date. As sometime publicity director of Mirror Group Newspapers (MGN), Felicity Green, put it: 'The Mirror Group should become a registered charity.'

Looking at the annual balance sheets, the hawks eyed one another as they estimated bids for a biting-the-biter takeover. Fortunately IPC had a reasonably friendlier alternative: they owed a large chunk of Reed International, manufacturers of newsprint, paint, plastics, packaging, and much more. Reed also had money. And so, in a reverse takeover, IPC became part of Reed International.

The unions, again the production unions in particular, continued to crack the whip and, sadly, were to do so until Robert Maxwell bought MGN and overnight imposed the disciplines that others had never been able to achieve – even if he did so with all the subtlety of a steamroller.

* * *

In 1959, not long after absorbing *Picture Post, Illustrated* folded: not so much because of the quality of the product, but because television was able to provide instant pictures of events with the added virtues of movement, sound and colour. Advertising – the life blood – was also drained by TV.

Hearing of my impending unemployment, Frank Owen asked me if I knew Arthur Christiansen. I didn't. Frank explained that although Chris was no longer editor of the *Daily Express* he was till a powerful man, with influence on the *Evening Standard* and *Sunday Express* as well as the *Daily*. (This, I discovered, was shortly before he vanished into a black hole in a forgotten building in Shoe Lane.) Chris offered me a job with the *Standard* features department: he assured me they were waiting for a man with my experience and ideas to take them into the sixties. I went to see the editor, Percy Elland. The reception was cool. It didn't take long to discover why: the paper resented having me imposed upon them.

So began one of the two most depressing years of my journalistic life. (The other was when Robert Maxwell arrived at Mirror Group Newspapers and fired his journalists almost by rote on the first of every month. Or so it seemed. I took early retirement rather than the aggravation.)

On the *Standard* the people with whom I worked were charming, but I was given jobs suitable for juniors: running the 'Mainly for Men' column, which meant going round the big stores to discover what new bits and pieces they had on sale for men. I insisted that this appear under the pen name Hugh Riley (a character in some book I'd been reading). Roy Wright, then the paper's features editor, was sympathetic. . . . Writing a Saturday column, 'Sunday in London' – about 250 words listing the attractions of Kew Gardens, the Zoo, Hampton Court, and so on. It came to an end when I wrote a piece suggesting they stay in bed . . . The only relief was when the literary editor, Harold Harris, gave me books to review. He also published a couple of my short stories.

When I said I wanted something better to do I was put on the Picture Desk to spend my days sizing up photographs for the next day's early, primarily racing, edition together with captions that did not dare contain a hint of wit: racing buffs, I was assured,

167

would not understand them. More important: neither would the picture editor.

Percy Elland died of a heart attack – giving the lie to the assumption that such deaths in Fleet Street are the result of drink and hard work – and was replaced by the cerebral, but charming, shy and extremely able Charles Wintour. But I could still see no jet waiting for me to pilot into the sixties, so I looked around and discovered that Newnes were looking for an editor for *Men Only*. I applied and got the job, which was to last until they turned it into a semi-erotic publication for teenagers in 1963 when, once again, I was looking for a job.

The *Standard* ran a paragraph about my leaving *Men Only* and Derek Marks, deputy editor of the *Daily Express*, telephoned to ask me to meet him and editor Roger Wood at the Savoy at 8 that night. I went to the bar, waited, and was then struck by the thought: 'Did Derek mean the pub next door, the Savoy Tavern? . . . Surely not . . . Not the editor of the Daily Express and his deputy.' . . . That's what he did mean.

Roger offered me a job, this time in overall charge of the future planning of the features department. Could I start on Monday? Since I hadn't had a holiday for a couple of years, would he mind if I first had a fortnight's break? Not at all. And so, on a handshake, it was agreed.

When I arrived home, Hugh Cudlipp rang. When I told him I'd struck a deal he immediately said: 'The *Daily Express*. When [not if] you get bored with it, give me a ring and come and have a chat. We're re-launching the *Sunday Pictorial* as the *Sunday Mirror* and I've always thought that one day we'd work together.'

During the fortnight my wife and I were in Paris, the gnome of the Cap D'Ail, Lord Beaverbrook, was playing one of his games of human chess. Among his whimsical moves, Roger Wood was fired and Bob Edwards, my old mate from *The People* in Sam Campbell's day, returned to edit the *Daily Express* for the dozenth time (or so it seemed). Fleet Street was always an unsettling merry-go-round.

Bob and his team arrived on the same day as me. It had clearly been worked out that the job I had come to do no longer existed (or someone else was to do it). I didn't have an office, I didn't have a desk. I was allowed to use a battered, cigarette-burned armchair in the features department – until a features sub came to use it at around 6 p.m. I thought: 'If this is the mighty Express Group in action, shove it!'

In a corridor I saw Bob, my pal for so many years. As I approached him, hand extended and ready with a merry, congratulatory quip, he gave me a thin smile, a thinner 'Hi!', the briefest of nods and strode on as I stood with my hand somewhat stupidly shaking space. Knowing his memory, he had probably forgotten who I was – or was suffering twitchy preoccupation.

Either way, it was evident that he was going to be of little help and so I resigned, explaining my much-enquired about entry in *Who's Who*: '*Daily Express* (one day)' – although, in all truth, it took a couple of days to reach Bob to tell him I was going. In the meantime I rang Hugh Cudlipp to ask: 'Can I come and have that chat?'

I joined the *Sunday Mirror* on its launch day in 1963, and what a bizarre issue it was! The lead story, by Lionel Crane, was about a naval officer who had been thrown out of the Navy some years earlier for allegedly thrusting a toothbrush up a fellow-officer's arse.

The editor of the *Sunday Mirror* was Reg Payne (although, in those early days, it was really run by Hugh Cudlipp). After a story (nothing to do with Hugh) claiming that a famous peer, well known on TV, was having a sexual relationship with one of the infamous Kray Brothers, Lord Boothby recognized himself and sued for libel. Cecil H. King settled out of court for vast damages. Reg Payne got the chop from the *Sunday Mirror* and, after a decent spell in the wilderness by way of contrition, Hugh employed him on Newnes to mastermind *TitBits* and the *National Geographic Magazine*. When Sam Campbell died and Hugh Cudlipp gave the editorship of *The People* to Bob Edwards, who had made his really – truly – honestly final appearance on Express Newspapers, Reg was made his deputy.

Reg's replacement on the *Sunday Mirror* was the great Michael Christiansen.

Almost by definition, eccentricity (no matter with how much brilliance it may be coupled) cannot be equated with the demands of even a benevolent bureaucracy. So the time came (1972) when the Mirror board were sufficiently irritated by Mike

Christiansen's maverick unpredictability to teach him a lesson: remove him from the editorship of the *Sunday Mirror* and make him suffer a short, sharp period of austere chastisement in a tiny black hole where he pretended to be concerned with the editorial side of the forthcoming new technology before being brought back to the real world as deputy editor, then editor, of the *Daily Mirror*.

Cruelly, only a few months after this last appointment, he suffered a stroke – of which, typically, he was unaware since it occurred as he drove himself back to London from Paris after a banquet of a lunch. He thought he had no more than an attack of dyspepsia, and so arrived at the office before collapsing and being rushed to Bart's. A medical examination concluded that it would be suicidal for him to continue on the *Mirror* – especially at the pace at which he insisted upon driving himself – and he was forced into very early, and extremely reluctant, retirement.

He was still in his fifties when he died of a heart attack. As I quoted in my address at his memorial service: 'One crowded hour of glorious life is worth an age without a name,' adding that Mike had certainly had his crowded hour and that those of us gathered at St Bride's were fortunate to have shared some part of it with him.

Mike's replacement on the *Sunday Mirror* was the peripatetic Robert J. (Bob) Edwards. A tall, slim man with a frizzle of now-grey hair over a large swoop of a nose, and a mouth that gleamed with a great whiteness of (sometimes gritted) teeth, Bob always looked magnificently fit and, to my knowledge, was indeed generally fit, although this has not prevented him from being a pulse-fingering valetudinarian for all the years I've know him.

When I was news editor of *The People* he'd ask: 'Anything doing?' If I replied 'No,' he'd say: 'In that case I'll amble out for a beans on toast to feed my ulcer.'

The first time I heard this I asked: 'What ulcer?'

'You never know,' he replied gravely. 'Better to be safe than sorry.' Thereafter he was to amble out with some frequency for haircuts and shopping and earned the nickname Amble Out Edwards.

Years later, when he again told me that he thought he had an ulcer, he chirped up enormously when I told him that as an editor he was now in a position not to have ulcers but to give them.

Since, unlike civil servants, bank managers and the like, editors are creative, or are in charge of creativity, it follows that no two are identical in their methods and attitudes. Bob Edwards' style was certainly the antithesis of Mike Christiansen's (quite apart from games of chance and whimsical decisions to hold a joint London/Manchester editorial conference at some half-way hotel adjacent to a golf course). Bob lacked Mike's spontaneity and impudence and flair for the outrageously unexpected. He was far more cautious, forever feeling the need for reflection and consultation. If his careful deliberations had their roots in insecurity, it was understandable when you consider the curriculum vitae of his ups and downs: he made the *Guinness Book of Records* as the man who had edited more British papers than anyone else. (He was also, therefore, the most experienced of Fleet Street editors.)

Members of the staff sometimes complained of what they called Bob's self-oriented arrogance: how he ignored them as he rushed to and from his office; how their hellos were responded to with thin smiles (if at all); how he rarely listened to what they said by way of small talk. The truth, as I had discovered on the *Express*, was that Bob was almost always preoccupied. His eyes were focused elsewhere as his brain whizzed round (there were those who claimed to hear it) while he pondered and excogitated and weighed his options over matters as disparate as how much to bid for a major series being auctioned and the suitability of a comma rather than a semi-colon in the second sentence of the fourth leader. He agonized.

A result was that his twitchiness communicated itself to the editorial, circulation and publicity teams which he led. As a tiny example, his tenseness was such that he'd drive me close to tearing my internal telephone from its roots on Saturdays when, after lunch, it rang virtually non-stop as Bob began to read his page proofs and complain about the absence of commas and the presence of literals – not realizing that he was reading Wednesday's early, uncorrected, pages.

But if he was not the impulsive and impromptu journalist as was Mike Christiansen, his caution made him the far safer editor, steering the *Sunday Mirror* along a far less erratic course. Then, as though negating it all, or to mischievously confound his critics, he ran the Royal Train story: how Diana spent some part of a night with Prince Charles on that locomotive. . . before they were married. There were the inevitable cries of outrage from the Palace and the rest of the media, some of the indignation of the latter being genuinely righteous. Bob, to his eternal credit, stood by news editor P. J. Wilson and P. J.'s reporters led by Wensley Clarkson, and refused to yield an inch, far less apologize. The *Sunday Mirror* was never proved to be in the wrong.

Curiously, though, the paper didn't publish the greatest scoop about the Royal Family for years: of Fagan, the intruder who found his way into the Queen's bedroom at Buckingham Palace. The story came from the *Sunday Mirror*'s crime reporter, Norman Lucas, who had it as a copper-bottomed exclusive from a senior officer at Scotland Yard. Norman was by no means the most prolific member of the staff, but when he did produce a tale it was often both accurate and exclusive. Over the final years of his career he suffered a great deal of domestic upset and illness and his contributions became progressively rarer. Then came what he intended as his journalistic swan song prior to early retirement or, more accurately, his exultant, thunderous paean – but, ironically, the *Sunday Mirror* didn't use it even though it reached the stage when art editor Roy Foster had designed a page one (continued on pages X, Y, and Z) with which to accommodate it.

Bob Edwards was off that week, tramping round his Oxfordshire village doing his tweed cap and green wellies bit. (Only pig farmers, he once confided, wore black ones.) Bob's deputy, Vic Birkin, who was in charge of the paper, telephoned to advise him of the story with which he was leading the paper, understandably pleased that we had obtained such a great exclusive. But instead of joyous acclamations, Bob, a bit sensitive about the Royal Family despite (or maybe in consequence of) his Invictus-style stand over the Royal Train, gave two instructions. The first was that members of the staff of the legal department be contacted (because of sod's law only a non-staff man was on duty that day) and asked: since Fagan has been charged, will we be in contempt of court if we publish? Their answers were a unanimous 'No' and the Group's legal manager, Arthur Wynn Davies, told one of his children: 'Wait until you see tomorrow's *Sunday Mirror*, all about the naughty man who sat on the Queen's bed.'

It was not to be, for Bob's second instruction was to obtain confirmation of the story away from Norman Lucas's police informant. Since the Buckingham Palace press office was closed that Saturday afternoon (and, presumably, none of its staff were at their homes) the story was killed.

It was left to the *Daily Express* to pick up the tale and provide editor Christopher Ward with the finest exclusive of his editorship of that paper. Norman Lucas shook his aching head, curled up in his duvet and was never heard of again on the *Sunday Mirror*.

Away from it all Bob could be great company and a superb raconteur, and even if the anecdotes with which he monopolized the lunch or dinner table were thrice-told tales of his experiences with Lord Beaverbrook, and thus Fleet Street stories (maybe leavened with reports on his health or reminiscences of his adventures as a signalman in the RAF), he was always guaranteed an appreciative audience. Oddly though, despite being a fine story-teller, Bob had a terrible memory for names apart from Lord Beaverbrook, most members of his family, the majority of the *Mirror* board and one or two others.

As editor of the *Sunday Mirror*, Bob had a key to the leather- and mirror-lined vertical coffin of a private lift known as The Chairman's Wallet. One day, awaiting its arrival from some high floor, and with his mind not pondering life's imponderables, Bob saw someone he half-recognized, and on a caprice not only said 'Hi!' but offered him a ride, asking: 'Which floor?'

A surprised: 'Same as yours, Bob.'

Through that dazzling display of teeth: 'Yes, of course . . . er . . .'

Passing the first floor Bob had the idea that the man was on his staff. As they approached the second floor Bob had the added inspired remembrance that not only was the man on his staff but worked in the sports department. On the fourth floor he had the name. As the doors opened at the fifth (*Sunday Mirror*) floor, Bob said with triumphant satisfaction: 'See you later, Wilf.'

'We buried Wilf Jones three fucking months ago,' sports writer Jack Wilson snarled.

When Bob tells the story he emerges as its hero, since he is enormously pleased with himself at having remembered that the man worked in the sports department.

Bob's great strength was his political knowledge and his capacity for interpreting and anticipating political events. It was a subject that had long interested him: he'd stood as a Labour parliamentary candidate and had written leaders for, and had edited, publications as polarized politically as *Tribune* and Beaverbrook Newspapers. He also knew a great deal about motoring.

Apart from sport, a weakness shared with many editors was his limited knowledge of show business despite its importance to the paper. But no editor can be well versed in every one of the diverse departments that constitute a newspaper, from politics to fashion to astrology to gardening to agony aunting to the City to medicine to book reviewing – and more. You employ experts – until they grow tired or bored or complacent or dry up or the readers don't like them any more and so have to be replaced.

Not that Bob was ignorant of all showbiz: he often referred to George Formby, whose story he ghosted for *The People* in Sam Campbell's day, and to the monologue-reciting comedian Billy Bennett (1887–1942) and his billing 'Almost a Gentleman'. Bob was also an enthusiast for the big band swing sounds of the Glenn Miller/Woody Herman era, and was something of an expert in that area.

So Bob generally left decisions about show business to others. Not that such decisions were hard to make. This was the era of Coronation Street's unassailability at the top of the charts, and for years it provided the basis for most of the *Sunday Mirror*'s show business series. When we ran out of Stars' stories to buy, we ran the memoirs of the script writers, the producer and probably Jean Alexander's milkman and Pat Phoenix's chiropodist. Plus their horoscopes and the horoscopes of the fictional characters portrayed by the stars. When we were drained of ideas, we repeated the cycle. Let me admit that I dreamed up, or was in some way responsible for, many of these series, including one about the supposedly magic ley lines, two of which intersected at the centre of the Street's rehearsal rooms and so guaranteed that the cast were accursed and doomed. ('We were right!' we chortled when some months later a darts player in the Rover's Return sprained an ankle.)

From time to time similar series about Dallas, Dynasty and Crossroads served as digestive punctuation marks – entremets, as it were, between 'Julie Goodyear's New Beefcake – World Exclusive' and 'The Truth About Hilda Ogden's Flying Ducks'.

The readers loved every word, since good soap opera clichés have the mindless appeal and indestructibility of bubble gum. And since these series sold papers Bob Edwards regarded them with tolerance (tinged with bemusement).

A punctuation mark with a difference came when Bob realized that he had on the staff a man unequalled in Fleet Street in his knowledge of his beloved era of the big bands. Show business writer Jack Bentley had been a star trombonist whose name is still to be found in reference books of British jazz greats, and who had played with such distinguished and still-resurrected names as Jack Hylton, Ambrose and Ted Heath (as well as the Irish Guards).

'Write a series,' Bob instructed. 'Fill it with anecdotes and memories about the great days of the British big bands. Geraldo and Oscar Rabin and that other one.' Jack did so. He had a large store of stories and told them well, with the help of that unrivalled features sub-editor, Brian Checkley.

Bob loved every word and decided to trail the series in that week's TV commercial. 'As background music we'll use Glenn Miller's "Tuxedo Junction",' he told Terry Sanders of the publicity department, the mastermind behind so many of the best *Sunday Mirror* commercials. Then, frowning as his memory again failed him: 'How does it go, Terry?'

'It's a bit before my time,' Terry apologized. 'I don't go back further than The Beatles.'

Various people were summoned. None was able to hum 'Tuxedo Junction'. Finally clenched teeth were followed by the heel of a hand slapping his forehead as a now-obsessed Bob said: 'Of course! Jack Bentley! He has to know.'

Picking up the phone he dialled Jack, whom he must have roused from a deep sleep. After some seconds: 'Jack? Hi! It's Bob ... *Bob* ... The fucking *editor* ... Hi! We're going to give your series the big treatment. It's in the commercial! ... Eh? ...

Yes, the TV commercial, and I want to use "Tuxedo Junction" as background music. Since you know 'em all Jack, remind me how it goes.'

Jack did know them all – or most of them. His musical repertoire was prodigious. His mind skimmed through the card index of memory of trombone parts, and after a longish pause he uttered a sort of gutteral coughing of a trombone sound as he remembered "Tuxedo Junction". But before he had a chance to translate it into a hummed melody, and doubtless because one human-voiced 'oompah' sounds much like another, Bob howled an anguished: 'That's "Chattanooga Choo-Choo!"' and slammed down the telephone.

Terry Sanders used one of those bits of non-copyright rhubarb. Nobody noticed.

FOURTEEN

Call A Strike – There's Rind On My Bacon

There were times when I fancied that Sam Campbell asked members of the staff what books they were reading, films and shows they were seeing, and music they were listening to, in the hope of flushing out closet intellectuals. Certainly, when I reviewed films one week when Ross Shepherd was on holiday, and wrote of *The Red Shoes*: 'a must for those who like ballet', Sam added to my copy 'and I don't' – the words serving as a sort of garlic and crucifix ritual to save me from damnation.

(There was a very bad movie about Fleet Street called *Front Page Story*, or somesuch. The guest critic who reviewed it for the *Daily Sketch* wrote 'This is not a good film,' and editor Herbert Gunn speedily deleted 'not', the script having been written by his wife, Olive. Since the guest critic was a well-known personality of the day, Bert Gunn received some very unwelcome publicity, which he tried to wriggle out of by putting the blame on the sub-editor who had handled the copy.)

It was impossible to stay for long in popular journalism in any sort of lively and creative capacity, particularly in the immediate post-war years, without being guilty of at least one dirty trick of which, later, you were not very proud. Mine occurred inevitably on *The People* when I was running the News and Features Desk. This would have been in the early fifties when Sam Campbell bought for the sports pages the memoirs of some hanger-on to the soft underbelly of the boxing underworld – matchmaker, crooked referee, second, trainer or somesuch.

In one instalment the writer claimed that heavyweight boxer, Jack Doyle, lost his second fight against Eddie Phillips because he was suffering from an anti-social (i.e. venereal) disease. Sam got this past the lawyer because, ignorant of boxing, he accepted the author's word that Jack Doyle was dead, and the sports department didn't argue, possibly because the men of consequence working there at the time were drunks. (Or maybe because Sam convinced everyone that an anti-social disease could mean influenza since it was so contagious.) Jack was, of course, very much alive and was to remain so until 1978. Since it was in the sports pages I knew nothing until I read the paper.

Jack Doyle, 'The Gaelic Nightingale' or 'Irish Song Thrush' because of his not at all bad 'When Irish Eyes Are Smiling' sort of voice, came from County Cork and joined the Irish Guards before turning professional boxer. In his prime he was very good looking, possessed a formidably powerful right hand and had a string of wins before fighting Jack Peterson for the British Heavyweight Title and being disqualified in the second round for low punching. He went to America where his only fight on record seems to be against Buddy Baer (brother of Max), who knocked him out in the first round. In America he married an actress called Judith Allen. When she divorced him he married Mexican starlet Movita, with whom he returned to England where they had a successful double singing act – until she left him in 1945 and married Marlon Brando.

Jack was a good, but not a great, heavyweight and the photograph of him knocked out in the second Phillips fight is a classic – Jack stretched completely horizontal just inside the ropes. Yet he remained immensely popular with the fans and made a considerable fortune between here and America. Somewhat reminiscent of my brother, there was no provision for the future, and the money went on drink, women, heavy gambling and a *Guinness Book of Records* queue of free-loaders. When I first met him, towards the end of the forties, he was still elegant in his double-breasted pale grey suits and carnation, but reduced to such cons as telling American tourists that he would get them into exclusive, members-only, Mayfair night clubs for £X. 'Just wait here,' he told them as he took the money and ran.

Yet he did have some regular income until the day he died: £25 a month from Movita as their divorce settlement, and £100 a month from the enormously wealthy American Dodge family on the promise that he would never again see their daughter Delphine, who had been cited in Judith Allen's divorce action.

I was sitting in the office late one evening when Jack arrived with a man in a three-piece suit, starched collar and not quite Old Etonian tie whom he introduced as his legal adviser. Unfortunately I knew him almost as well as I knew Jack, which included the awareness that he was by far a more accomplished petty crook. Since he may well be still alive and working to help Dublin's poor, I'll call him, somewhat unoriginally, Pat. He had been to prison for his part in a caravan swindle, when people were buying the things in the absence of proper homes.

At the time of this story Pat was making a reasonable, if dishonest, living from what used to be called champerty: a strictly illegal bargain in which he'd encourage some innocent to threaten a libel action and undertake to help him or her for 50 per cent of the profits. For instance, sitting in the reference section of the local public library, he'd comb the papers for suitable misprints. Seeing one that referred to Miss (instead of Mrs) Bloggins and her five children he would offer to represent her in obtaining compensation for such a monstrous inpugnment of her morality. (This was before the law of Criminal Libel only; the days when a misprint, even if accidental, was actionable.)

Pat had official-looking stationery – embossed copperplate – with 'Legal Adviser' over a Lincoln's Inn address and phone number (he had an answering service there) and wrote to the offending newspaper saying that he represented Mrs Bloggins and, since she was not greedily seeking punitive damages, she would settle for £100. It's surprising the number of times it worked, newspapers and magazines (particularly in the provinces) assuming Pat to be a solicitor and grateful his client would settle for such a reasonable sum.

So when I saw him accompanying Jack Doyle (for some reason he'd decided not to write), and after Pat explained with much hyperbole why they were there, I said to Jack: 'You and I are old mates. Right?'

'Right!'

'So you and I can talk. But I don't want this conman getting in the way.' When Jack nodded, I said: 'Pat, why don't you go down to the Enterprise and wait there until Jack joins you?'

Pat blustered and used some almost legal phrases, but Jack just pushed him through the swing doors to the lifts.

When the two of us sat at my desk, Jack said: 'It wasn't nice, was it, saying I had the pox?'

'Did you?'

Embarrassed and shuffling in his chair, Jack said: 'What if I did? It was years ago and you have no right to bring it up. Pat says I should sue, and that's what I'm going to do. I'll get thousands.' (He was absolutely right in his assessment of damages if the case came before a jury.)

I went into a spurious spiel about him having no money while Odhams had millions. 'All the money in the world. Add together the cost of the action, solicitors' and barristers' fees – and God knows they're greedy enough – Pat's cut, appeals, expert witnesses *such as the doctors and their records* – and so, what with one thing and another, how are you going to pay for it all?'

'Won't I get legal aid?'

'Not for a civil action.'

'B-but I'm innocent.'

'Not if you don't have the money to fight the case.'

'What do I do?'

'Settle out of court, Jack.'

'That's what Pat said. How much?'

'Whatever I can find you in cash. From the petty cash. Tonight. *Now!*'

Jack's eyes sparkled. Plainly he hadn't seen folding money for some time. Again: 'How much?'

'I don't know. I'll have a look.' I took the petty cash box from a filing cabinet, unlocked it and counted £11. 'Eleven quid.'

'Holy Mother of God! Is that all you've got?'

I turned the box upside down and shook it. 'That's all. No, hold on.' I added £2 from my own pocket.

'OK, then,' said Jack, eyes fixed unblinking on the money.

I sat at my typewriter and rattled out one of those ultra-elaborate-just-to-be-on-the-safe-side letters. 'I, Jack Doyle (address) accept in full and final payment of any claim I might have, now or in the future, against *The People* for their story in the issue of (date) about my second fight with Eddie Phillips . . .', and so on.

He signed and I gave him the £13. 'You off now to meet Pat at the Enterprise?'

'No bloody way! He said I'd get thousands and all I've got is thirteen lousy quid. Let's have a drink on our own.' We went to the Freemason's Arms and Jack wouldn't let me go until most of the £13 were spent (which meant that we, mostly Jack, shifted a vast quantity of drink).

A dirty trick, but at the time I was feted, even by rival popular press journalists who came to hear of my 'brilliant coup'. That's how it was in those days.

For a while Jack became an all-in wrestler, as did many boxers of the day when their careers were over. I continued to see him from time to time, particularly around Notting Hill Gate, scrounging drinks from anyone who recognized him – and many who didn't. The carnation was still there, but changed only weekly as he grew seedier, dividing his time between a Bayswater Road betting shop and a couple of local pubs. I gave him a few pounds from time to time – friendship and guilt – and for small fees he also played the guitar and crooned to lonely middle-aged women.

He made the headlines again in the sixties when he was arrested for shoplifting a pot of cottage cheese from what was then MacFisheries supermarket. He was fined a tenner and sold his life story for what must have been the dozenth time, on this occasion to the *Sunday Mirror*.

I last saw him on Christmas Day, 1977. I'd gone out to fetch something from my car as Jack came down the street, very puffed and shabby now, although with a carnation (dead) in his buttonhole. When I asked him where he was off to, he took a small tin of corned beef from a jacket pocket and said: 'My Christmas dinner.'

The encounter cost me a tenner.

He died almost exactly a year later in a Notting Hill basement. The irony was that collections for his funeral costs resulted in more money than Jack had known for some years. Enough, indeed, for a statue to be erected to his memory at his birthplace in County Cork.

For true wickedness on *The People* there was no one to equal Sam Campbell.

During their rivalry in the fifties the fortunes of *The People* and *Pictorial* see-sawed, but towards the end of the decade the *Pic* was just ahead with a sale of 5¼ million copies a week. Then came a series that could be described as show business, although it was not that which inspired Sam Campbell's interest: the material was also very dirty. It was 'My Wicked, Wicked Ways', the autobiography of Errol Flynn, who gave the story extra value by dying just before the manuscript was completed.

Sam knew it had been written, had negotiated for it, and was gleeful to have it in the bag; or thought it was there until Flynn's literary agent, Carlton Cole, arrived from America – and went to see Lee Howard, editor of the *Sunday Pictorial*. 'The story's mine!' . . . 'Oh no it isn't!' . . . 'Oh yes it is!' . . . and so on as injunctions were threatened, the only smiles being those on the cyanosed lips of Carlton Cole as he played one paper against the other. I'd left *The People* by then and was editing the old *Men Only*, but Sam Campbell was filled with delighted chortles when he told me the macabre end to the swash and buckle battle for the memoirs of the hero of the Spanish Main and Burma.

One evening, as Cole was yo-yoing between *The People* and *Pictorial*, Sam virtually kidnapped him and kept him up all night arguing, while feeding him endless cups of strong black coffee. The caffeine, plus the lack of sleep, plus the nagging and accumulated stress were too much for a man Sam knew to have a severe heart condition. As the dawn broke so did Carlton Cole. Utterly exhausted, he signed the contract (for a massive £40,000), tottered back to his hotel. . . and died. 'But we had his bloody signature, eh?' Sam cackled through his lupine grin.

'My Wicked, Wicked Ways' was the winner that added some 200,000 copies to *The People*'s sales and took it well ahead of the *Sunday Pictorial*. It was very sexy stuff for its time, with so-and-so slipping out of her panties and switching off the light, dot, dot, dot – and strong enough to earn *The People* a rebuke from the Press Council (which was fairly meaningless, since the most the Press Council can do is gnash its gums). Anyway, Hugh Cudlipp admitted that *The People* 'published far more purple passages than the *Pictorial* would have dared'. If Sam lacked chutzpah, he wasn't shy of gaining attention as a sort of journalistic flasher.

A few years later, in 1963, the *Pictorial* bought the Duchess of Argyll's story after she was somewhat sensationally divorced by the Duke.

The problem proved to be a confusion caused by the existence of two synopses of Her Grace's story. One, given to editor Lee Howard, contained very saucy stuff indeed. On the strength of it Lee was delighted to pay £55,000 (probably around half-a-million by today's standards) for the completed series. The second synopsis, the one that the Duchess saw, was for an infinitely gentler tale of debutantes and balls and the *haut monde* in general (very general as it transpired), and for her part the Duchess was also happy to agree to a payment of £55,000.

Understandably, completely innocent in the matter, hers was the synopsis to which she insisted upon adhering, and despite the best efforts of the *Pic*'s highly experienced Victor Sims, who ghosted the series, it simply was not possible to equate it with the story outlined in the Lee Howard copy of the synopsis. From the point of view of the Duchess of Argyll, how could it? I don't know what went wrong, except that somehow both the Duchess and Lee were misled. What *is* known is that there was no contractual loophole and the *Pictorial* ended up with what they reckoned to be a £55,000 non-event.

Meanwhile in Long Acre . . .

For some reason the Duke of Argyll's literary agent was Cyril James, a sometime star *Daily Mirror* writer (and married to one of the truly great women reporters, Hilde Marchant) but now seedy and puce-jowled and whose office was the saloon bar of The Albion at Ludgate Circus. Having acquired the Duke as a client – how was never revealed – and having aroused Sam Campbell's interest in his tale, Cyril was told that His Grace had no intention of going anywhere near anything as vulgar as a newspaper office to discuss the matter. While in London he was staying at the Ritz (being a bit hard up) but refused to allow even the editor of *The Times*, far less Sam Campbell and Cyril James, to visit him there. 'We'll meet at your office,' the Duke told Cyril.

Office? With the Welsh equivalent of '*oi veh*' Cyril scurried around and managed to borrow for the afternoon the basement cell that journalist, and now PRO, Frank Owen rented in a block opposite the Houses of Parliament.

After effusive greetings from Sam and Cyril, and a perfunctory nod of acknowledgement from the Duke, Cyril sat behind the desk with Sam on its left side, Argyll on its right. Since the desk was about the size of a table for one in the average Kebab house, and set in an area comparable to that of the same Kebab house's lavatory, their noses almost touched; if one of them tried to lean backwards away from the others he succeeded only in crushing a shoulder blade or spine against filing cabinet, mantlepiece or doorknob. The situation could not have been helped by Cyril's bronchial gasping and throat clearing.

By way of a conversational relaxant Sam said: 'Since I'm a Campbell and you're head of the Clan Campbell I suppose we're sort of cousins, eh chum?'

The Duke stared at him.

Fingering the knot in his tie, Cyril wheezed: 'His. . . um. . . Grace finds all this very distasteful, so would you address your questions through me . . . er . . . Sam?'

It was Sam's turn to stare as he replied: 'Sure, OK, Cyril. First things first, then: how much does His Nibs want for his tale?'

'His *Grace*.' Cyril frowned warningly. 'His Grace isn't interested in money, are you Duke?' (Argyll, who had managed to wriggle his head so that he was staring at the ceiling and not at his companions, did not deign to reply.) 'He doesn't care what you pay, as long as it's £5,000 more than the Duchess is getting from the *Pictorial*.'

After absorbing this and taking a quick look at the ceiling to see what might be up there other than discoloration and dust, Sam said: 'So what's he going to tell for the money?'

'Ah yes,' said Cyril, and proceeded to list in some detail the appalling allegations the Duke was to make against the Duchess. Even Sam winced from time to time as alleged horror followed horror, Cyril nearly rubbing away the knot in his tie and running out of phlegm, while the Duke, superbly impassive, continued to examine the ceiling, from time to time yawning with distaste at the vulgarity of it all. Encouraged by the Duke's lack of response, Cyril allowed his Celtic flair for Grand Guignol to run riot.

Finally, having heard enough monstrosities even for him, Sam said: 'OK, it's a deal.' Contracts were signed, and with a nod the Duke made his way back to the Ritz. And then – or so the story goes – to one of his clubs where he advised various members of the deal he'd struck and that he was in possession of a diary not mentioned in court and in which various names were listed. For a sum of money (cash) he was prepared not to mention a person or two. Rumour had it that men who had never met the Duchess and had been impotent for many a year rushed forward clutching bunches of tenners in order to upstage fellow members.

What is not apochryphal is the polarization between the series Cyril said the Duke would put his name to and what His Grace was actually prepared to sign. And the legal department, backed by counsel's opinion, assured Sam that it was useless to write to Odham's solicitors: the contract was foolproof.

When the final whistle went on this *People* v. *Sunday Pictorial* contest the score was a draw with one own-goal each.

The great dream of both papers was that after their circulation struggle the winner would then overtake the *News of the World* with its weekly sale of 6 million-plus. It was never to be, although years later (in 1981) the *Sunday Mirror* was within a whisker of doing so, primarily because, although all circulations were well down, the *News of the World*'s fall was the most dramatic. What would have resolved the matter was the *Sunday Mirror* going for the *News of the World*'s jugular (as they say in the sports pages) with its proposed colour magazine.

I had transferred from the *Sunday Mirror* to edit *Reveille* and while there in 1976 pioneered Fleet Street's new technology (a process that, between the purchase of the wrong machinery and the Mirror Board's craven terror of the print unions, was to mean *Reveille*'s last post).

Anyway, sometime after my return to the *Sunday Mirror* I was asked by chairman Tony Miles if I would take charge of costing

185

and producing a dummy for a *Sunday Mirror* colour magazine (the idea for such a magazine is claimed by too many people to list here), and when I accepted I was appointed its editor-elect. In deciding upon the magazine's character I worked out a completely new formula for such a publication.

The details don't matter now. What does matter is how everything went wrong from the very early days: too many people interfering with content and design and telling me whom I would or would not engage as staff, excitement with a new toy resulting in more chiefs that Indians, and, when you add the firewater, impulsive excitement that led to a shambles of a dummy... Plus an insistence upon keeping the product inside the Mirror complex and so having to estimate costs at Fleet Street national newspaper, rather than magazine, rates and so doubling basic outgoings.

The list of naive stupidities went on and on as people who lacked any knowledge of the problem (or even of magazines) postured in readiness for the TV cameras at a launch that never came. Reed International, our then masters, were not prepared to invest the necessary money and (to my knowledge) no Mirror director was willing to go anywhere near screwing his courage to the sticking-place.

And so, as Reed International prevaricated, it was left to Rupert Murdoch and the *News of the World* to produce a colour magazine and jet away over the rainbow.

*   *   *

Although I have been a member of the National Union of Journalists for many years, there were times when the power and arrogance – and often stupidity – of some of our Fathers of the Chapel (shop stewards) drove me near to tearing up my membership card (except that so doing would have meant my expulsion and, in consequence, inability to work). An example was when a mandatory meeting (one it was absolutely obligatory to attend) was called by the *Sunday Mirror* FOC Ronald Maxwell. The issue – and I do not exaggerate – was whether we should strike because the canteen staff failed to cut the rind from the bacon in the bacon sandwiches. The issue was dragged out by the militants before being defeated on the vote – the majority of *Sunday Mirror* staff did not eat canteen bacon sandwiches.

As *Reveille* started the new technology, making me Fleet Street's first photocomposition editor, it involved moving from our editorial offices in Stamford Street near Waterloo Station to Fetter Lane off Holborn in order to be close to the new technology in New Fetter Lane. The main Mirror building was sandwiched between, as it were.

The idea was to move on a Friday in order for all of us to be ready to start work at our new offices on Monday. Now the new technology made absolutely no difference to the overwhelming majority of the staff, this being long before direct input by journalists. So the secretaries would continue to shorthand and type, the reporters and writers to report and write, the photographers would continue to take their happy snaps, the messengers would continue to run messages, the librarian would do the same job, the men who retouched photographs would continue to retouch photographs as before – and so on. No changes in their jobs. The only people who suffered small alterations to their working patterns were the sub-editors, who had to learn a new set of symbols (with visual aids it took a full hour), and the art department, whose pictures and page measurements were now in centimetres instead of inches (rulers provided).

I don't remember the order in which the aggravations occurred. No matter. The removal men had delivered the tea chests and red plastic baskets in which items for removal were to be put. The secretaries decided not to empty their desks into these containers until they received extra, new technology, money. For the same reason the librarian refused to pack so much as a dictionary. The photographers wouldn't empty their filing cabinets. (With editorial manager Ken Udall, my deputy and the picture editor, I was to come in the next day to do the emptying.) The messengers joined in. Ken was under so much pressure that he had to call for a senior man from MGN's head office in Holborn to help him out. Then the NUJ joined in the demands for extra money. One by one they all did.

The removal men arrived. Mirror Group Newspapers moving

didn't involve just a phone call to Pickfords (or somesuch) who then came and did the job. Members of a branch of one of the unions had to carry things to the front door and hand them over to the removal men. (At the other end the process was reversed.) From my office I heard one of the union men say to his colleagues: 'Why should we be left out? Let's go over to Holborn and get our share of these technicologicals.' So they downed furniture and walked out.

As she went to the lavatory a secretary snagged the sleeve of her dress on a tea chest nail and demanded compensation for an amount that startled me: I didn't know our secretaries were dressed by Dior.

In the end, needless to say, MGN gave in to everyone.

Later that evening, utterly drained, I was in my office sitting on the carpet with a can of beer – the furniture had gone at last – when a phone rang. I reached across for it. It was all I needed to complete my day: Lord Longford calling to tell me at some length that the front-page story in the previous week's issue about Moors killer Myra Hindley was rubbish . . . And why. I switched my brain to hold and said 'Really?' every few minutes, probably for long after he'd rung off.

Union power made employing people quite hazardous. Having taken them on, it was virtually impossible to fire them unless they were caught with their hands in the till or selling secrets to our enemies. I recall on *Reveille* being persuaded by my then deputy to take on a writer who proved to be illiterate and apparently dyslexic. And a very strange man indeed, who had heard of a union trouble-maker who was so good a negotiator he was given a job on management and rose to great heights. So this man started to cause trouble, hoping to catch the chairman's eye. He did – and the eyes of his fellow trouble-makers in the Group. He was so crassly inept that, far from being promoted, both sides of the negotiating table prayed for a fatal accident.

It was the print unions that gave the Mirror Group the excuse to kill off *Reveille*. (It wasn't making money, and having been used as a technological test-bed was in the way in terms of the limited skills of a composing room staff that would have to handle the *Daily* and *Sunday Mirrors*, *The People* and *Sporting Life*.)

There were two men whose jobs disappeared when *Reveille* switched from hot metal to the new technology. Being kind-hearted in certain areas, the management said they could stay on until they died or retired. So they did – doing absolutely nothing. Finally one died – at the age of 82. (Being a shift worker, age didn't seem to matter.)

The union concerned – led by militants – demanded he be replaced in his non-existent job! Understandably, the management refused. The union went on strike. After *Reveille* failed to appear for several weeks, it was closed, and I returned to the *Sunday Mirror* as an assistant editor.

There were times when I supported strike action and occasions when I didn't. In the 1960s when, in order not to be disruptive, mandatory meetings were held after office hours in an upstairs room of The White Swan in Fetter Lane, one drawback was the drinking time downstairs before the meeting. This particular evening involved more than bacon sandwiches, but I didn't think it justified a strike. I was sitting next to Bernard McElwaine, who fell asleep during the preliminaries. Then the arguments of both sides, during which I nudged Bernie from time to time to stop him snoring. Next the vote. 'Those in favour of a withdrawal of labour?' Many hands were raised. 'Those against?' I raised my arm, and, since it was going to be a very close decision, I raised Bernie's, holding it up by the elbow.

To the day he died I don't suppose Bernard McElwaine knew how he had averted a strike on the *Sunday Mirror*.

FIFTEEN

If You're Dead
Please Let Me Know

Some years ago there was tragedy at Bolton football ground when overcrowding on the terraces led to a crush that killed 33 spectators and injured 400. The news caused panic on the *Sunday Pictorial*. They had no Northern office at the time and thus no staff reporter on hand to cover the event. In some desperation the News Desk riffled through the card index in search of a freelance who might be at home that Saturday afternoon. Calm returned when the sports department told the editor and the News Desk that a man was there: the reporter they had sent to cover the game. After signs of relief the news desk waited . . . and waited . . . and waited as the reporter failed to telephone. When they could wait no longer they ran a story cobbled together from Press Association and radio reports and inventive genius.

Sometime that night the reporter was contacted at home with the not unreasonable question: 'Why didn't you file a story?'

An astonished: 'There wasn't one to file, was there?'

'Eh?'

'There was that terrible crush, wasn't there? Umpteen people were killed, weren't they?'

'Exactly!'

'Well then.'

'Well then what?'

'They cancelled the match. So there wasn't anything to report, was there?'

For years the man went around aggrieved at having been peremptorily fired, his rancour aggravated by his inability to think of any rational explanation for his dismissal.

Although the reporter wasn't Menachem (Freddy) Lee, it could have been. Freddy was brought from Berlin as a young teenager just before the war by his cousin Morrie Klopps, a Birmingham fishmonger who, my mother once worked out, was second cousin by marriage of Rosie Goldberg in Hackney who was an in-law of Aaron Wagner who was somehow related to Max Lee who was married to my Aunt Esther. So Freddy had to be Family.

Certainly Uncle Max welcomed him with open arms and tear ducts, for he was utterly convinced that everyone called Lee was not only, like himself, originally Lefkowitz, but was also some sort of a cousin. Looking back, it is hard to believe that Jenny, Peggy, Bernard, Christopher, Laurie, Robert E. and Gypsy Rose all had their origins in the loins of Max Lefkowitz's uncles in Gora Kalvaria, but Max's certainty was absolute. I must have had some scepticism even as a child, since I can recall asking him about Mr Lee who owned a Chinese restaurant in King's Road, Hammersmith. It took him the time to roll and light a cigarette to arrive at the explanation. 'We was a very big family, and when we left Poland not everybody came to London. Some went to America, Leeds, all over. So why not China where he learned the cooking and then came to London? I must visit him, find out if he's from my grandfather's side or from one of the brothers. Might do business together.'

'But he's a real Chinaman,' I protested. 'I've seen him.'

Obsessive certitude is never nonplussed for long. After a few puffs at his cigarette, Max said: 'Maybe his father went to China and married a local Yiddisher girl (Why not? There's Jews everywhere, God be thanked) and he resembles the mother. So no more questions; I got important business to see to . . .'

An ex-waiter, Uncle Max described himself as caterer, and he did organize the occasional small wedding and bar mitzvah. A biggish man with the complexion of moist putty, completely bald, but with hair growing from ears and the rounded tip of a generous nose, he wore the most enormous and shapeless shoes I have ever seen. This, he lamented, was the legacy of his years as a waiter in Warsaw, which left him with corns the size of apples, grapefruit-like bunions, ingrowing toenails that reached to his heels and callouses as big as pot-scourers. From the stories he told, an entire intake of chiropody students could have trained and graduated on Uncle Max's feet. (At home he was seldom seen, even at mealtimes, without his feet soaking in a basin of water, which his wife insisted he cover with a towel. Apparently, from the ankles down, he was the Elephant Man.)

Between catering arrangements he hobbled around London involved in mysterious deals. He regarded himself as an entrepreneur of enormous perspicacity and cunning – buying here, selling there – but the few enterprises I did learn about carried the stigmata of doom. I remember the afternoon he arrived at the Askew Road bakery staggering under the weight of a large and elaborately wrapped parcel. After mopping his face with a handkerchief, he said breathlessly: 'I got hold of a real bargain today.' Dropping his voice: 'But I got to sell quick.'

Uncle Sam nodded understandingly. 'Quick sales and small returns, eh? Like in the baking.'

Uncle Max shook his head. As he untied the parcel: 'No, it's not that. I got to sell quick because they're suit lengths. And what material! Sixteen-ounce cloth. I got from my cousin, Sidney. I had to pay a bit more than the proper price, but a bargain. Look. Feel. I got fifteen lengths, so I brought along three. One each. For you I'll let have at cost. A suit from cloth like this'll last you a lifetime. What you say?'

'Where's the bargain?' asked Uncle Lew.

'At more than the proper price a bargain?' asked Uncle Sam.

'How can cloth over the odds be a bargain?' asked Uncle Dave.

Uncle Max groaned with impatience and rolled his eyes. After peering furtively about him he whispered: 'No clothing coupons.'

The rest of us looked at one another and then back at Max who asked: 'What's the matter?'

'Clothes rationing ended nearly three months ago, *shmok*', Uncle Sam screamed.

From time to time, long and tedious reports of Freddy Lee's progress filtered through. Which is how I knew that he had become a freelance journalist working for various trade magazines in the

Midlands, and then the heart-sinking news that he was coming to London to try his luck in Fleet Street. I was depressed because I was aware that I would be expected to put Freddy (of whose talents I knew nothing) on the road to stardom within a fortnight. 'After all,' said my sister Sylvia, 'he is Family. I know Freddy Lee is a common name, but this one is really Menachem, also Uncle Max's . . .'

'Yes,' I interrupted quickly, happy to take her word for it rather than attempt to follow her into a cat's cradle of twigs attached to the convoluted branches of the family tree. I assured her I'd do my best.

Freddy came to see me one Saturday at the *Sunday Mirror*, a small, apologetically smiling man with a nervous sniff who resembled an American tourist on a Bayswater-based package holiday, for it was threatening rain and he not only carried an umbrella and raincoat, but wore galoshes and had a plastic cover on his plastic hat. Monty Court, the news editor (now the distinguished editor of *Sporting Life*), had agreed to give Freddy a reporting shift on my say so, and when I introduced them Monty stared at Freddy's rainwear in disbelief, then looked at me, at first suspiciously as though I was playing a practical joke, then with eye-narrowed hatred.

Among the events of the day that Monty's staff and Saturday casuals were covering was a march by black students from the Embankment to a mass rally at Speakers' Corner in Hyde Park. Leading the demo was a briefly notorious, now long-forgotten, Nigerian firebrand with deadlocks and wispy beard who aroused no little fury among Britain's white population (and some embarrassment among the black) with his screamed 'Kill everybody white' attacks, his detestation of all things British, and his paranoiac loathing of former British colonies that had meekly accepted the hand-over of independence rather than (as a matter of principle) cut a few thousand white throats in the process.

Such is the transience of such notoriety I cannot remember his name, nor can Monty Court. He will doubtless turn up in one of those 'Where Are They Now?' mini-features tucked away among the classified ads. He was a minor character at best. What made the march worth covering was the tip the *Sunday Mirror* had been given that the National Front intended to disrupt it with savage violence. So pairs of reporters and photographers were deployed along the route.

When he'd completed his briefing, Monty Court noticed Freddy Lee. With a sigh he went up to him and said: 'There're going to be a demo. Some mad coloured gentlemen. You can cover the Speakers' Corner end. Just don't get in the way of the reporters who arrive with the marchers, unless they happen to be from *The People* or *News of the World*. Get there early . . . Like now . . . Hover . . . Absorb the background . . . Um . . . er do *something*.' Apart from being an ebullient news editor, Monty was a keen sportsman, which he now demonstrated by adding: 'As for me, I'm off to strike a blow for freedom,' meaning that he was going to place a Yankee or Canadian or Heinz or some other complicated and improbable combination of wagers at the betting shop in Fetter Lane.

The demo was a non-event journalistically since the National Front put in only a token appearance supplied by jeering teenagers, and Mike Christiansen had no intention of devoting space to the march for its own sake. Monty Court was about to cross to the racing desk to discover how his each-way Bulgarian (or whatever) was doing, when he saw Freddy Lee arrive in the office. 'OK?' Monty asked. 'Get anything?'

'I'm a bit late because I got a long interview with their leader.'

'Big deal,' said Monty, completely underwhelmed.

'He's going to live in a cave on the Welsh coast. He says it's his mission as instructed personally by Jesus Christ. He's seen the light.' Consulting his notes; 'All was revealed to him at Mount Pleasant. He . . .'

'Hold on!' Monty interrupted. '*Mount Pleasant*?! The Post Office sorting office up the road?'

After more scanning of notes: 'Er, yes, . . . He couldn't afford to go to Mount Sinai so he went to Mount Pleasant, where Jesus came to him and told him he must end his evil ways and purify himself by meditation in a cave in the desert before spreading his message of universal love. But he can't afford the desert so he's going to the Gower Peninsular in Wales. Lots of caves and sand, apparently, and it's the thought that counts.'

'B-but what . . .' Monty gulped. 'What about revolution and the wickedness of the whites and how the blacks shall inherit the world through blood and violence.'

'He has seen the light. Doesn't believe in violence. Mass baptism. That's the beginning of wisdom.'

With a 'Well I'll be . . .', Monty grabbed the house phone and told Mike Christiansen, who immediately began to think of a page one lead turning to a couple of inside pages.

Monty Court was nobody's fool, and although he sent for library cuttings for background information, he delayed getting reporters to phone around for reaction from public figures while he attempted to equate the dreadlocked Nigerian throat-cutter with an anchorite in a Welsh cave – via a visitation from Jesus Christ outside the Mount Pleasant sorting office. An appalling possibility came to him, and as Freddy Lee settled down to type his story Monty shouted a window-rattling 'Oi!' and beckoned him over. 'What was chummy's name again?'

Freddy replied with someone completely different from the leader of the demo.

'Sit!' Monty ordered. After phoning Mike to advise him to hold his horses for a while, he growled at Freddy: 'I should have known better than to trust a man who walks around with his hat and shoes covered with French letters . . . Let's start at the beginning . . .'

Freddy had gone to Speaker's Corner where he saw a black man just coming to the end of excitedly addressing a large crowd waving banners bearing revolutionary slogans. No other reporter rushed up to the speaker when he'd finished, so his interview was a scoop . . . Except that the march was still at the southern end of Whitehall. Freddy's man was the founder and leader of The True Israelite Church of St Didymus the Martyr (or something similar), the crowd of banner-waving blacks filling in time as they awaited their marching comrades.

Having told Freddy, reasonably politely in the circumstances, that if he had any decency he would go home, pour a large scotch, then lock himself in an outside lavatory with a Webley revolver and one round of ammunition, and having established that his Super-Swindon (or whatever) had not produced a single winner, Monty Court went to the Stab for a large Dewars, a game of darts and a snarl. He was joined there by Mike Christiansen who had taken the contretemps with his usual philosophic shrug. I went across as well, in part to apologize to Monty for Freddy Lee, whom I was now convinced was indeed Uncle Max's cousin.

Freddy didn't blow his brains out: he went into public relations.

*   *   *

Public relations officers and publicists operate on various levels. At the top of the public relations industry are those earning vast sums for Hollywood and City-style super-hypes. Below are layered strata that include operators like Wesley Clapton who had a gift of an account since it instructed him to make certain that turkeys – as such, no brand names – were well mentioned by the media at Christmas. As he sent complimentary turkeys to every journalist in Britain, he admitted that an infinitely tougher challenge would have been to attempt to prevent the beasts from being mentioned, priced and photographed at that time of year – in the manner of the impossible situation faced by publicist Nigel Nielson who was employed by Aristotle Onassis to ensure, among other matters, that the shipping millionaire's name was kept out of the press.

The most unfortunate are those PROs employed to write hyperbolic handouts for such products as a new brand of seaweed-based pimple cream, and act for such people as 7-year-old psychics and whisky-wrecked Country and Western Unknowns making farewell tours of the Cairngorms.

Their handouts carry the hopeful footnote: 'For further information contact (name and telephone number).' In my experience they were rarely (if ever) telephoned because their material was rarely (if ever) read, good journalists preferring to be contacted personally with offers of newsworthy exclusives. What have helped the handout writers are the burgeoning free sheets delighted to plug almost anything if the copy is offered at no cost and helps fill the spaces between advertisements with material that makes a change from ecstatic plugs for local restaurants and the library's revised opening hours.

For some years after *Reveille* ceased publication, envelopes containing these mimeographed handouts continued to arrive at its former offices addressed to me and my departmental heads. Indeed, not only was the paper dead, but some of the executives named on the envelopes (if a departmental title was granted the courtesy of a name) were also long dead and half-forgotten. Until I could ho longer be bothered, I wrote a letter on the anniversary of *Reveille's* demise to our trade paper, *UK Press Gazette*, lamenting the inefficiency of those public relations people who not only were too lazy to update their lists of Fleet Street executives every year, but hadn't read the papers, or listened to the radio or watched TV (or bought *UK Press Gazette*) and so didn't know of *Reveille's* going. My letters were published but the bumf continued to arrive. (If the PROs, and not their clients, had been footing the bills it might have been a different story.)

Those PROs who did manage to stir themselves into a posture of defence did so by writing to *UK Press Gazette* protesting that it was up to *me* to advise *them* that *Reveille* and I (if applicable) were dead: they had more important things to do, they implied, than listen to or watch or read the news.

Inevitably, I received a letter from Freddy Lee. I know which Freddy Lee it was quite apart from 'It was nice to see your letter in UK Press Gazette. You may remember me, the former Menachem Lee, a cousin of Uncle Max Lee (may he rest in peace), who you kindly gave a shift to one Saturday on the Sunday Mirror.' It had to be him when he continued: 'What I'm wondering is whether you might have a vacancy for a staff reporter on *Reveille*.'

A multi-millionaire who relished being in the limelight but needed no PR services was Nubar Gulbenkian, son of Calouste 'Mr Five Percent' Gulbenkian (who made a colossal fortune as an oil entrepreneur and earned his nickname because he made certain of getting 5 per cent from every firm with which he was involved). Having spent the war in Portugal, Calouste inaugurated a charitable Foundation with its headquarters there and named a group of trustees to run it when he died, as he did in 1954. That led to the troubles with his son, Nubar.

Nubar Gulbenkian was a big, broad man with bushy black eyebrows and a fierce grey moustache over a great spade of a grey bread. (The eyebrows and moustache were brushed upwards except during Lent when they were brushed downwards).

Gulbenkian wore a monocle and in his buttonhole an orchid which was changed daily. He was not the sort of person you'd miss on a blind date under the clock at Waterloo Station. He rode to hounds and when in London travelled in a chauffeur-driven taxi that carried carriage lamps, its exterior panelling decorated with wicker lattice-work. A story, surely apocryphal, was that when asked why he travelled in a taxi rather than a Rolls, he explained the far greater manoevrability of a cab in London, adding: 'I'm told that it can turn on a sixpence – whatever that might be.' He subscribed to a cuttings agency so as not to miss anything said about him. A shrinking orchid he was not.

He had diplomatic status here as an honorary commercial attaché to the Iranian Embassy, and it was in this capacity that I met him at some diplomatic reception when I was on *Illustrated*. We chatted, and that was that – until, a couple of days later, Gulbenkian phoned me on *Illustrated* with a long and bitter attack on certain of the trustees of the Gulbenkian Foundation and told me of the legal actions he was taking against them. Most of it involved such technical high finance I was utterly lost. I told him so, adding that it was not really a story for *Illustrated*. 'No, no no,' he assured me 'I don't want a story in your magazine.' I believe I could hearing him shuddering at the thought. 'I'm only interested in stories in *The Times* and *Evening Standard* diary. I just wanted a chat.'

Of all the hundreds of people he knew I never understood why Gulbenkian picked on me as someone to whom he could pour out his bitterness about the running of the Foundation when the safety-valve of emotion was over-pressurized. He could afford counsellors and psychiatrists by the dozen. Or perhaps it was because he found it easier to talk over the telephone to a virtual stranger who didn't understand much of what he said and so was unable to argue with him. Whatever his motive, he must have trusted me.

The calls continued at irregular intervals for several weeks. Then stopped. I never saw him or heard from him again.

The giving of Christmas presents such as turkeys, booze and cigars by PROs was at its height during the days of post-war shortage. I remember Tony Helliwell telling me one Christmastide of arriving home much too late and much too drunk, and as a peace offering handed to his wife, Pina, a goose he'd been given by the PRO for boxing promoter, Jack Solomons. Furious, she hit Tony over the head with it, her rage sufficient to cause the bird to burst. 'I didn't mind too much at the time,' said Tony. 'In my other hand I had two turkeys.'

Even today perks can be liberal, since an editorial mention is a far better bet than an advertisement that relatively few are likely to read.

In 1973, a brilliantly argued memo from Hugh Cudlipp, then chairman of IPC Newspapers, was circulated to Mirror Group Newspaper staff. Headed EDITORIAL INTEGRITY, and subtitled 'A re-statement of our principles,' it said in part:

'Every member of our editorial staff should be free from any imputation of persuasion by commercial interest. Therefore:
1) As a general rule, no member of the editorial staff should accept facility trips of any kind. The only exceptions will be where there is no other means of obtaining a desirable story or pictures. In such cases, the Editor's permission to accept the facility offer must be obtained.
2) All members of the editorial staff should exercise the greatest discretion in accepting gifts from people or organisations with whom they deal in their journalistic work. When gifts of more than a nominal value are proffered, they should be politely returned.'

Since Hugh's declaration of intent was issued in time for Christmas, various PROs were baffled by the mass return from the Mirror Group of trumpery, logo-bearing plastic pens and diaries – who was to define 'nominal value'? – as well as (presumably) boxes of Lew Grade-size Havana cigars. Then, honour having been satisfied, at least as far as the troops on the editorial floors were concerned, the situation eased back to normal.

One of the best and most popular show business publicists was a blackberry-nosed butterball who handled many big stars and, although by definition he had to be part salesman, part conman, he also had a genuine love of newspapers and journalism. This

199

led to something of a *cause célèbre* when he arranged to write a column of pop gossip for a national newspaper. He wouldn't plug his own clients, nor did he want payment: he was an *amateur* of journalism in the true meaning of the word.

The person with whom he negotiated rationalized: 'A pop column is being supplied. Free of charge. From the paper's point of view it is worth £X a week. So I will open my own bank account using this man's name and get the accounts department to pay a weekly £X into it. The sum is reasonable so there will be no management questions, and the man isn't going to complain since he's doing it for free.'

Simple, and the journalist paid himself a nice weekly cheque until the day when the PRO had to telephone the paper's editor to say: 'I love doing the column, and I'm happy to do it free of charge. But I'm fucked if I can see why I'm now being asked by the Revenue to pay some thousands of pounds in tax for the privilege!'

I've not named the men, nor the paper, since the journalist recovered from his sacking and is said to be doing well again.

In public relations.

Newspapers have their publicity departments but, prior to TV and radio chat shows, journalists and their stories were virtually unknown outside of a newspaper's own readership, or word-of-mouth publicity, or advertising, or pejorative references by rivals. A way round the problem was to find, or be offered, alternative methods of publicity. One outlet was sponsorship, but other papers often removed prefixes from such events as the *Daily Mail* Ideal Home Exhibition, *Daily Express* Boat Show, *Daily Herald* Brass band Championship, *The People* Pigeon show and *Reveille*'s Glamorous Grannie Competition.

One or two readers with long memories might recall a mercifully brief series of variety shows on TV produced by Jack Hilton and introduced by Tony Helliwell, complete with his one-size-too-small trilby hat. Apart from the not inconsiderable problems of a completely new medium and its techniques, Tony had to go on sober, which meant that he was nervous and overwhelmed and suffering his inferiority complex (he wasn't very tall unless he was drunk, and his trilby was rarely raised to save him revealing his baldness). And so, for the viewers, the scourge of the spivs proved to be a curiosity of disastrous inarticulation. (Unlike brother Gerald drinking the hospitality room dry before making an ass of himself in front of the cameras on a BBC quiz show.)

When editor of *Picturegoer*, Connery Chappell introduced the magazine's Film of the Month, and persuaded companies to screen 'Winner of Picturegoer's Film of the Month' on their trailers. It was a brilliant idea. People were then going to the cinema once or twice a week, so Connery had enormous captive audiences. When I edited *Men Only* I devised a publicity scheme whereby High Street outfitters would have bold displays with the sell: 'As Featured in This Month's *Men Only*.' The trouble was that our then masters, Newnes, had forgotten to apportion a publicity budget for *Men Only*, so the big sell was reduced to handwritten postcards sellotaped to the insides of windows.

A Mike Christiansen stunt was to commission, for a large sum, David Bailey, the *enfant terrible* of sixties' photographers, to snap every member of the *Sunday Mirror* editorial staff. Mike's plan was three-pronged. One was to offer other papers and magazines, *absolutely free*, pictures taken by Bailey of diarist Quentin Crewe, cartoonist David Langdon, Cyril Kersh (who?), Mark Kahn (eh?), Lionel Crane (huh?), and so on, in exchange for a mention of the *Sunday Mirror* in the captions. There were no takers apart from local papers, which ran 'Llandrindod Wells boy makes good' stories, but with 'now a distinguished Fleet Street journalist' substituting for a mention of the *Sunday Mirror*.

There weren't even many of these, which explains the failure of Mike's second ploy: to use Bailey's pictures to accompany by-lined stories in the *Sunday Mirror*. The snag was that Bailey had photographed us with so much dramatic light and shade that his pictures would reproduce on newsprint only as smudges unless an entire page was devoted to each one. Which, in turn, led to the blunting of the third prong: Mike wanted to fill the long, oblong front window of the Mirror building, and the area behind it, with Bailey's pictures, so that passers-by could enjoy a free, exclusive exhibition of the great man's photographs – but the mischievous Bailey had snapped us in outrageously distorted close-ups which, added to their light and shadow, caused publicity director Tommy Atkins to say with absolute justification: 'No bloody way. People will think the *Sunday Mirror* is manned by escapers from bottles in Hammer Films' Chamber of bloody Horrors.'

Arthur 'Tony' Helliwell was often urged by Odhams executives to write books for both his and *The People*'s greater glory and the swelling of their bank balances. The only one he agreed to was *The Private Lives of Famous Fighters*, a compilation of boxing stories he'd written under a pseudonym composed of his Christian names, Arthur Williamson. It was very well done, but memorable now only because the material was stolen – literally verbatim – by a journalist for a paperback. Tony was too kind, or lazy, to do anything about it.

Duncan 'Tommy' Webb wrote books. They concerned the cases he covered as a master crime reporter and contained passages on the lines of 'Sucking at my pipe I saw that the left trouser leg had been severed and sewn below the knee. My keen, trained gaze did not miss the fact that there was only one shoe and that clutched in the dead man's hand was a tobacco pouch bearing the initials XY. This contained tobacco and a packet of a well-known brand of cigarette papers. These items, together with a copy of *The Cab-driver's Gazette*, moved me to say with some confidence: 'The victim was one-legged taxi driver who rolled his own cigarettes.'

'"By Jove, sir, I do believe you're right!" gasped the grateful Chief Inspector.

'Always happy to help Britain's bobbies,' I smiled, then added: 'A cabbie with the initials XY.'

'A week later the Yard arrested the lover of the wife of one-legged taxi driver X—— Y——. Six months later he was hanged.

'That was the seventeenth case in which my trained eye had resulted in a miscreant being brought to justice . . .'

Tommy Webb really did write such books. He wasn't the only one: it was a sort of occupational disease among crime reporters. Ironically, however, the only book written by Fred Redman of the *Sunday Pictorial/Sunday Mirror*, the finest investigative journalist of them all, was on how to seek advice for domestic problems. This was when, as pension time approached, he was nudged into running the Mirror Group's Readers' Advice Service

A literary enterprise by Tommy Webb involved the Odhams books department when it jumped on the post-war paperback bandwagon. Tommy, who had been gathering background material ready for the trial of acid bath murderer George John Haigh, telephoned the head of Odhams Paperbacks to say: 'I've got an instant paperback for you. About Haigh. The manuscript is nearly done. I've almost completed my investigations. It needs only a few final paragraphs.' He was about to add: 'The verdict, the appeal, the hanging,' when he was interrupted by 'Very kind of you, old boy, but I don't think there's much interest today in First World War generals, what?'

Odhams Paperbacks lasted about a fortnight.

There were strange masters at Odhams long before my day. As the magazine building was an old wool warehouse, the one occupied in part by *The People* at the south-east corner of Long Acre and Endell Street had once been the Queen's Theatre. On the south-west corner was the New Building with its handsome neo-Georgian facade, built just before the war to accommodate a proposed evening newspaper. The plan was aborted by the war, with the assistance of a basic design fault: it was physically impossible for reels of newsprint to be transferred from their lorries into the building to feed the printing machines.

*   *   *

Despite the size of the Odhams press publishing empire, the men who ran it were primarily printers and accountants, and when they visited an editorial floor it showed. With expressions of bewilderment or near-rage. No matter how many times they had been there they could never come to understand how desks with typewriters on them could earn money. Now if the space was occupied with a few printing and binding machines ... Their nails dug into their palms as they controlled urges to take rulers from their pockets and make measurements. (God alone knows the extent of the suffering caused by that unusable machinery in the basement of the New Building.)

It was much the same on *Men Only* at Newnes, which I edited from 1960 to 1963. There were times when the attitude of the board seemed gratuitously offensive. For instance, it was only when the deal was a *fait accompli* that I was told by a director called Hocking-Baker that *Lilliput* was folding and that its title

203

would be incorporated with *Men Only*'s and that if I wanted to take over any of *Lilliput*'s contributors or unpublished material I had two days in which to make up my mind. Nor was there any consultation or advance warning before another director, Walter Williams, told me that *Men Only*'s printing was changing to web-offset. I was simply instructed that it would happen with the next issue, and that if I wasn't already a master of the web-offset system I had a weekend in which to remedy this unfortunate omission.

I came to realize that the Newnes board were not arrogant, but ignorant: since they all seemed to be printers and accountants, they had little time for, in my opinion, the editorial staffs who gave them the material to print and profits to count.

The Newnes chairman who engaged me was Charles Morris. He seemed to be a nice, beaming little man, although I earned his displeasure when he saw an early copy of one issue and had someone relay to me the message: 'This cannot go on sale to the public. It contains filth. The chairman has ordered its destruction.'

Cannot go on sale? . . . Filth? . . . To be destroyed? . . . I was horrified. Then terrified. What monstrosity had crept into *Men Only*? Was it something like the misprint in *The Times* when Queen Victoria, instead of passing over Westminster Bridge, pissed over it (so the story goes). One can smile now, but it was truly frightening at the time to receive such a message from the chairman. With my staff I combed and re-combed the issue in search of the offending material. Without success.

I spent sleepless nights and anxious days wondering about both my crime and my future, but there was no further message from Charlie Morris. Directors to whom I spoke (grey men in baggy grey suits) were evasive, possibly because of ignorance. Ultimately I discovered the answer, via a secretary.

Blasphemy.

In a cartoon, which showed a parson in his pulpit saying: 'World Without End . . . Touch Wood.' It may not have been all that funny, but blasphemy? For this you'd pulp an entire issue? The answers are, Yes if you're a fundamentalist Christian, and I still think that I should have been advised of the chairman's piety when I joined.

The day came in 1963 when I was told (again with no consultation) that the board had decided that they did not like the pocket-sized format of *Men Only* and its contents: a balanced mix of fiction, off-beat features, cartoons, picture stories, columnists, reviews, and so on. I designed a dummy for a new magazine, which I presented, not to the main board, but to a group of trainees: 'tomorrow's men,' who spent the entire time looking bemused or playing with their pocket calculators. I don't recall a journalist among them.

It was a training exercise. Minds had been made up: Newnes were going to increase the page size of *Men Only* and fill it cover to cover with cut-price tit and bum pictures. Virtually no reading matter: just girls. Barrel-scraping nastiness.

I left.

Life has its ironies. Newnes were now part of the International Publishing Company and its chairman, Cecil H. King, took one look at the new product and did something of a Charlie Morris. 'I do not wish to be associated with such a publication,' he pronounced. So *Men Only*'s title was sold for peanuts to the *News of the World*, who sold it to club owner Paul Raymond, who carried the project to its logical conclusion, as it were, by tucking it into the copycat *Playboy* market.

Epilogue

Memory is a rose-tinted distorter designed to save us from unpleasant recall. How many rainy days of our youth can we remember, unless there was a special wedding–birthday-style occasion involved? Which is why the old insist that the weather was better when they were young. Memory has filtered away the rain, as it filters the more horrendous aspects of the days 'when we were poor, but . . .'

And so on.

When I was young, veteran journalists lamented the passing of the good old days. As Dickens and Kipling must have done when they were journalists. So, probably, did the editor of the *Stanford Mercury* in 1695. The man who subbed the Theban hieroglyphics doubtless hankered after them, too.

So if I have managed some amusing reminiscences about Fleet Street it is not because of nostalgia for the good old days.

There never were any.

But, by God, I certainly enjoyed them.